THE PROBLEMS OF SUFFERING AND EVIL

JOHN COWBURN

THE PROBLEMS OF SUFFERING AND EVIL

MARQUETTE STUDIES IN PHILOSOPHY
NO. 72
ANDREW TALLON, SERIES EDITOR

© 2012 Marquette University Press
Milwaukee, Wisconsin 53201-3141
All rights reserved.
www.marquette.edu/mupress/

Library of Congress Cataloging-in-Publication Data

Cowburn, John.
  The problems of suffering and evil / John Cowburn.
     p. cm. — (Marquette studies in philosophy ; no. 72)
  Rev. ed. of: Shadows and the dark : the problems of suffering and evil.
  1979.
  Includes bibliographical references and index.
  ISBN-13: 978-0-87462-805-0 (pbk. : alk. paper)
  ISBN-10: 0-87462-805-9 (pbk. : alk. paper)
 1. Good and evil. 2. Suffering—Religious aspects. 3. Theodicy. I.
  Cowburn, John. Shadows and the dark. II. Title.
  BJ1401.C65 2012
  231'.8—dc23
                                                                    2012004480

This book is a greatly revised and extended edition by
John Cowburn of his *Shadows and the Dark*
(London: SCM Press, 1979).

♾The paper used in this publication meets the minimum requirements of the
American National Standard for Information Sciences—
Permanence of Paper for Printed Library Materials, ANSI Z39.48-1992.

MARQUETTE UNIVERSITY PRESS
MILWAUKEE

The Association of Jesuit University Presses

Preface

In the nineteen-seventies I wrote *Shadows and the Dark: The Problems of Suffering and Evil*, which was published in 1979. In the forty years since then I revised it extensively and Parts 2 and 3 of this book are a greatly altered second edition of that book. Part 4, which is more than a third of the book, is new. I have made the subtitle of my 1979 book the title of this one.

Often, especially in the Introduction, I will present theories with which I do not agree, omitting to attribute them constantly to their authors. I have found that students sometimes quote something which they attribute to me, omitting to mention that it is someone else's idea, and I wish to state clearly here that this book contains sentences which, though written by me, do not express *my* ideas.

In footnote references, facts of publication are omitted: they are in the bibliography at the end of the book. Biblical quotations are from the New Revised Standard Version, unless another translation, such as the New Jerusalem Bible (NJB), is named.

I have tried to be inclusive in my language, often saying "he or she" where I would once have said "he". However, I still use "he" and "his" where "he or she", "his or her" and so on would occur more than twice in a few lines.

There are many cross-references. Many of these are meant for people who, without reading the whole book, will go to see what I say about this or that topic, and I refer them to passages which I have presupposed, or in which I later qualify what I say in the passage which they have found.

Contents

Part One

Chapter 1: Introduction ~ 16
  Theoretical and practical thought ~ 16
  Definitions of terms ~ 17
  The thesis of this book ~ 17
  Non-religious thought ~ 18
  This book ~ 18

Chapter 2: Forms of Christian Optimism ~ 20
  An Extreme Philosophical View ~ 20
  The idea that evil is non-being and cannot be willed ~ 20
  Criticism of this theory ~ 21
  A Theological View ~ 22
  The theory ~ 22
  A short history of this theory ~ 23
  The idea that what God wills is the universe as a whole ~ 27
  The analogy of a play ~ 29
  Criticism of This View ~ 30
  Some literary rejections of the view that all is for the best ~ 30
  That the theory is incredible ~ 32
  A basic flaw: free will ~ 32
  Criticism of the play analogy ~ 33
  The whole and the part ~ 33
  The inhumanly cheerful repression of anger & grief:
    the denial of tragedy ~ 34
  Permission ~ 35

Chapter 3: A Version of the Fall & Redemption ~ 37
  The Fall ~ 37
  Merits of the theory ~ 38
  Criticism of the theory ~ 38

Chapter 4: Extreme Pessimism ~ 41
  The world as meaningless ~ 41
  The world as evil ~ 42
  The rejection of religion ~ 43
  The Marquis de Sade ~ 44
  How pessimists live ~ 46
  A comment on this pessimism ~ 48

Part Two: The First of My Two Theories

Chapter 5: Free Will & Chance: Indeterminism ~ 51
    Three kinds of event ~ 51
    Necessary or predetermined events ~ 51
    Free acts ~ 51
    Chance ~ 52
    The unpredictability of particular events ~ 53
    Probability ~ 55
    Necessity & predictability in large numbers ~ 56
    The words "theory" and "evolution" ~ 57

Chapter 6: Evolution ~ 59
    The scientific picture of evolution ~ 59
    Chance in particular events in evolution ~ 60
    Necessity in large numbers in evolution ~ 61
    The Rise theory ~ 62
    Entropy ~ 62
    The principal deficiency of the evolutionary theory: moral evil ~ 63
    Teilhard de Chardin ~ 64

Chapter 7: God & Evolution ~ 67
    Two suppositions ~ 67
    Intrinsic possibility and impossibility ~ 67
    The past cannot be changed ~ 68
    God and evolution ~ 69
    The divine foreknowledge: some history ~ 70
    The divine foreknowledge questioned ~ 72
    My position ~ 75
    The idea that God is "outside time" ~ 75
    Probability of particular events ~ 76
    Necessity in large numbers ~ 77
    The divine sensitivity ~ 77

Part Three: The Second of My Two Theories: Moral Evil

Chapter 8: Moral Evil ~ 81
    What moral evil is ~ 81
    Subjectivity ~ 82
    Moral evil is real ~ 82
    Kinds of immoral act ~ 84
    An immoral action ~ 84
    Immoral attitudes ~ 84
    Other people's actions ~ 84
    Serious and unserious immoral acts ~ 85
    The personal choice ~ 87

Contents

  The abiding intention ~ 88
  The evil moment ~ 89
  Laws ~ 89
  Moral and legal obligations ~ 91
  Legal and moral order ~ 93
  Legal positivism and the connection between law and morality ~ 94

Chapter 9: The Content & Effects of a Morally Evil Act ~ 95
  The Content ~ 95
  The explicit and implicit content of decisions ~ 95
  The destruction of the self ~ 95
  The rejection of love ~ 97
  Hurting other persons ~ 98
  The will to destroy ~ 99
  The will to evil ~ 102
  The Effects of Moral Evil ~ 105
  The after-effects of immorality in the agent's subjectivity ~ 105
  The experience of guilt ~ 105
  The sense of meaninglessness, vanity, absurdity ~ 106
  Sadness ~ 107
  Outsiderhood ~ 108
  The fear of punishment ~ 108
  The effects of immorality in the outside world ~ 109
  Some people are hurt, in many cases seriously ~ 109
  There is destruction of moral order ~ 109
  The evolution of morality is set back ~ 110
  Moral evil and nature ~ 110
  Evil leads to more evil ~ 111
  The evil in the world ~ 113

Chapter 10: The Mystery of Evil ~ 116
  Moral evil is not non-being ~ 116
  How is moral evil possible? Incomplete explanations ~ 118
  Flaws in the person's nature ~ 119
  Flaws in the environment ~ 120
  Influence of particular other people ~ 121
  How can moral evil have a place in the scheme of things? ~ 122
  Moral evil is ultimately inexplicable ~ 123
  Explaining Hitler ~ 126
  The horror of moral evil ~ 127
  Moral evil is inexcusable ~ 128

Chapter 11: God & Sin ~ 129
   The idea that sin is non-being ~ 129
   Our relationships with the divine persons ~ 130
   The explicit and implicit rejection of God ~ 133
   The idea that immoral acts are willed by God ~ 134
   Paul Claudel ~ 136
   Sin mysticism ~ 138
   Two defences which implicitly deny foreknowledge ~ 139
   The idea that God permits sin ~ 139
   The Free-Will Defence ~ 140
   This defence and some modern philosophers ~ 140
   The rejection of all this ~ 141
   The divine foreknowledge of sins ~ 146
   That the divine persons are hurt by sins: the divine sensitivity ~ 147
   Risk ~ 150
   Teilhard de Chardin ~ 151

Chapter 12 : Corporate Guilt & Original Sin ~ 152
   Solidarity ~ 152
   Good things done by members of a group to which one belongs ~ 152
   Good things done to members of a group ~ 153
   Bad things done to members of a group ~ 153
   Bad things done by members of a group ~ 154
   The analysis of guilt by solidarity ~ 154
   Not personal complicity ~ 155
   Not "We would have done the same" ~ 155
   Not "We might do the same in the future" ~ 155
   Not a feeling which comes from our own similar experiences ~ 156
   What solidarity-guilt is ~ 156
   The Fall and original sin ~ 156
   The doctrine ~ 156
   A proposed modern theory: moral immaturity ~ 158
   A second proposed theory: "All human beings sin" ~ 159
   A third proposed theory: the environment ~ 160
   What I propose: solidarity-guilt ~ 160

Part Four: The Remedy for Moral Evil

Chapter 13: Judging & Excusing ~ 163
   Excusing oneself and others where there has been no fault ~ 163
   Judging oneself where there has been fault: admission of guilt ~ 165
   Judging others where there has been fault ~ 167

Chapter 14: Repentance, Forgiveness & Reconciliation ~ 168
   Repentance ~ 168
   The admission of guilt ~ 168
   Repentance: what it is ~ 169
   Repentance has a moral motive ~ 170
   That repentance ends moral guilt ~ 170
   That repentance is not demeaning ~ 171
   That repentance can be easy or difficult ~ 172
   The "firm purpose of amendment" ~ 173
   Restitution ~ 174
   Forgiveness ~ 174
   What forgiveness is not ~ 175
   Forgiving is not excusing ~ 175
   Forgiving is not forgetting ~ 175
   Forgiving is not condoning ~ 176
   It does not spring from admission of one's own moral weakness ~ 176
   Forgiving is not demeaning ~ 177
   What forgiveness is ~ 177
   The past and the future ~ 178
   The idea that repentance is not necessary for forgiveness ~ 178
   That repentance is necessary for forgiveness ~ 180
   Not forgiving ~ 182
   Where the wrongdoer is elsewhere ~ 183
   Forgiving can be easy or difficult ~ 184
   Forgiveness of oneself ~ 184
   Reconciliation ~ 184
   Pragmatic truces between individuals ~ 184
   False routes to reconciliation ~ 185
   Understanding and excusing ~ 185
   Forgetting the past ~ 185
   Letting bygones be bygones ~ 185
   True reconciliation ~ 186
   Examples of reconciliation ~ 187
   Reconciliation requires repentance and forgiveness ~ 189
   Repentance and forgiveness must normally be expressed ~ 189
   Reconciliation is for ever ~ 190
   The idea that the post-reconciliation relationship is better than before ~ 190
   The idea that at reconciliation may not completely restore the relationship ~ 191
   When attempts at reconciliation fail: not forgiving ~ 192
   The reconciliation of an individual with a group, or of groups ~ 194
   Pragmatic truces between countries ~ 195
   The repentance or regret of a group ~ 195
   Forgiveness by a group ~ 196
   Group reparation ~ 196

Chapter 15: Divine Forgiveness & Other Theological Matters ~ 199
    The divine forgiveness needs repentance ~ 200
    The controversy concerning attrition ~ 201
    God's attitude towards unrepentant sinners ~ 201
    Our obligation to forgive ~ 202

Chapter 16: Retributive Justice ~ 204
    Revenge ~ 204
    Punishment: the social fact ~ 206
    That punishment is a civil act ~ 207
    Retributive justice ~ 207
    Support for retributive justice ~ 209
    Primitive human beings ~ 209
    Literature ~ 209
    Philosophers ~ 210
    Lawyers ~ 211
    People in general ~ 214
    Particular cases ~ 214
    Christian thinkers ~ 215
    Rejection of retributive justice ~ 216
    Empiricism ~ 216
    Determinism ~ 217
    An idea of liberal democracy ~ 218
    Humanitarian considerations ~ 218
    Punishment and revenge ~ 219
    That punishment is basically revenge, and a good thing ~ 219
    That punishment is basically revenge, and a bad thing ~ 220
    That punishment is not revenge ~ 221
    Some cases of non-punishment ~ 222
    Reasons for this ~ 224
    A moral judgement on this non-punishment ~ 224
    Mercy ~ 225
    Mixed cases ~ 227

Chapter 17: Expiation & the Victim's Need for Justice ~ 231
    Expiation ~ 231
    People who have believed in expiation ~ 231
    Primitive human beings ~ 231
    Plato ~ 232
    Literature ~ 232
    Psychlogists ~ 233
    Others ~ 235
    Group expiation ~ 235
    The right to punishment ~ 236

The Victim's Need for Justice ~ 236
Examples ~ 237
The need of the victim: what is its source? ~ 239
Is it a need for revenge? ~ 239
Is it a need for deterrence? ~ 240
It is a need for justice ~ 240

Conclusion

Chapter 18: Some Theological Reflections ~ 242
    The evolutionary theory ~ 242
    Bright and dark mysteries ~ 242
    The present situation ~ 244
    The Bible – vengeance? ~ 245
    A suggestion ~ 246
    Our part in our redemption ~ 248
    The "last things" ~ 248

Bibliography ~ 249

Index ~ 260

Part One

Introduction

1 Introduction

Theoretical and practical thought

There is a difference between pure or theoretical thought and thought about practical matters, many of which are serious.. Kant wrote a book about pure philosophy (*Vernunft*) and another about practical philosophy. In a somewhat similar way, we distinguish between physics on the one hand and engineering on the other, and between chemistry and cookery. In the religious sphere, we (Catholics, at any rate) distinguish between theology, which is pure or theoretical, and spirituality, which is concerned with living a good Christian life.[1] "Spiritual", as in "spiritual father" and "spiritual reading", is the adjective corresponding to "spirituality". A *theological* question is: What does it mean to say that a consecrated host is the body of Christ? A *"spiritual"* question is: How should we prepare to receive communion and how should we pray when receiving communion? Often, in seminaries theological lectures are given in classrooms to groups of students, whom the lecturers may rarely meet. There are two libraries, a remote library of theological books, supervised by a professional librarian, and an accessible, unattended library of "spiritual" books. There are two different teams of priests: one team gives theological lectures and marks examination papers, while the other gives talks in the chapel and counsels the seminarians individually. Sometimes there are two separate buildings, one called a "college", with a theological library and offices for lecturers, and the other called a "seminary", with a different library and a team of spiritual directors.

Another distinction can be made between another pair of styles, or kinds of talk and writing, for which I will use the terms "academic" and "popular". As the word "academic" suggests, the first style is virtually normative in universities, but it is also the style of highly educated

---

1 Nowadays a world-view such as environmentalism, which is not materialistic, is sometimes called a spirituality. I do not object to this but shall use the word in its religious sense.

persons elsewhere, who read scholarly books, periodicals and magazines, and watch or listen to high-level interviews late at night. It involves footnotes, bibliographies and references to many authors, including some who lived centuries ago. The other or "popular" style is that of "the general public"..

Definitions of terms

"Bad" as an adjective is applied to things which are disordered or cause suffering or distress, whether they were anyone's fault or not. For instance, we talk of bad weather, bad luck, a bad accident and bad writing, and if we speak of a bad man we mean someone who is wicked. If one reads a death notice which says that a man has died at the age of thirty and does not say whether he died a natural death, was murdered or committed suicide, we may say, "That's bad", meaning that, however it happened, we regret it.

I shall use the word "evil", both as a noun and as an adjective, for serious moral wrongdoing and its results. This is how the word is usually used now, though sometimes the word is used of hurricanes and earthquakes, which are unusual. It is not used for unserious or commonplace troubles. I shall sometimes speak of "moral evil", though for me the expression is tautologous.

I shall use "misfortune" and "natural trouble" for things which are bad, but no one's fault, and hence not evil.

The thesis of this book

The basic thesis in this book is that causes of distress, or bad things, are of two different kinds and need to be studied separately. In Part Two I shall consider what I call misfortunes and in Parts Three and Four I shall consider evil. The title of this book, which has "problems" in the plural, is meant to indicate that it deals with two problems.

In many lectures and books what is called "the problem of evil" belongs to pure philosophy or to theology. It may be formulated as the question: "Is the proposition 'God exists' logically compatible with the proposition 'evil exists'?" It is an obvious mistake, and one often made by philosophers, to limit the problem in this way; but it is equally a mistake to dismiss the intellectual problem as remote from life, for sense must be made of life if we are to cope with it emotionally and engage in efficacious action. I shall face the intellectual problem I mentioned, and I shall also deal with repentance, forgiveness and retributive justice. Also, I shall draw on some works of literature such as Shakespeare's plays and Dostoyevsky's novels. Of course, Iago and the characters in *The Brothers Karamazov* never existed; but Shakespeare and Dostoyevsky thought a great deal about what goes on in the minds and hearts of men and women who commit or are hurt by evil deeds, and they put this into their works, which can be quoted here.

Non-religious thought

In general, I shall work in a Christian or, to be more precise, Catholic context. However, now and then I will mention what others think about the problems which I discuss. Let me say a word about non-religious writing that deals with them.

Many people in the West have no religion at all. They see the universe as it is and make no attempt to explain it by means of a being or beings outside it. They have discovered certain "laws", such as the law of gravity, and if you ask them to explain an event, they show how it follows from a universal law, and that is that. If you ask them to explain the universal law, they reply that it just is.

Concerning the practical problem, when there is question of a common and foreseen event which causes suffering, people begin by endeavouring to prevent it or to lessen its effect. When all else fails, a certain fatalism may come into play, they accept the disaster "philosophically" and they say, "There's no use crying over spilt milk", or something similar.

This book

This book is for thinking Christians who are intellectually puzzled and emotionally affected by the disorders of our world, and who wonder whether they should accept them or take action to remedy them. They may also be troubled in their faith in God. When Christians wrote about the problem of evil they often drew on metaphysical speculation, so that they were more philosophical than strictly theological. I shall quote "spiritual" writers like Alphonsus Rodriguez and Jean Pierre de Caussade, who had great influence on Catholic religious and others. I shall also refer, usually critically, to what Austin Farrer calls Christian folk-wisdom, and to what is or was said by preachers of hellfire sermons.

Introduction

Someone to whom I showed a draft of this book said that there are too many examples of family life gone wrong. He said that I seem to be obsessed by such relationships. In reply I said that I wanted to give examples of serious wrongdoing, I do not know any murderers, burglars or swindlers, and I do not expect any readers of this to know any, either, but I, and I expect some readers, at least know of broken marriages and of divisions between parents and children, so I often use these as examples Also, for the most part I wanted to avoid cases where the law would normally be brought in.

Finally, this book is not, I hope, morbid. If it hurts to read some of its pages, as it hurt to write them, it is my hope that the end result will be a degree of intellectual clarity, appropriate emotions, and confidence in action: in a word, my aim is not to hurt but to heal.

2 Forms of Christian Optimism

AN EXTREME PHILOSOPHICAL VIEW

The idea that evil is non-being and cannot be willed

I will now outline, and dismiss from consideration, a theory which used to be taken seriously in neo-scholastic circles. In my opinion, it was neo-scholasticism at its worst. Plotinus said: "Evil cannot have any place among Beings or in the Beyond-Being: these are good. There remains only, if Evil exists at all, that it be some mode, as it were, of the non-Being".[1] This influenced Augustine, who said: "Evil is not a positive substance: the loss of good has been given the name of evil".[2] Thomas Aquinas maintained that every being and only being is good and when students like me were taught neo-scholastic philosophy, one of the first "theses" was: *Omne ens est bonum*, or "Every being is good", which (as we were taught) implied that evil was non-being. Antonin Gilbert Sertillanges, an important early neo-scholastic philosopher, said that the more all-embracing one's view of reality is, the more the notion of evil disappears.[3] This theory can be explained as follows. Light and dark may at first appear to be equally real, positive things, which cannot co-exist; and it may seem that at nightfall darkness drives out light and at dawn light drives out darkness. In truth, however, light is energy and darkness is not an opposing energy but the absence of light. Similarly, good and evil may seem to be two opposite forces, equally real, locked in an eternal conflict, as the Manicheans believed, but (according to the theory which I am expounding) goodness is being and evil is a form of nothingness. These thinkers set out to show how all evils turn

---

1 Plotinus, *Enneads*, I 8 3. Hick discusses Plotinus in *Evil and the God of Love*, pp. 46-49. He says that there is some conflict in Plotinus.
2 Augustine, *The City of God*, XI, 9.
3 "Plus l'homme s'élève à une intuition du tout et de son infinie complexité secondaire, plus la notion du mal disparait." (Sertillanges, *Le problème du mal*, vol. 2, p. 50).

out on analysis to be as it were holes in being: blindness, for instance, is lack of sight and stupidity is lack of intelligence.

If a man is in a deep cave and his light goes out, he will find himself in darkness. If he tries to find the source of the darkness, he will not find it because there isn't one – nothing emits darkness in the way that lamps emit light. The thinkers whose view I am quoting maintain that the will's object is always being, that is, reality, which implies that just as darkness does not have a source, so evil does not have a cause and is not willed. Thomas Aquinas said that "evil as such cannot be intended or in any way willed or desired";[4] Desiré-Joseph Mercier said: "The direct term of an action is never evil" and "evil as such is never willed";[5] and William Temple said: "That any man ever chose evil, knowing it to be evil for him, is to me quite incredible"[6].

The proposers of this theory concluded that while on the one hand God is the ultimate cause of every being and event in the universe, he does not will or cause evil, because it is non-being and therefore not willed. For instance, Germain Grisez says: "The creator causes states of affairs which involve evil, but does not cause evil, since evil does not require a creative cause".[7] Hence if we have an encounter with something that seems bad, we should say to ourselves: "God did not cause this. No one did".[8] This seemed to solve the problem.

Criticism of this theory

It seems to me that some Christians, especially teachers of various kinds, who had difficulty reconciling the suffering and evil in the world with the omnipotence and benevolence of God found in pagan authors the idea that evil is non-being and thought that it solved the problem. This perhaps worked with students and others who had had little experience of life, and who, when even newspapers did not exist, did not know much about what was going on in the world and

---

4 Thomas, *De Malo*, 1 3 c.
5 Mercier, *Métaphysique Générale*, p. 245.
6 Temple (1881-1944), *Nature, Man and God*, p. 362.
7 Grisez, *Beyond the New Theism*, p. 294.
8 This is similar to what Mary Baker Eddy, the founder of Christian Science, said: "Evil has no reality" and "Evil is but an illusion". The way to combat evil, she said, is to make people see that there is no such thing. But the context is totally different.

consequently were open to an unrealistic, "metaphysical" theory. But one cannot state it to someone whose child has just died of leukaemia, it should not have been taught to people who, later in life, were going to try to help such persons, and certainly today, when we all know about the Holocaust, the drug and refugee trades, and AIDS, we find it utterly absurd to say that only what is good is real, or that it is a mistake to attribute reality to disorder of any kind. Also, if someone casts a person into a totally dark room and leaves him there, it is wrong to say that, because darkness is not a being, nothing has been done to him.

A THEOLOGICAL VIEW

The theory

The theory which I am going to present has two fundamental doctrines. One is that God is omnipotent, which I take to mean that God is the creator of all that, besides himself, has actually existed, exists now or will exist, that he is the ultimate cause of all that has happened, is happening or will happen; and that he has total control of the universe. The other doctrine is that he is benevolent towards all his creatures This implies that of every person and thing that exists, the fact is that it is good that he, she or it exists, and of everything that happens it is good that it happens.

According to scholastic philosophers, the basic principles of being are potency and act. God is pure act and all creatures are combinations of potency and act (there is no such thing as *pure* potency). From this it follows that there is no passivity or receptivity in God, and this implies that God cannot *receive* knowledge from creatures. If an architect who lives in Melbourne designs a building which is built in Albury, his idea of it, even before it is built, is clearer than that of anyone who later goes to look at it, and God's knowledge of the universe is like that. (There is this difference between the architect and God: the architect can go to Albury and add received or passive knowledge to the creative knowledge which he already has, whereas God cannot passively receive any knowledge from his creatures.) Since all God's knowledge comes

Marquette University Press
New Title Announcement

The Problems of Suffering and Evil

By John Cowburn, SJ

ISBN 978-0-87462-805-0
Paperback | 265 pages | $27.00

Order Information
Toll free from US and Canada: 1-800-247-6553
Direct: +1 419 281-1802 Fax: +1 419 281-6883
www.marquette.edu/mupress/

We hope you find the accompanying book interesting enough to have it reviewed in your pages. If you do publish a review please send a copy or a link to:

Marquette University Press
P.O. Box 3141
Milwaukee, WI 53201-3141
maureen.kondrick@marquette.edu

Thank you

from within himself, there is nothing which God does not know, and because he is pure goodness, everything is good.

A short history of this theory

In the Middle Ages, Thomas Aquinas maintained that because God is the universal cause of all created beings, his will is always done.[9] This was already a Christian view, and after the Reformation it remained so. Leibniz (1646-1716), a German Protestant, said that of all possible worlds "God must needs have chosen the best",[10] and he is often quoted as having said that everything is for the best in this best of possible worlds.

In 1609 Alphonsus Rodriguez (1538-1616) published *The Practice of Christian and Religious Perfection*, which was read by thousands of people (including me) for centuries. In it he said that while it is agreed that "the evils which happen by natural causes, or from irrational creatures, as sickness, hunger, thirst, heat, and cold, come from the hand of God" and contribute to our greater good and profit, some people think that "the evils which happen by means of man ... come not from God's hand, nor are directed by the order of his providence", and hence may not be good for us; but, he said, in every vicious or sinful action "the cause of the action is God".[11] Of great natural disasters he said:

> We are to look upon these chastisements as the effects of his holy will; which, by a secret and hidden judgement, has decreed them, for certain purposes, conducive to his greater glory and service.

In seventeenth-century England, Milton, who was a Puritan, said:

> What th' unsearchable dispose [disposition]
> Of highest wisdom brings about,
> And ever best found in the close.

He found this verified in Samson's death:

---

9 "Dicendum quod necesse est voluntatem Dei simper impleri" (*Summa theologiae*, 1 19 6 the whole article).

10 Leibniz, *Theodicy*, 8, p. 128.

11 Rodriguez, *The Practice of Christian and Religious Perfection*, ch. 2.

> *Nothing was here for tears, nothing to wail*
> *For in his death there was nothing but well and fair*
> *And what may quiet us in a death so noble.*[12]

When people believe that everything that happens was willed by God and is therefore good, and something goes seriously wrong for them, they are often troubled but if they hold on to their belief, and accept it in their hearts, whereas their friends expect them to be in despair, they are at peace with what has happened. For this they may be admired for the strength of their faith. This is possibly why this view is widely accepted, though I doubt whether many people took it to the wild extreme of a woman in France who, according to Ronald Knox quoting Bossuet, endowed a series of Masses to be said "in thanksgiving to God for having decreed her salvation or damnation, as the case might be".[13]

In the eighteenth century, optimism was highly fashionable, and in *An Essay on Man* Alexander Pope put into verse some ideas which Lord Bolingbroke (1678-1751) had given to him in writing:

> *All Nature is but Art, unknown to thee;*
> *All Chance, Direction, which thou canst not see;*
> *All Discord, Harmony not understood;*
> *All partial Evil, universal Good:*
> *And, spite of Pride, in erring Reason's spite,*
> *One truth is clear: whatever is, is right.*[14]

It seems that during this century, in educated circles it became common to deny divine revelation, and hence Christianity, and to affirm belief in a non-personal supreme being, which the Masons represented with a compass and set-square and which would probably be represented today by a computer, programmed to govern all events.

In the middle of this century (to be precise on All Saints Day, 1 November, 1755), an earthquake occurred in Lisbon which caused a mental distress all over Europe.[15] At about half past nine in the morning there was a rumbling noise and a trembling of the earth, followed by a pause. Then the earth shook for two minutes, bringing

---

12 Milton, *Samson Agonistes*, last speech of Chorus.
13 Knox, *Enthusiasm*, p. 273.
14 Pope, *An Essay on Man*, Epistle I (1732), section X.
15 See Kendrick, *The Lisbon Earthquake*.

down buildings and doing other damage. After a second pause, there was another shock, which did further damage. By this time the air was thick with dust and no one could see what was happening. A quarter of an hour later this dust was beginning to settle and it was seen that fires had broken out. They spread. The waters of the Dagos became agitated and began to rise. At half past ten or eleven o'clock an aftershock did serious damage to the western parts of the city and brought down a church in which people had taken refuge, while waves of water broke over the quays and foreshore and did damage there. In the course of the morning thousands of people were crushed to death and hundreds died in the fires. This shook the belief which many people had in God's benevolence and complete control. However, within a short time it was said that it had been a blessing in disguise.

In Portugal, a Franciscan friar preached and later published a "consolatory sermon" in the form of an address given by Jesus to the Portugese people, in which he told them that they should be proud of having been singled out in such a special way by divine providence. In Lisbon, a Jesuit, Gabriel Malagrida, who like me had probably had to read Rodriguez in the noviceship, made himself a nuisance to the civil authorities, because while they were trying to get the city rebuilt as quickly as possible he said that by means of the earthquake God had told people to turn their minds away from the things of this world and give themselves entirely to prayer. (He, poor man, was later found guilty of heresy and in 1761 he was publicly strangled).

In the eighteenth century someone wrote a book which was passed from hand to hand in a convent for over a century, after which it was shown to Henri Ramière, a French Jesuit, who published it in 1861 as *L'abandon à la providence divine* (the English translation, published in 1933, was called *Self-Abandonment to Divine Providence*). For over a century it was attributed to Jean-Pierre de Caussade (1675-1751) and letters attributed to him were added to it.[16] Two principles were stated:

> First, that there is nothing so small or apparently trifling, even the fall of a leaf, that is not ordained or permitted by God; second, that God is sufficiently wise, good, powerful and merciful to turn the most seemingly disastrous events to the good and profit of those who are capable of adoring and humbly accepting all these

---

16 It seems not to be known who actually wrote this work.

manifestations of his divine and adorable will. Is there anything more consoling in religion than these two principles?[17]

It was said:

> The soul that sees the will of God in the smallest things or in the most distressing and fatal events, accepts them all with equal joy, gladness and respect.[18]

That was said over and over again, in different words. One should perhaps remember that the author was writing private letters, not a book for the general public. He was urging enclosed nuns to obey with gladness all the rules of the order, to obey all decrees of superiors (however foolish they seemed), and to accept any misfortunes which might befall them in the convent. Fortunately, this idea did not catch on.

In the nineteenth century, Browning wrote the often-quoted line:

> *God's in his heaven, all's right with the world.*

Also in the nineteenth century there was a revival of scholastic philosophy in the Catholic Church, and it was virtually imposed on all Catholic tertiary institutions. With it came a revival of this optimism, which became the Catholic doctrine. In *Foundations of Thomistic Philosophy*, published in French in 1927, Antonin-Gilbert Sertillanges said:

> In order to have a right idea of Providence, we must know whether God's will is always obeyed. We give an affirmative answer to this question, because God is the cause of universal being, and all being must obey his law. A cause infallibly attains its effect, unless impeded by something which is not subject to it. Since God is the cause of all things, nothing can escape his causality, and therefore nothing can impede the complete realisation of his effects.[19]

If I fire an arrow at a target and a gust of wind carries it off course so that I miss, this is because while I can aim the arrow I cannot control the air. But because God controls everything,

---

17   Caussade, *Self-Abandonment to the Will of God*, letter 10, p. 123.
18   Ibid., book 1, ch. 2, p. 20.
19   Sertillanges (1863-1948), *Foundations of Thomistic Philosophy*, p. 141.

his action always attains its end. Everything he created is according to his pre-established plan, which includes even contingencies [seemingly chance events] and free acts.[20]

In the twentieth century, Peter Geach, an English philosopher who may have been influenced by scholastic philosophy, said that God is like a world champion chess player playing games with amateurs: the amateurs think that they are working out their own moves, but in fact

> God is the supreme Grand Master who has everything under his control. Some of the players are consciously helping his plan, others are trying to hinder it: whatever the finite players do, God's plan will be executed. ... God cannot be surprised or thwarted or cheated or disappointed.[21]

I am sure that he believed he was simply putting in words what all Catholics believed, and so was Cardinal Suhard when he said:

> Events themselves are a means of recognising the will of God. Providence speaks through facts. As long as events are in the future, they remain the mystery of divine good-pleasure. But once they have happened, they reveal to us God's decision.[22]

More recently, Ernesto Cardenal, a Latin-American poet, said:

> Everything that happens is a sacrament of God's will. ... Every historical event is as sacred as the sacred Scriptures, because it is also an expression of the will of God.[23]

> We should gladly accept everything that happens because everything that happens, however unpleasant it appears, is for our good.[24]

The idea that what God wills is the universe as whole

A certain kind of cleric might, with a confidence which was probably just good acting, have maintained that all is well and should be accepted as ultimately beneficial, but the necessity for explanations, even qualifications, was felt and one idea which went round was that while everything that happens is willed by God and is therefore good,

---

20 Ibid., p. 148.
21 Geach, *Providence and Evil*, p. 58.
22 Suhard, *Collected Writings*, p. 12.
23 Cardenal, *Love*, p. 105.
24 Ibid.

everything is not necessarily beneficial to every individual person. Rather, everything is good for *the whole* – in the end, for the created universe from its beginning to the end which is ahead of it. Augustine said: "Every part which does not fit into its whole is evil"[25] and in the *Summa Contra Gentiles* Thomas Aquinas said:

> A particular being exists for the good of the whole of which it is a part; it is a means by which the good of the whole is obtained. So God wills every particular being in the universe for the good of the universe.

He went on: "God wills man's existence in order that the universe may be complete", and he said: "The good of the whole universe is what God primarily wills and intends".[26] Lest anyone thinks that Thomas was talking about things, not persons, I will quote this: "Among all creatures, rational creatures are most principally ordered to the good of the universe".[27] In the eighteenth century Bolingbroke, whom I mentioned earlier, said that the universe must not be judged by what happens to individual beings, and Soames Jenyns said:

> The universe resembles a large and well-regulated family, in which all the officers and servants, and even the domestic animals, are subservient to each other in a proper subordination; each enjoys the privileges and perquisites peculiar to his place, and at the same time contributes, by that just subordination, to the magnificence and happiness of the whole.[28]

Another thinker of that time criticised Voltaire because, he said, "he considers the unhappiness and destruction of a certain number of individuals as an evil in the universe".[29] In an article which he wrote a year after the Lisbon earthquake of 1755, Kant said that we are a part of

---

25 *Confessions*, ch. 8; quoted by Thomas Aquinas in *Summa Theologiae*, 2-2 47 10 ad 2.

26 Thomas Aquinas, *Summa Contra Gentiles*, 1, 86. In the *Summa Theologiae* he said: "The good of the whole universe is properly intended by God" (1 15 5 c).

27 Ibid., 1 27 2 c.

28 Jenyns, *A Free Inquiry into the Nature and Origin of Evil*, quoted in Lovejoy, *The Great Chain of Being*, p. 207.

29 Grimm, quoted in Vereker, *Eighteenth-Century Optimism*, p. 146.

nature, and divine wisdom is concerned with the whole.[30] In an article about optimism he said that he was going to try to understand "that the whole is best, and it is for the sake of the whole that everything is good".[31] He was at that time, in his pre-critical phase, being unoriginal and repeating what most educated people were saying.

There is a certain plausibility about this. When a violinist plays a great melody, for instance, there is little beauty in each note, taken separately, but the melody as a whole is beautiful; and a great symphony may have moments of dissonance in it and a great play may have events which, taken by themselves, are distressing, but we enjoy the symphony and the play as wholes, and if someone were to want to remove those moments we would insist that they be kept in.

To anyone who thought in this way, a very layered society, with a downstairs class subservient to an upstairs class, miners suffering horribly as they produced coal for upper-class people, and Africans and Asians working for Europeans in servile ways, seemed perfectly natural. In some religious orders there were lay brothers and lay sisters who were thought to exist in order to serve the priests and choir sisters. Also, when women were deemed to be inferior to men in intelligence, prudence and other virtues, a society in which women were expected to serve their superiors, men, seemed quite in order. To anyone who had this mind-set, it seemed natural that decisions should be made by the superior people. Social equality and equal participation of everyone in the making of decisions seemed monstrous, and if life was hard for many, that was natural and in order.

The analogy of a play

When a play is performed, it has natural troubles such as sickness, and the characters unthinkingly make mistakes; also, they make free decisions into which they put much thought, and sometimes they deliberately do wrong. If I am in the audience, I see characters making

---

30 "Wir wissen, dass der ganze Inbegriff der Natur ein würdiger Gegenstand der göttlichen Weisheit und seine Anstalten sei. Wir sind ein Teil derselben und wollen das Ganze sein." (Kant, "Geschichte und Naturbeschreibung der merkwürdigsten Vorfällen des Erdbebens, welches an dem Ende des 1755sten Jahres einen grossen Teil der Erde erschuttert hat", *Werke*, vol. 2, p. 472.)

31 Kant, "Versuch einiger Betrachtungen über den Optimismus" (1759), *Werke*, vol. 2, p. 37.

decisions of their own free will. However, the play was written by an author and the characters always do what he or she decided. This can be seen as providing an analogy with real life, in which we make free decisions and at the same time always do what God has decided we will do. (Otherwise, he would not know what we do, for he knows what we do only by being conscious of his own decisions.)

The author of a play is not blamed for either mistaken or immoral decisions made by his or her characters, but the characters are blamed for what they do. This, too, provides an analogy with real life, in which people make immoral decisions, for which they are blamed and punished, but God, like the author, should not be blamed.

Suppose that a theatre manager has to select a play to be performed in his theatre, and suppose that he considers several plays and finally says, "We'll do *Hamlet*". From that single decision flow many events, before and during the play. Similarly, prior to creation God considered millions, perhaps an infinite number, of possible universes, each with its own history from start to finish, and he chose the one we are in now. Prior to his decision, he faced possible universes, one with everyone well behaved all the time and another with Adam sinning and being thrown out of the Garden of Eden, Christ coming to die for sinners and so redeeming them, Christ founding his Church and so on and so on; and he chose this universe. He was like a theatre manager who could have chosen to stage an escapist comedy but chose to stage a drama, and we are like actors who have small parts in a great play and who, when they have not read the whole play, should trust the author.

CRITICISM OF THIS VIEW

Some literary rejections of the idea that all is for the best

One of the great attacks on total optimism is Voltaire's novella, *Candide*, which was written after the Lisbon earthquake, about which Voltaire also wrote a poem. In it Dr Pangloss – the name means something like Dr Explainaway – suffers one disaster after another and keeps coming up for more, saying "The worse the disaster, the better, because a proportionately greater good must come of it to counterbalance the greater harm done". "Private misfortunes," he says, "contribute to the general good, so that the more private misfortunes there are, the more we find that all is well".[32] He is made to appear utterly ridiculous, and "Panglossian" has become a derogatory term for this kind of optimism.

A more recent attack is that of Albert Camus, who wrote *The Plague* (1947), which is about an outbreak of bubonic plague in Oran. It is an analogy of the German occupation of France from 1940 to 1944. In another book Camus said that the Christian faith "presumes the acceptance of the mystery and of evil, and resignation to injustice".[33] In *The Plague*, a Jesuit, Père Paneloux, says of the plague that

> since it was God's will, we, too, should will it. Thus and thus only the Christian could face the problem squarely and, scorning subterfuge, pierce to the heart of the supreme issue, the essential choice. And his choice would be to believe everything, so as not to be forced into denying everything.[34]

That is, he had to believe that everything is for the best and accept it, since to do otherwise would have been to deny Christianity in its entirety. In the novel, Dr Rieux, who stands for Camus himself, treats people, including children, dying in agony and he says: "Until my dying day I shall refuse to love a scheme of things in which children are put to torture".[35] Clearly, he believes that the existing world is such a scheme and while he refuses to love it he does all he can to make it a less horrible place.

Dostoyevsky's *The Brothers Karamazov* (1880) contains a famous passage which expresses agony because the speaker cannot reconcile

---

32 Voltaire, *Candide* (ca. 1789), ch. 4. I find it interesting that optimism is represented in *Candide* not by a priest, as in *The Plague* by Camus, but by a secular thinker, who represents eighteenth-century deists. *Candide* has been made into a musical with music by Leonard Bernstein (1956, revised 1988).
33 Camus, *The Rebel* (1952) p. 56.
34 Camus, *The Plague*, p. 184. In Resistance circles Camus became a friend of a Dominican priest, Père Bruckberger, and he probably based his idea of Christian teaching on what Bruckberger said, attributing Bruckberger's ideas to a Jesuit.
35 Camus, *The Plague*, p. 178.

what he has seen with what he thinks is the Christian belief. In it Ivan Karamazov says that children suffer and he says to Aloysha:

> Tell me frankly, I appeal to you – answer me: imagine that it is you yourself who are erecting the edifice of human destiny with the aim of making men happy in the end, of giving them peace and contentment at last, but that to do that it is absolutely necessary, and indeed quite inevitable, to torture to death only one tiny creature, the little girl who beat her breast with her little fist, and to found the edifice on her unavenged tears – would you consent to be the architect on those conditions? Tell me and do not lie!

Aloysha replies: "No, I wouldn't".[36]

That the theory is incredible

It is simply not believable that all turns out to be, in the end, for the best. Some afflicted people say that, as Christians, they believe that all is for the best but they do not understand how their afflictions can be. They are heroic, but underneath what they say there may be a subconscious hostility to God. Others simply decide that they do not believe what they have been taught and abandon Christianity altogether, choosing to live like Dr Rieux.

A basic flaw: free will

I will deal with this later, when I affirm free will at some length and make it the basis of a different theory. I will also affirm chance, which is similarly incompatible with this optimism. Omnipotence was defined above in such a way that it implicitly denied free will. I will deal at length with chance later.

In the theory which I outlined, human persons make bad choices *because God has so decided*. The ultimate responsibility is God's. Also, the theory implies that after I have done something, whatever it was, I should say to myself that it was precisely what God decided would happen, and it was what he wanted to happen, therefore I should not in any sense be sorry I did it. If it was not what he decided, according to this theory he would not even know about it. Moreover, if I have to make a difficult decision I should say to myself that whatever I decide to do will be what God wills, which means that, instead of thinking

---

[36] Dostoyevsky, *The Brothers Karamazov*, book 5, chap. 5; Penguin edn., pp. 287-288.

and praying for hours and consulting many people, I can do anything at all and go and play golf. This cannot be right.

Criticism of the play analogy

When we see a play, we distinguish in our minds between two human beings, the actor and the character, a real person and a fiction. For instance, if an actor whom we admire is playing a murderer, we can detest the murderer and then, at the end of the play, applaud the actor, whereas we would not applaud a real-life murderer. We are real persons, not characters in a play, and there is no analogy.

Also, if an author attends a performance of a play which he himself has written and in which a character is a despicable villain, he may be appalled at one level by what he sees happening on the stage, and despise the character, while at a deeper level be pleased to see what he wrote being well performed. Going backstage after the production he may tell the man who played the villain how much he had enjoyed his performance. We surely must not imagine God, when he saw that Adam had eaten the apple, being superficially angry and dismissing Adam and Eve from the garden, while at a deeper level saying to himself, "This will set the stage for me to send my Son to redeem mankind, which is why I willed it".

The whole and the part

I said earlier that it has been said that it is the universe as a whole, not any individual person, that matters to God and should matter to us, and that this enables us to accept all troubles. It is, however, now accepted that every person has value in himself or herself. When a soldier is killed, we ought not to say that ultimately his death does not matter, because what matters is the country as a whole, and if a young person dies of a drug overdose we ought not to say that while that seems bad we can be sure that in the long run it will turn out to have been for the best. If a young man becomes a drug addict, despairs and kills himself, I would not tell his parents that God willed the addiction and death because in some mysterious way they have been beneficial to the universe as a whole, which is what matters.

The inhumanly cheerful repression of anger and grief: the denial of tragedy.

When a very old person dies peacefully after a happy life, we may feel a certain sadness but we feel – we not only think, we feel – that the death was natural or right, and we are easily consoled. If he or she has had a long and painful illness, or has had dementia, and at last dies, we are sad but we say – for by this time we have accepted the sickness itself and we start from there – that the death was a happy release and we feel relief both for the sufferer and for his or her family and friends. Other deaths, however, are totally different from these and from deep within us there rises a shout of protest, which we stifle, and deep sadness fills our hearts. It is like this when a happy, healthy child suddenly dies or when a young married person with children is happy and healthy one week and dead the next. It is even more like this when a young person dies of an overdose and no one knows whether it was an accident or suicide. If at times like these a priest tells people that what happened was God's will and therefore for the best, he does them a great wrong, for instead of consoling them he adds guilt to their grief, or else he forces them to repress their feelings and so delays their attainment of peace. Whatever we say or do on these occasions, let us like Jesus himself begin with tears, for something dreadful has happened and it is "a time to weep" (Eccl 3:4): the time "when the bridegroom will be taken away" has come and it is the time to fast (Luke 5:35), that is, to mourn. Optimism is blind to all struggles of conscience, pains of guilt and dramas of repentance, forgiveness and reconciliation; it takes all substance out of the ideas of salvation and redemption; in short, it embodies a pathetically glossy, untragic view of human existence, and to assert it is to be like the monkeys which cover their ears and eyes and "hear no evil, see no evil".

Many writers on tragedy have said that there can be no such thing as a Christian tragedy. For instance, David D. Raphael says that whereas tragedy "treats evil as unalloyed evil; it regrets the waste of human worth of any kind, and does not think that innocent suffering can be justified", the religion of the Bible "is optimistic and trusts that evil is always a necessary means to a greater good"; it "praises submission" and "commends resignation".[37] This may be true of some popular Christianity, which denies tragedy and regards the tragic sense as

---

37 Raphael, "Tragedy and Religion", p. 55.

pagan; it implies that tragedies are fantasies which have no relation to real life, whereas fictions with happy endings are true to life; but there is a place for tragedy in "the religion of the Bible".

Permission

We have seen that some Christians have maintained that in the long run all events are for the best, so if something unpleasant occurs we should say to ourselves that *eventually* we will see that more good than harm came of them. We also saw that that is Panglossian and incredible. A way out would be to deny that God has total control of events and to say that the event was not in his control, so that while the event was unpleasant he should not be blamed for it. Some authors solved the problem, it seems to their own satisfaction, by saying that God does not himself *cause* all events but merely *permits* those which, to keep using this term, are unpleasant. Thus they put a certain distance between God and these events. They add that when he permits something to happen he is not like a headmaster who knows that a teacher *may* excessively punish a certain student and decides to stand back and let him do whatever he chooses to do. If he did that, he would have no control over the event. He is like a headmaster who, when he decides to let the teacher do as he chooses, knows for a fact either that he will punish the student excessively or that he will not do that. He permits unpleasant events to happen when he knows that they will have predominantly good consequences in the long run. Consider this example:

> A man is driving his car past an old weatherboard church one evening and sees that a fire has broken out in it. It is still small and he could stop his car, go in and put it out. However, he quickly judges that it would be to the good if that church were to burn down and be replaced by a modern one. He therefore decides to let the fire continue. He drives on and, sure enough, the church burns down and, with money from the insurance and an appeal, a better church is built.

According to what I might call "the permission idea", God is analogous to this man. For instance, just as he does not start the fire but lets it continue because the destruction of the church is desirable, so God does not as a rule send hurricanes to destroy cities, but when he sees that a hurricane is approaching a city, if he sees that more good than harm will come of its reaching the city, he permits it do so.

3 A Version of the Fall & Redemption

The Fall

The Bible has a story of the creation of the first human beings, Adam and Eve. According to it, they lived in safety and prosperity in what was called the Garden of Eden. It needed some work, which was enjoyable, as work is in a garden, and (though this is not mentioned) they did not need to be afraid of animals or any other aspect of nature. They seem to have had a sort of sunny sexual innocence, thanks to which they were nude without embarrassment. However, God told them not to eat any of the fruit of a particular tree, and they ate some. At once "the eyes of both of them were opened and they realised that they were naked" (Gen 3:7). They had lost their innocence and, when he discovered what had happened, God made clothes for them. The Fall had occurred. I will now go beyond this story to the "theory" behind it.

The authors of Genesis believed in what we call retributive justice, and to have regarded it as something which seems to have bound even God, who necessarily punished Adam and Eve by expelling them from the garden and sending them into a world in which the man would have to work hard to survive, the woman would experience pain when she gave birth to children, and they would suffer in various ways. Augustine said that all unpleasantness (that was not his term) is either sin or punishment for sin. The intellectual problem of reconciling divine control with the existence of evil and suffering was solved by means of retributive justice.

Adam and Eve had children, who, besides being born into the fallen world, inherited their lack of innocence and the need to wear clothes. They also inherited their guilt, because of which they themselves needed to be punished. All later descendants inherited this guilt. Moreover, they have committed sins of their own, or personal sins. Fortunately, the story does not stop there. God the Father decided to send his Son to suffer and so to satisfy the demands of justice and restore the relationship between the divine and human persons.

Merits of this theory

The extremely optimistic theory which I outlined in chapter 2 (not the first part) had an idea of God which was basically Aristotelian, metaphysical and impersonal. It was a complete contrast to the idea of the gods which was current in Athens at the time, and which I feel sure no thoughtful Athenian took seriously. The Fall-and-Redemption theory has a more personal, I might even say a more human, idea of God. Things happen against his will and he reacts to them. I will say here that I regard this as a great merit of the theory. Also, instead of maintaining that all is for the best, holders of this theory let evil be evil.

Criticism of the theory

For one thing, it is now known that much suffering has natural causes which were active long before there were any human beings. For instance, earthquakes are caused by movements of plates deep in the earth which were causing earthquakes long before the first human beings appeared, and it is safe to say that there were bushfires in Australia before there were human beings here or anywhere else.

For another, the couple in the Book of Genesis are more or less like us in intellectual ability. They are able to understand a command and to make a moral decision. It was surely millenia before human beings reached this stage. Also, some people are born with deformations which, if they are punishments for sin, cannot be for any personal sins and cannot be for original sin, either, since it is presumably the same for all, which the deformations are not.

As it was often presented, this theory included a selection by God of those who are finally redeemed. Augustine maintained that not all human beings are saved. He said that only some are saved and that they manifest God's mercy and forgiveness, while others are unredeemed and, when they die, go to hell, thus manifesting God's justice. He said that whether a particular man or woman is saved or not depends entirely on God's choice – it depends in no way on him or her. Fortunately, this has not become a general belief. Nobody knows how many, or what proportion of human beings, go to heaven or hell, but it was and is generally believed that it depends on them.

3 ※ A Version of the Fall & Redemption

Finally, in practice some Christians have been so insistent on sin and hell that their version of Christianity has been frightening, and far from good news. They quote Jesus, who said: "The gate is narrow and the road is hard that leads to life, and there are few who find it" (Matt 7:14). In many popular presentations of Christian, especially Catholic, beliefs, hell was far more vivid than grace, and fear was felt more strongly than hope. The most famous sermon of this kind is probably the one given by a Jesuit in James Joyce's *A Portrait of the Artist as a Young Man*. Redemptorists used to be famous for their hellfire sermons, which were usually the highlights of their missions. Fr Furniss (I am not making this up) had probably preached many of them and he decided to put a long one into a book. He wanted to instil fear of hell into his child-readers, to make them avoid sin, and for this reason he laid it on when he described hell in a book for children called *The Sight of Hell* which was published in the nineteenth century. In it he took the children, his readers, on an imaginary tour of hell, from which I quote:

> See! On the middle of that red-hot floor stands a girl; she looks about sixteen years old. Her feet are bare. She has neither shoes nor stockings. ... Listen! She speaks. She says, "I have been standing on this red-hot floor for years. Day and night my only standing-place has been this red-hot floor. ... Look at my burnt and bleeding feet. Let me go off this burning floor for one moment, only for one single short moment." ... The fourth dungeon is the boiling kettle. ... In the middle of it there is a boy. ... His eyes are burning like two burning coals. Two long flames come out of his ears. ... Sometimes he opens his mouth, and blazing fire rolls out. But listen! There is a sound like a kettle boiling. ... The blood is boiling in the scalded veins of that boy. The brain is boiling and bubbling in his head. The marrow is boiling in his bones. ... The fifth dungeon is the red-hot oven. ... The little child is in this red-hot oven. Hear how it screams to come out. See how it turns and twists itself about in the fire. It beats its head against the roof of the oven. It stamps its little feet on the floor. ... God was very good to this child. Very likely God saw that it would get worse and worse, and would never repent, and so would have to be punished much more in hell. So God in his mercy called it out of the world in its early childhood.[1]

---

1   J. Furniss, *The Sight of Hell*, quoted in Lecky, *History of European Morals from Augustus to Charlemagne*, (1869), vol. II, pp. 223-224, footnote.

On Fr Furniss's principles, if God had really wanted to be kind to those children, he could have called them out of the world when they had just been baptised, so that they would not have had to be punished at all in hell but would, instead, have gone straight to heaven. It seems to have occurred to Fr Furniss that what he had described was hard to reconcile with the goodness of God, he said that "God was very good to this child", and he tried to explain how that could be. As a result, he only made things worse. This, I admit, is an extreme example, but perhaps at all times there have been Christian preachers whose main aim was to inspire fear.

4 Extreme Pessimism

The world as meaningless

At the other extreme from total optimism, there is utter pessimism. There is, first, the view that there is no inherent pattern or design in the universe, or certainly not in the things that happen to people. Events follow each other, sometimes bringing good to persons and sometimes bringing bad, without any reason. Moreover, whatever we say, do or become will ultimately be swept away, so that in the end nothing really matters. Life, in this view, is in the end

> a tale
> Told by an idiot, full of sound and fury,
> Signifying nothing[1]

and the world is "a senseless and detestable piece of work".[2] James Thomson wrote:

> The world rolls round for ever like a mill;
> It grinds out death and life and good and ill;
> It has no purpose, heart or mind or will.[3]

In Somerset Maugham's *Of Human Bondage*, Philip – who stands for Maugham himself – realised that

> there was no meaning in life, and man by living served no end. It was immaterial whether he was born or not born, whether he lived or ceased to live. Life was insignificant and death without consequence. ... What he did or left undone did not matter. Failure was unimportant and success amounted to nothing.[4]

Bertrand Russell wrote:

> That Man is the product of causes which had no prevision of the end they were achieving; that his origin, his growth, his hopes and

---

1 Shakespeare, *Macbeth*, 5 5 25-27.
2 Voltaire, *Candide*, ch. 23, p. 110.
3 James Thomson (1734-82), *The City of Dreadful Night*, section 8.
4 Somerset Maugham, *Of Human Bondage* (1915), ch. 106, p. 809.

fears, his loves and his beliefs, are but the outcome of accidental collocations of atoms; that no fire, no heroism, no intensity of thought and feeling, can preserve an individual life beyond the grave; that all the labours of the ages, all the devotion, all the inspiration, all the noonday brightness of human genius, are destined to extinction in the vast death of the solar system, and that the whole temple of Man's achievement must inevitably be buried beneath the debris of a universe in ruins – all these things, if not quite beyond dispute, are yet so nearly certain, that no philosophy which rejects them can hope to stand. Only within the scaffolding of these truths, only on the firm foundation of unyielding despair, can the soul's habitation henceforth be safely built.[5]

Jean Rostand, a French scientist, said:

> The human race will die out just as dinosaurs and stegocephalia died out. Little by little the small star that serves as our sun will lose its power to give light and heat. ... Then, of the whole civilisation, human or superhuman – its discoveries, philosophies, ideals, religions – nothing will persist. ... In this tiny corner of the universe the odd adventure of protoplasm will be finished forever.

He said that "the adventure" may have run its course in some other worlds and be beginning in others,

> everywhere sustained by the same illusions, provocative of the same torments, everywhere just as absurd, just as vain, as doomed from the outset to ultimate failure and to infinite darkness.[6]

The world as evil

An even gloomier view than this one is that the universe is inherently destructive, malign, vicious or in a word evil. According to Paul Ricoeur, Greek tragedy embodied an idea that could not be openly expressed – that the gods who rule the world are wicked, or that there is an inherent malice in being.[7] Una Ellis-Fermor writes of "Satanic dramas" in which it is implied that particular evil events are but manifestations of the inherently evil nature of the universe: Marlowe, she says, "did not question the nature of the world-order. He saw it steadi-

---

5   Russell, "The Free Man's Worship" (1903), in *The Basic Writings of Bertrand Russell*, p. 67.
6   Rostand, *The Substance of Man*, pp. 60-61.
7   Ricoeur, *The Symbolism of Evil*, pp. 211-226.

ly and saw it evil".[8] In Shakespeare's *Troilus and Cressida*, she says, the existence of a principle of order in the cosmos and in human affairs "vanishes, revealing destruction as the principle underlying all life".[9]

The rejection of religion

Some writers have said in effect that because God is responsible for all the pain in the world, they want to have nothing to do with him. Byron's Cain, talking to Lucifer, wonders why he and Lucifer exist and says:

> *To produce destruction*
> *Can surely never be the task of joy,*
> *And yet my sire [Adam] says he[God]'s omnipotent:*
> *Then why is Evil – he being Good? I asked*
> *This question of my father; and he said,*
> *"Because this Evil only was the path*
> *To Good". Strange Good, that must arise from out*
> *It's deadly opposite.*[10]

Lautréamont's Maldoror (1868) says to God:

> If, when you please, you send cholera to ravage cities, or death to carry off in its claws – without any distinction – the four ages of life, I do not wish to ally myself with so redoutable a friend.[11]

In *The City of Dreadful Night* (1874), the Scottish poet James Thomson said:

> *Who is most wretched in this dolorous place?*
> *I think myself; yet I would rather be*
> *My miserable self than he, than he*
> *Who formed such creatures to his own disgrace.*[12]

And so on for page after page. Some authors have even become anti-theists,

---

8   Ellis-Fermor, *The Frontiers of Drama*, pp. 141-142.
9   Ibid., p. 70.
10 Byron, *Cain*, II,2,282-289. My inverted commas.
11 *Lautréamont's Maldoror*, p. 68.
12 James Thomson, *The City of Dreadful Night*, section 8.

Souls that dare look the omnipotent tyrant in
His everlasting face, and tell him that
His evil is not good![13]

The Marquis de Sade

Baudelaire said that in discussions of evil one always come back to Sade (1740-1814) and to him we now come.[14] Until the eighteenth century, optimism was generally based on belief in a benevolent personal God; in the eighteenth century many thinkers talked about an impersonal absolute being or about Nature, to which they attributed a sort of unemotional benevolence. Sade then entered and said: "I bow to evidence only, and evidence I perceive only through my senses; my belief goes no further than that, beyond that point my faith collapses".[15] And when I look at nature, he went on, "is there any limit to the injustices we see her commit all the time?" I see how animals live, and how savages in a state of nature live. I observe that man's inborn and hence most natural impulses are violent and lustful. And I say: Take nature for your guide, imitate her, do what she impels you to do, yield to your passions which are the means Nature employs to attain her ends:

> Must we not yield to the dominion of those [inclinations] Nature has inserted in us? ... Were Nature offended by these proclivities, she would not have inspired them in us; that we can receive from her hands a sentiment such as would outrage her is impossible, and, extremely certain of this, we can give ourselves up to our passions whatever their sort and whatever their violence, wholly sure that the

---

13 Byron, *Cain*, I,1,138-140 (spoken by Lucifer).

14 Sade, after whom sadism is named, is best known as a pornographer whose writings are still probably the most extreme of their kind. For years the publication and distribution of his books were illegal but they were printed secretly and sold to members of particular circles. Mario Praz, *The Romantic Agony*, first published in Italian in 1933 and later translated into other languages and published in several editions, told of his influence and made him more widely known. Now, however, his works are sold openly and many books have been written about him. A number of films have been made and *Salo* (Pasolini, 1974), which is one of the most banned films of recent times, is based on one of his books.

15 Sade, "Dialogue Between a Priest and a Dying Man", in *Justine, Philosophy in the Bedroom and Other Writing*, p. 168. Sade was attacking the fashionable deism of his time.

discomfitures their shock may occasion are naught but the designs of Nature, of whom we are the involuntary instruments.[16]

This means that to be true to Nature we should do many things that are now regarded as crimes. If Nature could talk it would say to us:

> Idiots, sleep, eat, and fearlessly commit whatever crimes you like whenever you like: every one of those alleged infamies pleases me, and I would have them all, since it is I who inspire them in you. ... If there exists a crime to be committed against me it is the resistance you oppose, in the forms of stubbornness or casuistries, to what I inspire in you.[17]

In Nature, argues Sade, there is no love or kindness, and so these ought to be sedulously avoided. "You mention, Eugenie, ties of love; may you never know them!" For "nothing is more an egoist than Nature; then let us be egoists too, if we wish to live in harmony with her dictates".[18] The wolf which devours the lamb acts according to Nature, and the man who understands nature "no longer fears to be selfish, to reduce everyone about him, and he sates his appetites without inquiring to know what his enjoyments may cost others, without remorse".[19] Sade takes the reasoning a stage further when he argues positively for cruelty to others. "Cruelty, far from being a vice, is the first sentiment Nature injects in us all."[20] Savages are cruel until civilisation teaches them kindness, thus rendering them unnatural – "Cruelty is simply the energy in a man civilisation has not yet altogether corrupted; therefore it is a virtue, not a vice".[21] And in sexual experiences, it is "very essential that the man never take his pleasure except at the expense of the woman".[22]

---

16   Sade, *Justine*, p. 607. French does not have the word "it" and the translator has chosen to use "she" and "who" of Nature where he could equally well have used "it" and "which". Simone de Beauvoir says that "there was nothing new in the view that Nature is evil". Sade, she says, had read Hobbes, who had lived almost two centuries earlier, and who said that nature is full of violence and that man is a wolf to man, and others had expressed similar views. (De Beauvoir, *The Marquis de Sade*, p. 58.)

17   Ibid., p. 609.

18   Sade, *Philosophy in the Bedroom*, pp. 285-286.

19   Sade, *Justine*, p. 608.

20   Sade, *Philosophy in the Bedroom*, p. 253.

21   Ibid., p. 254.

22   Sade, *Justine*, p. 604.

So far, what Sade has done is to maintain as devoutly as anyone before him that Nature is the ethical norm, but then he goes his own way and observes that Nature is cruel and concludes that cruelty is good. He now changes his ground and says that Nature is inherently, profoundly evil. He writes:

> A God exists. A hand has created all I see, but for ill. ... It is in evil that he created the world, it is by evil that he keeps it in being, it is for evil that he perpetuates it, it is impregnated with evil that the creature should exist, it is to the womb of evil that it returns after its existence is over. ... I see eternal and universal evil in the world.[23]

He concludes that we ought to do evil, and his heroes and heroines hurl themselves into evil, seen as evil. A woman cries out:

> Oh, Satan, one and unique god of my soul, inspire thou in me something yet more, present further perversions to my smoking heart, and then shalt thou see how I shall plunge myself into them all.[24]

How pessimists live

That is one way of living in a world that is meaningless or even malevolent. There are others.

Some people, seeing the world as meaningless or evil, fall into despair and say with the chorus in Sophocles' *Oedipus*: "I call none happy who beholds the light", or "Not to be born were of all things the best; but, if born, to die as soon as possible". They say:

> *This life itself holds nothing good for us,*
> *But it ends soon and nevermore can be.*[25]
>
> *This little life is all we must endure,*
> *The grave's most holy peace is ever sure;*[26]

and they commit suicide or are kept alive only by a biological drive that they do not have enough strength of will to resist.

Others seek a solution in art. Nietzsche writes that man sees the horribleness and absurdity of being and is nauseated. Also, he sees

---

23 Sade, *Juliette*, quoted in Praz, *The Romantic Agony*, ch 3, # 5, pp. 104-105.
24 Sade, *Philosophy in the Bedroom*, p. 272.
25 James Thomson, *The City of Dreadful Night*, section 16.
26 Ibid., section 14.

that action is useless. At this point, Nietzsche says, art approaches to save him. As only it can, it twists his insights into representations with which he can live; the sublime, which is the artistic subjugation of the horrible, and the comic, which is the artistic discharge of the nausea caused by the absurd.[27]

Yet others maintain their dignity and achieve a certain nobility by defiance. In "The Free Man's Worship" Bertrand Russell urged man,

> undismayed by the empire of chance, to preserve a mind free from the wanton tyranny that rules his outward life; proudly defiant of the irresistible forces that tolerate, for a moment, his knowledge and his condemnation, to sustain alone, a weary but unyielding Atlas, the world that his own ideals have fashioned despite the trampling march of unconscious power.[28]

Some authors maintain that this is the essence of tragedy. In a tragedy, they say, and I agree with them on this, something goes wrong for a person not because of some purely contingent circumstance but because of some deep if dimly perceived necessity: we miss the meaning of *King Lear*, for instance, if we think that it shows how great is the need for adequate homes for old people.[29] The tragic hero, these authors go on to say, defies and resists this necessity even as it crushes him, and so is great, even sublime, in his fall. The greatness of his opponent is greatness of physical power; his own greatness is greatness of spirit.[30] Thus tragedy "shows human effort to be sublime, a fit match for the sublimity of nature and nature's gods".[31] "Tragedy exalts man in our eyes."[32] The tragic attitude, according to this view, is expressed in exemplary fashion by Anouilh's Antigone and by the old rabbi in Maxwell Anderson's *Winterset*, who says:

> *and Mio – Mio, my son – know this where you lie,*
> *this is the glory of earth-born men and women,*
> *not to cringe, never to yield, but standing,*

---

27   Nietzsche, *The Birth of Tragedy*, end of # 7.
28   Russell, "The Free Man's Worship", in *The Basic Writings of Bertrand Russell*, p. 72.
29   Steiner makes this remark in *The Death of Tragedy*, p. 128.
30   Raphael, *The Paradox of Tragedy*, p. 27.
31   Raphael, "Tragedy and Religion", p. 55.
32   Raphael, *The Paradox of Tragedy*, p. 31.

> take defeat implacable and defiant,
> die unsubmitting.[33]

Finally, some people simply live in contradiction. On the one hand, they believe that nothing has meaning or value; on the other hand, they live and act as if some people or things do matter. One of Faulkner's characters says:

> You get born and you try this and you don't know why only you keep on trying it and you are born at the same time with a lot of other people, all mixed up with them, like trying to, having to, move your arms and legs with strings only the same strings are hitched to all the other arms and legs and the others all trying and they don't know why either except that the strings are all in one another's way like five or six people all trying to make a rug on the same loom only each one wants to weave his own pattern into the rug; and it can't matter, you know that, or the Ones that set up the loom would have arranged things a little better, and yet it must matter because you keep on trying or having to keep on trying and then all of a sudden it's all over.[34]

A comment on this pessimism

If in the long run nothing has lasting value or meaning, then in the last analysis there can be no morality and even the torture of a child does not finally matter. Camus says:

> If we believe in nothing, if nothing has any meaning and if we can affirm no value whatsoever, ... the murderer is neither right nor wrong. One is free to stoke the crematory fires or to give one's life to the care of lepers. Wickedness and virtue are just accident or whim.[35]

When anyone who holds this view contemplates crematory fires or lepers, he necessarily judges that it is meaningless to endeavour to do anything about them. Pessimism destroys action.

Also, the pessimistic theory of tragedy is not verified by many of what are indisputably the world's great tragedies. Shakespeare's tragedies, for instance, suppose not that the universe is absurd or even

---

33 Anderson, *Winterset* (1935), near the end, p. 133.
34 Faulkner, *Absolom, Absolom!* (1936), p. 127.
35 Camus, *The Rebel* (1952), p. 13.

malign but rather that it has a certain order or rightness: and they do not glorify the defiant shouting of "No" to being. Those who maintain that defiance is the essence of tragedy usually go on to say that therefore there can be no Christian tragedy. However, it is not Christianity but pessimism that excludes tragedy.

Part Two

The First of My Two Theories

5 Free Will & Chance: Indeterminism

Three kinds of event

I am now going to present two theories which differ both from the over-optimistic theory which I summarised earlier and from the Fall-and-Redemption theory. First (in this Part) I shall offer an explanation of misfortunes or natural troubles, that is, of suffering that is no one's fault. Then (in Part Three) I shall deal with the problem of moral evil. In both Parts it will be necessary for me to mention free will, about which I have written a book. I cannot assume that everyone who reads this book will have read it and I shall therefore, in this introductory chapter, offer a brief explanation of what I mean by it.

Necessary or predetermined events

Some events are necessary, which means that it is impossible that they not happen. For instance, that the sun will rise tomorrow is a necessary event. It used to be maintained, by determinists, that all events are necessary, even if we do not, in every case, know whether or when they will happen.

Free acts

Free will supposes multiple possibility. That is, if I am shopping and looking at two shirts, one red and one blue, it is possible for me to buy the red one and it is also possible for me to buy the blue one (it might also be possible for me to buy neither or both, but let that pass). More seriously, if an unmarried man has met an unmarried woman whom he likes, and who he has reason to believe likes him, it is usually possible for him to ask her to meet him somewhere and it is also possible for him to decide not to have anything personal to do with her. (Determinism is the belief that only one of these alternatives is possible, and that the agent is mistaken if he thinks that they both are.)

The situation which I have described changes when a person makes a decision or choice, one way or the other, and makes one alternative the thing which is going to happen and the other something which before the choice was possible but as a result of the choice will not happen. This choice involves *responsibility*. If a series of actions followed necessarily one from another, and an investigator follows the causal chain back, when the search comes to a situation in which various things were possible and a person chose one of them, that person will be held responsible for what happened.

Chance

For a long time, science, which was mainly physics, dealt with non-living beings and chance was denied. Then biology became a respected science. It quickly became apparent that animals in the wild did not look a bit like the planets going round the sun, never deviating from their courses, and researchers who worked with animals found that they could not be controlled like the inanimate things which were to be found in physics laboratories. Also, it was found that it was by chance that a pregnant animal produced a male or female off spring, and, especially where human beings were concerned, it was found that there is chance in the inheritance of qualities. Jacques Monod said:

> Pure chance, absolutely free but blind, at the very root of the stupendous edifice of evolution: this central concept of modern biology is no longer one among other possible or even conceivable hypotheses. It is today the sole conceivable hypothesis, the only one compatible with observed and tested fact.[1]

Finally, the indeterminacy principle was discovered around 1924 and it is now assumed in science, including physics, that it is intrinsically necessary that the material universe has chance in it.

If human beings have free will, there must be chance, because, first, free will entails multiple possibility and hence the denial of determinism, and, second, as a result of free acts things happen which no one decides; so that many events are random. For instance, if people play cards, the dealer does not decide what cards to deal to each player. Also, if two people, acting quite independently, decide to attend a conference, where they meet, their meeting was neither predetermined

---

1 Monod, *Chance and Necessity*, p. 110. This was published in France in 1990.

5 ॐ Free Will & Chance: Indeterminism

nor freely decided on: it happened by chance. Finally, the letters of our alphabet were not predetermined, nor were they the result of rational planning: at least in part, they are products of chance.

The unpredictability of particular events

Suppose that it is a fact that a certain person is in the library, and that I do not know this. If someone asks me where he is, I reply either that I do not know or, if he is usually in the library at that time, that he is *probably* there. In this case, my ignorance or uncertainty is purely subjective. If, however, I was with the person in the library ten minutes ago and am asked where he was then, I know for a fact that he was there and if I am asked where he was ten minutes ago I reply with certainty that he was in the library. My knowledge is subjective, since it is in my mind, but it is not *purely* subjective..

A question is: Is it possible to have *certain* knowledge of a future event? If an event will necessarily happen, and I know that, I can foreknow and predict it with certainty. Take, however, the case of a free act, and let us consider this example:

> Sydney is 16 hours ahead of New York when it is summer in Sydney, so that in January when it is 5 pm on Saturday in New York it is 9 am on Sunday in Sydney. I am in New York on a certain Saturday at 5 pm, I switch on a television set and find myself watching the final of the Australian Open Tennis Championship. A clock is visible on the screen and from the commentary I realise that there has been some trouble with a satellite and the match has in fact not yet been played. It will start at about 10 pm, New York time. I settle down to watch it and at a break point I see an Australian player going for a wild serve and losing a game. I happen to know the player's father, I ring him on his mobile phone and tell him what is going to happen that afternoon in Sydney. He promptly tells his son. What happens? Does the player, forewarned, not serve wildly? This is impossible, because I saw him doing it.. Will he, knowing he is going to miss, serve widly? That, too, is absurd. The conclusion is that the story is impossible, or, more generally, that it is impossible to know fo certain what an event which involves free will is going to be, when it is possible to use the knowledge to affect the event.

Now let us consider a case in which there is no one who (like me in the above example) knows what a free person is going to do. Suppose that on Friday in a free act I am going to vote yes or no, and that today, on

Thursday, I have not yet made up my mind. Let us also suppose that it is true today that tomorrow I am definitely (as opposed to probably) going to vote yes. I do not know – perhaps no one knows – that that it is true, but it is. If when Friday comes I vote no, I will cause what was true on Thursday to have been false then, which is impossible. Therefore, on Friday there will not be multiple possibility. But for me to have free will there must be. Not only must I think that I face more than one possibility, there must actually be more than one possibility. Therefore it cannot be certainly true on Thursday that I will vote yes on Friday. It will also not be certainly true that I am going to vote no. In general, if I have not yet made a free choice, it cannot be certainly true or false beforehand that I will make it one way or the other. I not only say that I cannot know what I am going to do: I say that it is intrinsically unforeknowable.

Logicians sometimes maintain that a statement with an intelligible content either has or has not a truth-value, so that any statement, including statements about what people are going to do, is either true or false, whether or not anyone knows which. They say that we may not know which until the decision has been made, but after it has been made we know whether the prediction, when it was made, was true or false. However, while it is true to say of Helena in *A Midsummer Night's Dream*, who exists only as a character in the play, that she is tall, because this is mentioned in the play, it is neither true nor false to say that she has brown eyes, because the colour of her eyes is not mentioned.. Also, if I sing, "I dream of Jeanie with the light-brown hair", the word "I" does not mean me or anyone else and the statement is neither true nor false. Therefore it is not true that every statement with intelligible meaning is either true or false, and while a statement like "When Jim's son reaches school age, he will send him to a private school" has an intelligible content, it is neither true nor false.

Like free acts, particular chance events (as defined above) are intrinsically unpredictable. I maintain, for instance, that the weather is to a large extent *objectively* indeterminate, so that if a couple are going to get married in three months time and I am asked what the weather will be like then, I can answer not only that I do not know what the weather will be like on that day, but that, *objectively* it is possible that it will be fine and also possible that it will be wet. Also, a particular radioactive atom can emit an alpha particle today, or it can keep its alpha particles for a year or more and then emit one: both these things are possible and what happens is, as we say, left to chance and unpredictable.

Jacques Maritain says that Henri Bergson wanted to safeguard the unforeseeableness of becoming, not only the absolute unforeseeableness of free acts and the relative unforeseeableness of contingent [random] happenings in the course of nature, but also what he calls the "radical unforeseeableness" of every moment in the universe. "This feeling of unforeseeableness," Maritain goes on, "is a highly philosophic feeling and one which we should not let lie quiescent within us".[2] Reinhold Niebuhr says:

> In both nature and history each new thing is only one of an infinite number of possibilities which might have emerged at that particular juncture. It is for this reason that, though we can trace a series of causes in retrospect, we can never predict the future with accuracy. There is a profound arbitrariness in every given fact, which rational theories of causation seek to obscure.[3]

By "rational theories of causation" Niebuhr means various forms of determinism and one might add: "and also theological theories of predestination and providence".

Probability

Many philosophers have regarded probable knowledge as an inferior kind of knowledge. However, when there is question of a free act or a chance event, *probable* knowledge is all that is possible, and it is not inferior to anything. If, for instance, a person has always been scrupulously honest and is asked to do something dishonest, he will probably refuse. Even if he subsequently behaves dishonestly, it will still be true that he was *probably* going to be honest. The same applies to statements about future chance events. For instance, if a tyrant gives a man, who has had no experience of archery, a bow and tells him to fire an arrow at a target, saying that if he scores a bull's eye he will be set free whereas if he misses he will be killed, a spectator might say, "He will probably miss". If the man scores a bull's eye and someone says to the spectator, "You were wrong", the spectator can reply, "No. If I had said

---

2 Maritain, *Redeeming the Time*, p. 72.
3 Niebuhr, *Beyond Tragedy*, p. 8

he was going to miss, I would have been wrong. But I said that he was *probably* going to miss, and that was true then. Later, the improbable happened."

The principle of indeterminacy does not mean that if a free act or chance event is going to occur, its occurrence and non-occurrence are always equally likely. This is sometimes the case – generally speaking, if one tosses a coin it is equally likely to come down heads or tails – but very often, one alternative is far more probable than the other. *Probable* predictions are frequently possible, and in life we are constantly estimating probabilities and basing our actions on our estimations. Sometimes probability can be expressed as a percentage – for instance, if a certain operation has been successful in 62% of the times it has been carried out, a surgeon may tell a patient that the probability of its being a success in his case is 62%.

Necessity and predictability in large numbers of events which by themselves are indeterminate

We can go further. At times particular events are free or happen by chance, but where large numbers of events are concerned a certain necessity and predictability (usually approximate) comes into play.

If there are children and fragile drinking glasses in a house, it is not necessary and predictable that at a certain time a particular glass will be dropped by a particular child and break, but it is usually certain that during their childhood years some of the glasses will be dropped by children and will break. Also, of no boy or girl in his or her final year in secondary school is it possible to say, with absolute certainty, that he or she will go to a university next year and study medicine, but it can be said that many students will do that.

When a child is growing up, many things are decided by the parents, who exercise their free will. Also, an enormous number of things happen by chance – for instance, a boy may by chance meet someone who teaches him chess. At the same time, it is predetermined that he will grow and develop physically, mentally and emotionally: this is necessary and predictable.

Also, if a car travelling at high speed crashes into a wall, necessity and chance are both involved, and if a spectator sees the event happening he knows, immediately before it happens, that an accident is going to happen but not exactly what damage will be done, how many people will be hurt, and how badly.

5 & Free Will & Chance: Indeterminism

There are times when there is what is called a statistical necessity. For instance, while it is not certain either that any particular child (say a couple's first child) will be a boy or that it will be a girl, it can be certain that, where there is no interference, half the babies born in a big city in a year will be boys, Also, consider this fictitious case:

> Let us suppose that another man and I play the following betting game (this is pure fiction). We agree to toss a coin 200 times, and before each throw he will put $2 on a table, I will put $1, if it comes down heads he will take the $3 and if it comes down tails I will take the $3. It will come down heads about 100 times and tails about 100 times. (I tossed a coin 200 times and it came down heads 97 times and tails 103 times.) This, I maintain, is certain. When the game ends, I will have put down exactly $200 and I will have picked up $3 about 100 times.. He will have put down exactly $400 and, like me, he will have picked up about $300. However, I, having put down $200, will pick up about $300 and so win about $100, whereas he, having put down $400, will pick up about $300 and so lose about $100.

This is a case of each particular throw being a chance event, with heads and tails being equally probable and neither of them certain, but before the game began it was certain that in 200 throws I would win about $100. What the exact amount would be was a matter of chance. Mendel discovered that it is a law of nature that if the pollen of a large number of flowers of a certain kind of plant is mixed, about a quarter of the next generation of flowers will have one colour and about three quarters will have another colour. (We speak of Mendel's Laws).

Finally, it can be certain that something will be invented sooner or later but not that it will be invented by a particular person at a particular place and time. For instance, after the steam engine was invented, it was certain that sooner or later the train would be invented, but it was not certain that any particular person would invent it at any particular time.

The words "theory" and "evolution"

"Theory" in a scientific sense means what has been accepted by almost the entire scientific community, so that we talk of the Copernican theory, which is that the earth goes round the sun, the gravitational theory, which is that there is a force of attraction between two bodies proportional to the product of their masses and inversely proportional to the square of the distance between them. One talks also of the atomic theory and (to come to the point) of the theory of evolution. At times non-scientists think that a theory is something which has been suggested but is not yet certain, and they say that evolution is "only a theory", but in scientific circles a theory (as distinct from a hypothesis) has been accepted as certain, and if I refer to the theory of evolution I will mean that it is certainly true.

After Darwin's books were published, the word "evolution" meant the development of animals, up to and including the earliest human beings. Pierre Teilhard de Chardin wanted a term for, at one end, the development of the universe from its beginnings, and, at the other end, the progress in human society which is going on now, and he invented the term "cosmogenesis" for the whole long process from particles to human beings as we are now, but I propose to use the term "evolution" for it.

6 Evolution

The scientific picture of evolution

It seems to have been assumed that mountains and oceans have always been what they are now, and that while animals and plants die the species have always existed. Then in the nineteenth century people became aware of change in nature. It may have started in geology, when sharp-eyed men noticed layers in exposed rock faces and concluded that the sloping strata had once been horizontal, which meant that mountains and plains had once had shapes quite differen from the shapes they had then, and for the most part still have. In the middle of the century Darwin revealed that animal species had evolved. This, with many additions, has become part of what every educated person in a civilised country knows, but it was surely a tremendous shock when it was discovered.

It is, I think, generally thought that from particles came atoms, from which came molecules, from which came compounds. Also, large non-living beings have existence-spans: stars are born, burn and then die. Even mountains were thrown up and have been worn down. Individual living beings have shorter life-spans: they are at first tiny, they grow until they reach maturity, after which they are killed or they decline into old age and die. When they reach maturity, they reproduce themselves so that, generally speaking, many species continue to exist.

The first living beings were one-celled and, compared with most present-day living beings, extremely simple. They were followed by colonies and then by multicellular beings. Their descendants were often not exact reproductions of their predecessors but gene mutations occurred which caused changes to appear, which sometimes enabled them to deal with the problems of new milieux. Within each species, there was development through the generations, and new species appeared which were superior to their predecessors. In some cases, the beings which did not incorporate the new developments survived, but in other cases they became extinct. The first living beings were all aquatic but eventually living beings appeared which were able to survive out of water and live on the land, obtaining oxygen from the air rather than from the sea-water: this was a tremendous step.

Over an immense period of time the land-dwelling living beings changed and at last there came another tremendous step, when from a change in some primates the first human beings appeared. Human beings then developed, by changing not so much physically as psychologically. The noises which they made evolved into language, they made dwellings instead of sheltering in caves or other natural retreats, and from being hunter-gatherers they developed agriculture and herds. At first they existed in groups like those of the primates, then they made more complex societies, with institutions. Millions of years later they evolved conceptual thought and morality, they wrote, they counted and measured, they made whole cities and nations, the family as we know it appeared, and the societies like those of the primates evolved into monarchies, which evolved into democracies. This development is still going on, as human thought evolves, as scientific and other discoveries are made, as moral obligations are more and more widely understood, and as democracy is constantly improved.

In various disciplines, different processes of development are studied. In the science faculties of universities, the evolution of human beings from simple marine living beings is studied in zoology, and the development of highly civilised human beings from early human beings is studied in anthropology. In the arts faculties, the development of civilised human beings is studied in the history departments. Finally, the behaviour of present-day human beings is studied in the psychology and political-science departments. I wish to maintain that these are phases of a single process of development. I think that in Pierre Teilhard de Chardin's time the word "evolution" meant the evolution of animals to human beings, as in "the theory of evolution", and he used the term "cosmogenesis" for the whole process.

Chance in particular events in evolution

For a long time Newton was the world's leading scientist, and physics was the leading science. Physics was deterministic (for instance, it was possible to deduce the period of a pendulum from its length, and once one had calculated it, one knew that nothing else was possible), and it came to be believed that belief in free will or chance was unscientific and hence incorrect. It seems to me that zoologists were the first scientists to reject determinism and affirm chance. I earlier quoted Jacques Monod, who said:

> Pure chance, absolutely free but blind, at the very root of the stupendous edifice of evolution: this central concept of modern biology is no longer one among other possible or even conceivable hypotheses. It is today the sole conceivable hypothesis, the only one compatible with observed and tested fact.[1]

In 1924 the physicist Heisenberg discovered indeterminacy in atoms, so that it became established that randomness is a fact of nature.

Necessity in large numbers in evolution

I said earlier that when there is chance in individual events there is often necessity in large numbers of events: for instance, if a woman becomes pregnant, it is a fifty-fifty chance that it will be a boy and a fifty-fifty chance that it will be a girl, but if a thousand children are born in a city in a month, it is certain that approximately five hundred of them will be boys and approximately five hundred will be girls. Also, when a boy is growing up an enormous amount is not predetermined but happens by chance (for instance, he happens to have an unmarried uncle with whom he forms a close friendship, the uncle teaches him how to play chess and he becomes a champion chess player), while at the same time there is much that is necessary and predictable in his physical, mental and emotional development. I venture to say that while, as Monod says, blind chance is at the root of evolution, there is a certain necessity in the appearance at unpredictable times of new species. To put it crudely, there is a resemblance between the evolving universe and a child growing up.

Timothy Anders says: "There are many widespread myths and misconceptions about evolution, but none is more popular than the idea that evolution is basically a good thing".[2] I can understand opposition to the notion that every invention or cultural change makes the world a better place; but I do not believe that the idea that evolution is basically a good thing is a myth or misconception. While many scientists abstain from value judgements and confine themselves to saying that living beings evolved from non-living things, that human beings evolved from primates and that human beings gradually developed spoken languages, agriculture, herds, written language and so on, without making any value judgements about this, I believe that we can make the

---

1 Monod, *Chance and Necessity*, p. 110. This was quoted above, p 44.
2 Anders, *The Evolution of Evil*, p. 25.

value judgement that evolution was and is basically "a good thing". It has involved setbacks and the suffering of particular people; at times it has gone in different directions at the same time, and one line has led to genuine progress while the others have proved to be dead ends. Indeed, the word "evolution" means change *for the better*, and if people say that they believe in evolution or the theory of evolution, they imply a certain hopefulness. The evolutionary theory which I am presenting here is that in spite of setbacks and mistakes, in general the world is better than it was when there were no living beings, better than it was when all life was in the sea, and it is now becoming a better place.

The Rise theory

In Chapter 3 I talked about the Fall theory as an explanation of what is wrong with the world. By contrast, the theory which I have been proposing is a Rise theory. Instead of postulating a paradise, from which we have fallen, in the distant past, it postulates a better world in the distant future..

The theory explains much of the unorder in the universe and much of the suffering we undergo and see. The Fall theory maintains that all "natural" ills are results of the act of disobedience which brought about the Fall, but as I said we now know that earthquakes, to mention only them, are caused by factors which existed long before there were human beings capable of disobedience. Also, we know that evolution involves chance mutations and other events, many or even most of which have been harmful: the advent of AIDS is perhaps an example of this. It is simply not believable that if (for example) a child dies, or hundreds of people die in bushfires, this is going to turn out to have been for the best, which is why God allowed it to happen. On the contrary, we are entirely justified in regretting and lamenting it. After all, when Jesus encountered suffering people, he did not tell them that what had happened was God's will and should be accepted. He wept with them.

Entropy

It is now established in the physical sciences that in every physical event some energy passes from a higher level to a lower level, so that afterwards there is less energy at the high level and more at the low level, which seems to mean that eventually everything will be at the same energy level, there will be no more events, and there will be no life anywhere. This is entropy. If I understand this correctly, the sciences which study life have discovered evolution, a process which exists in the universe and which consists in the appearance in it of higher and higher forms of life. Entropy is not the ultimate truth.

The principal deficiency of the evolutionary theory: moral evil

Many writers on the problem of evil have what I might call a scientific mentality and are blind to moral evil, which is to say, *evil*. In a book on the eighteenth century Vereker says:

> The moral freedom which characterised human sin found no place in the new doctrines. The defect in man which corresponded to sin was that his knowledge of nature and history was confused, disorderly and fragmentary,'[3]

that is, not moral. In the twentieth century some authors endeavoured to explain the Holocaust by saying that it manifested "a less highly evolved form of humanness". This, however, will not do and the great defect of the theory which I have been expounding, when it is presented as a complete explanation of reality, is that it does not even begin to take account of deliberate, wicked, malicious wrongdoing and its physical consequences: it is not a solution to the problem of *evil*. I shall return to this point later, after analysing moral evil, but even at this stage it is surely evident that if a little boy dies because he contracts some disease which we are as yet unable to cure, or because he accidentally locks himself in a small space and there suffocates, we can perhaps reasonably tell the parents that human beings, especially children, are by nature fragile, that it is part of the human condition to be in fairly constant danger, and that it is inevitable that from time to time, in spite of every reasonable precaution being taken, a child will die by sickness or accident. We will redouble our efforts to find cures for diseases and to make the world a safer place for children to play in, but in the meantime such things will happen. However, if an unscrupulous manufacturer wickedly makes an appliance the safety of which he guarantees, though it is not safe and he knows it, and if a child's death is caused by this appliance, then one cannot speak to the parents in the same way: this incident could and should have been avoided. Also, if a child is viciously mistreated and as a result is later, as an adult, psychologically disturbed, this is someone's fault. Neither can we say that just as there must be hundreds of musicians who fail

---

3 Vereker, *Eighteenth-Century Optimism*, p. 157.

to become great virtuosi for every one who succeeds, so there must be hundreds of criminals for every honest man or woman, and hundreds of adulterers for every faithful husband or wife. Therefore I do not offer the theory which I have stated as an explanation of all evil, or indeed of *evil* at all. I offer it as a solution to the first kind of disorder, and will in Part Three come to the second kind.

Pierre Teilhard de Chardin

Darwin published *The Origin of Species* in 1859 and *The Descent of Man* in 1871, they caused a sensation all over Europe, and a sort of war broke out. On one side were Christian clerics and laypeople who believed in the literal truth of the first chapter of *Genesis* and refused to accept the evidence, such as it then was, for evolution. On the other side were scientists like Thomas Huxley who were enemies of religion and used evolution to discredit the Bible. Before World War I, Pierre Teilhard de Chardin was a Jesuit scholastic whose hobby was geology. In 1912, by which time he had been ordained, his superiors ordered him to study it seriously in Paris. I suspect that they expected him to disprove evolution, scientifically. He, however, soon became a strong believer in it and an attractive and vigorous promoter of it. He ran into intense opposition in Catholic circles – after all, there was a war on and he was on the side of the enemy – and he was sent to China to get him out of the way. He did not back down but maintained more and more strongly, first, that the Church would sooner or later accept evolution, as it had accepted the Copernican theory. He maintained, second, that just as the ideas of heaven above the earth and hell below it had had to be revised, so the ideas about Adam and Eve needed to be revised, and this would lead to an immense advance in our understanding of the faith. In essays and in a book, *The Phenomenon of Man*, he developed his idea of an evolutionary Christianity. He was forbidden by his superiors to publish any of these writings but they were published after his death in 1955. They became best-sellers in many languages, and Christian books which were in favour of evolution were said to be Teilhardian.

To come to what is known as the problem of evil, he said in 1933:

6 ⁂ Evolution

> In this new [evolutionary] setting, while evil loses nothing of its poignancy or horror, it ceases to be an incomprehensible element in the structure of the world and becomes a natural feature.[4]

Towards the end of his life he was even more emphatic. In 1948 he wrote:

> Our ingrained habits of thought are such that we still automatically maintain that the problem of evil is insoluble. And yet, why should this be so? In the old cosmos, which was assumed to have emerged from the hands of the Creator, it was only natural to find it difficult to reconcile a partially evil world with the existence of a God who is both good and omnipotent. But with our modern view of a universe in a state of cosmogenesis [evolution] ... how can so many well-ordered minds still persist in failing to see that, intellectually speaking, the only too familiar problem no longer exists?[5]

And in 1951 he wrote:

> When cosmogenesis is accepted, then ... not only is there a solution to the problem of evil, but the problem itself ceases to arise.[6]

In 1948 the Jesuit General, Janssens, thought that it might be possible for *The Phenomenon of Man* to be published, perhaps with some alterations, without being at once condemned by the Holy Office, and he arranged for Teilhard to visit Rome and meet his critics there face to face. In Rome, Teilhard seems to have been told that he had overlooked moral evil, and he wrote "Some Remarks on the Place and Part of Evil in a World in Evolution". This, dated Rome, 28 October 1948, now forms an appendix to the book. Here he admitted that there might be more disorder in the world than his evolutionary theory accounted for, but he said: "On this question ... I do not feel I am in a position to take a stand". That was as far as he was prepared to go, and it was not far enough.[7]

Teilhard saw and experienced suffering: his sister had Pott's disease from 1903 until her death in 1936; he was a stretcher-bearer in World War I; he was misunderstood, denounced, made to live in

---

4 Teilhard, *Christianity and Evolution*, p. 82.
5 Teilhard, *Activation of Energy*, pp. 196-197.
6 Teilhard, *Activation of Energy*, p. 259.
7 See Mooney, *Teilhard de Chardin and the Mystery of Christ*, pp. 106, 122-145, 208.

exile from Paris, not allowed to hold academic positions in the Institut Catholique or the Collège de France, and permitted to publish only scientific articles. But his sister's sickness was nobody's fault; he does not seem to have seen war as a manifestation of sin at work in the world, or to have been aware of moral evil in the political and social sphere; and the opposition he encountered in the Church came from men who were ignorant, timid or prejudiced, but who were doing what they believed to be right. From 1926 to 1946 he lived in China and for some years he was in a city that was under Japanese occupation. While I am sure that he saw and heard of brutality, though during World War II probably he had only sketchy information about what was going on in Europe and thought that what was happening in Asia was explicable as primitiveness. Also, as a geologist he was aware of physical unorder, waste and failure in the world, but not of moral evil. Many of his colleagues were atheists, and he thought that this was unfortunate, but he did not think that it was their fault and generally speaking he encountered in the scientific community intellectual honesty, disinterested dedication to research, and co-operation between scientists of different nations. It need not, then, altogether surprise us if, while he was deeply aware of suffering, he was blind to moral evil. But it was a great fault and almost all commentators on his work have made this criticism of him. I quote Tresmontant:

> There is, in human evil, a remainder which cannot be explained either in terms of the multiple nature nor yet by the temporality of the genesis in progress. The perversity of the concentration-camp butchers cannot be explained simply in terms of the Manifold! ... Teilhard seems not to distinguish sufficiently between physical evil, which is susceptible of a natural explanation in terms of the unfinished state of creation, and the evil that springs from the sin of man.[8]

---

8   Quoted in Smulders, *The Design of Teilhard de Chardin*, p. 290; see also p. 141 and p. 289 n. 42. There is a little about Teilhard's theological ideas on p. 122.

7 God & Evolution

Two suppositions

In the previous chapter I omitted all reference to God, though since the beginning the controversy concerning evolution has been to a great extent religious. I will now enter this field but before I do so I will state and explain some things which I will assume to be true.

INTRINSIC POSSIBILITY AND IMPOSSIBILITY

There is an important qualification to the statement that God is omnipotent. God cannot do things which are intrinsically impossible and these are most obviously those which are logically impossible. At the risk of being too obvious, let me tell a story to make clear what this means.

> A man went to an architect, said that he had bought a block of land, and produced a map which showed the block, with its dimensions. He then said that he wanted the architect to design a one-level house for him, to be built on this block, and he gave the architect a list of rooms which he wanted the house to have, with their measurements. The architect did some calculations and said that the areas of the rooms, added together, came to more than the area of the block, so that the house which the man had requested was impossible. "I knew that there would be a problem," said the man, "but I was told that you are a good architect and I expect you to be able to solve it." "Look," said the architect, "it is not a question of how good an architect I am. The house you have described just could not possibly be built on this block of land." "You mean that you can't solve the problem, don't you?" said the man, "I'll just have to keep looking until I find an architect who can." "No," said the architect, "I do not mean that I lack the ability to design the house you want. I mean that it is inherently impossible."

God himself could not cause the plan of a house which, when built, would have rooms the areas of which would add up to more than the area occupied by the house. Also, he could not cause to appear on a piece of paper the last digit of expressed as a decimal (there isn't one). None of these "cannots" implies any limitation in God, nor does it amount to a denial of his omnipotence.

There are other things which are not so obviously *logically* impossible but which are intrinsically impossible. God cannot do them, either. For instance, though God is omnipotent, he cannot decide to cease to exist. The Father cannot decide not to generate the Son, the Father and the Son cannot decide not to spirate the Holy Spirit, and the three divine persons cannot be against one another. I wish to maintain here there is no possibility of a universe without persons, by which I mean without intelligent beings with free will, ever existing. Also, it would be impossible for God to create human beings who would have free will and would always do whatever he, in a prior decision, chose to have them do.

THAT THE PAST CANNOT BE CHANGED

Suppose that a play is in rehearsal, that its director is also its author, and that it is being rehearsed in sequence with a certain amount of scenery. Suppose also that in Act I one of the characters, following the script, angrily defaces a portrait which is hanging on the wall. Suppose then that the actor who has to do this objects, that the author yields and that the incident is cancelled. When the rehearsal ends, the stage hands clean the portrait, so that it is on the wall, undefaced, in the rehearsal of Act II. During this, an actor who was not on stage in Act I says: "Shouldn't that portrait have been removed, since it was defaced in Act I?" The author-director replies: "We've deleted that incident and the portrait should still be there". If that sort of thing were possible in real life, if a husband was killed in a car accident, his wife would be able to pray: "Please change that and cause the accident not to have happened". She would not be asking God to wipe out all traces of the accident so that anyone later investigating it would find no mention of it in newspapers, and no one (not even she) would have any memory of it, so that it would *seem* not to have happened. She would be asking for it not to have happened. That, I maintain, is intrinsically impossible so that even God cannot rewrite past history and if the woman whom I mentioned were to make that prayer, she would be wasting her time.

God and evolution

God made the world, and he made it as it necessarily is. Sometimes people talk of God creating human beings and *giving them* free will, as if there could have been human beings who did not have free will. I maintain the God could not create human beings who did not have free will, any more than he could give a man the design of a one-storey house which, when built, would have rooms which had areas the sum of which would be less than the area occupied by the house as a whole. I also maintain that the only universe which can exist has randomness in it. Laplace said that if we knew the position and velocity of every particle in the universe at any moment, and if we knew the laws of nature, we would be able to write a history of the entire universe from its beginning until now, and from now until the end of time. I maintain that not only is the existing universe not such a universe, as Laplace thought, but that such a universe is intrinsically impossible, so that God could not have created a universe in which Laplace's dream would be realised. It used to be said that for God there is no such thing as chance. John Houghton, an English physicist, said:

> Because the scientific description of some event may involve chance and probability, it does not follow that a theological description of the same event in terms of God's activity need also involve chance.[1]

I disagree with this, and I agree with Teilhard, who said:

> Not through inability, but by reason of the very structure of the nil to which he stoops [I would rather say: because of the nature of matter], God can proceed to creation in only one way: he must arrange, and, under his magnetic influence and using the tentative operation of enormous numbers, gradually unify an immense multitude of elements.[2]

By "tentative" Teilhard means "indeterminate". Just as human parents, when they have children, do not know precisely what their sons and daughters will decide to do and all that will happen to them when they are adults, so God, when he creates human beings, does not know with absolute certainty what will happen to them and all that they are are going to do. Einstein is reported to have said that God does not play dice with the universe. This was not meant to be a theological

---

1 Houghton, *Does God Play Dice?*, p. 122.
2 Teilhard, "My Fundamental Vision" (1948), *Toward the Future*, p. 197.

statement but a poetic way of saying that there is no free will or chance in the universe. He was wrong. On the one hand, if a woman has a child who is a girl, this is not because God decided to give her a girl. It happened by chance. On the other hand, if 1,234 women in a city give birth to 597 boys and 637 girls, this is not because God chose to give almost equal numbers of boys and girls, but slightly more girls than boys, to pregnant women. It is because that is how chance works. Today I went to the funeral of a contemporary who died of cancer. This was not because God willed his death by cancer and not mine.

However, there is in the universe a natural tendency to evolve, as a result of which, though particular events happen by chance, in the interplay of many creatures over millions of years there has been continual improvement. There were chance mutations in genes, some of which led to advances while others led to defects, and God did not intervene. For instance, he did not move a few aquatic beings from the ocean and give them the ability to survive on land. This did not happen because at a certain moment he intervened, but because it was in the nature of the universe that it should happen, sooner or later. Exactly when and where it happened was a matter of chance, but that it happened was necessary. It is true that I am denying that evolution was caused by God continually intervening in nature. I affirm that the universe which God has created reflects his nature more or less as children reflect their parents' nature, so that eventually intelligence and free will appeared and progress is going on.

The divine foreknowledge: some history

As I said earlier, scholastic philosophers used to maintain that God, being pure act, cannot receive knowledge from outside himself, and knows that creatures exist, and what they do, only by being conscious of his own volitions (which they call decrees). The big problem here is that of foreknowledge, since according to this theory the divine knowledge is causally prior to all the events in the universe and hence may be called *fore*knowledge.

Thinking that the future can be known, the Old Testament writers assumed that God knows everything which, from our point of view, is going to happen. The Book of Wisdom says that wisdom "knows the past, she forecasts the future" (Wis 8:8 NJB) and particular future events are foretold. In the New Testament it is constantly said of events that they had been predicted. This has always been difficult to reconcile with belief in free will, not to mention chance. Most Christians believed both in free will and in divine foreknowledge of *all* events, and either struggled to find a way of reconciling their beliefs or they put the matter into the too-hard basket.

In the late Middle Ages, to be precise in 1465, Peter de Rivo held a public discussion on the question of whether, after Jesus had said that the apostle Peter was going to deny him, it was possible for Peter not to deny Jesus, thus causing Jesus to have been mistaken. In the discussion, Peter de Rivo maintained that statements about future free acts, including Jesus' statement about Peter's denial, are neither true nor false. Definite statements about future events, he said, can be made only about necessary events. (The same reasoning would lead to the same conclusion about Jesus' predictions of his passion.) A vigorous dispute ensued, into which people from other universities were drawn. It went on until in 1474 a number of Peter's doctrines were condemned in a papal bull as scandalous and deviating from the path of the Catholic faith; and in 1476 in Rome Peter signed a retraction of things he had said.[3] Which did not solve the problem, and later speculation brought about his condemnation.

In the sixteenth century, in what is known as Second Scholasticism, a Spanish Dominican, Domingo Bañez, proposed a theory in which he endeavoured to reconcile divine control of events with human free will. He maintained that God gives every being, before it acts, an impulse which causes it to do a particular thing, and a human decision is free because the being is determined *not by its nature* but by God to act in a particular way. The Jesuits in Spain and Portugal, who had been trained in the *Spiritual Exercises* of Ignatius Loyola, which are all about "making an election" which is an exercise of free will, objected that the Dominicans were implicitly denying free will, and a controversy ensued.

A Portugese Jesuit, Luis de Molina, presented an opposing theory according to which God knows, prior to his decision to create

---

3 Two of the statements which were declared to be errors and which Peter retracted were: "That for the truth of a proposition about the future it is not sufficient that the thing will be, but it is required that it be impossible to prevent it" and "That it is necessary to say one of these two things: either that in credal statements about the future there is no present and actual truth, or that what they say cannot be prevented even by a divine power" (Denziger-Schönmetzer, *Enchiridion Symbolorum*, ## 629, 626).

anything, what every free being *would* do in every possible situation, and so, when he decided to create a particular universe, knew exactly what everyone in it *was definitely going to do*. It seems to me that if a yacht-builder studies a new design of a hull and is unable to calculate how a yacht with such a hull would behave, he may build a scaled-down model hull, test it in a tank and, if the results are good, build a full-size yacht knowing how it will behave in different circumstances and being guided by that knowledge. In a similar way, according to Molina God observed hypothetically-existing men and women and so learned what they would do if he were to create them and put them in various situations. In the light of this knowledge he created particular beings (including us) and put them (again including us) in particular situations.

The conflict became public and scandalous. To obtain some peace, the Vatican reserved the decision to itself and ordered the parties to keep quiet. Years later, after Bañez and Molina were both dead, the pope did not declare than either of them was right and the other was wrong. Instead, he declared that since both the Dominicans the Jesuits professed belief in divine providence and human free will, neither were heretics and both positions could be held and taught, which they were, for centuries.

The divine foreknowledge questioned

There are indications in the Bible itself that the predictions which God makes are not simple statements of fact. When David asks God whether Saul will come down, God says that he will; David then asks whether the townsmen will hand David over to Saul, and again God says yes, they will; whereupon David leaves and it does not happen (1 Sam 23:10-13). Evidently God did not tell Daniel about events which he, God, was seeing happen or had decided would happen, since they didn't. In Ezechiel, it is predicted that Nebuchadnezzar will attack and destroy Tyre and that it will never be rebuilt; three chapters later Nebuchadnessar fails to take Tyre (Ezech 26:7-14; 29:17-20) and it is still there.

Also, there are passages which say that God regrets a decision which he has made. For instance, in Genesis we read that "the Lord was sorry that he had made humankind on the earth, and it grieved him to his heart" (Gen 6:6). In 1 Samuel it is said that "the words of the Lord came to Samuel: 'I regret that I made Saul king'" (1 Sam 15:11) and that "the Lord was sorry that he had made Saul king over Israel (1 Sam 15:35). This makes sense only if when he made his decision God did not know what was going to come of it. Also, in Exodus God tells Moses what to do "if they [the people] will not believe you" (Ex 4:8), which implies that prior to his decree of creation of the world he did not know what the people in it were going to do.

In at least three important works, *De Veritate*, the *Summa Contra Gentiles* and the *Summa Theologiae*, Thomas Aquinas said that "a contingent event", such as a free act, in the future cannot be known with certainty by anyone; hence, he said, God does not know these events as future.[4]

In the twentieth century, some progressive Catholic theologians expressed doubts about the divine foreknowledge of human free acts. In his encyclical of 1950 on "modern errors" Pius XII said: "Eternal and infallible foreknowledge of the free acts of human beings is being denied",[5] and he said that this was "contrary to the declaration of Vatican I" and therefore unacceptable. This seems not to have ended discussion, since in 1975 William J. Hill said: "Contemporary serious thought is practically unanimous in denying to God an infallible knowledge of the future, precisely because there is as yet no such thing, either within the existing temporal order (obviously) or within what has traditionally been known as the eternity of God".[6] Jacques Maritain said that "the impossibility of being foreseen with absolute certainty" is a "property of the free act as such", and added: "whatever comprehension or supercomprehension of causes one may have".[7] That is, even God cannot foresee free acts with absolute certainty. Charles Journet (a Swiss theologian, who was made a cardinal) said that God sees things "at the very instant when they come into existence to co-exist with him. He does not know in advance."[8] In the twentieth century, Anthony Kenny said that "if God is to have infallible knowledge of future human actions, then determinism must be true",[9] and

---

4   Thomas Aquinas, *De Veritate*, 2 12; *Summa Theologiae*, 1 14 13.
5   Pius XII, *Humani Generis*; Denziger-Schönmetzer, *Enchiridion*, # 3890.
6   Hill, "Does God Know the Future? Aquinas and Some Moderns", p. 7.
7   Maritain, *God and the Permission of Evil*, p. 16.
8   Journet, *The Meaning of Evil*, p. 177.
9   Kenny, *The God of the Philosophers*, p. 121. For "determinism must be true" read "the Free Will doctrine cannot be true".

the converse is also true: if we have free will, as we do, God cannot have infallible knowledge of future human actions. JR Lucas observed that God cannot foreknow our acts unless they are predetermined and hence not free;[10] I maintain that they are free, and hence I deny foreknowledge.

In Protestant circles, too, the idea of divine foreknowledge has been questioned. In 1987 the evangelical theologian William Lane Craig said: "There is a disturbing new trend among some evangelical theologians to deny the biblical doctrine of foreknowledge and to explain away biblical passages supporting this doctrine, simply because the rational attack on it seems to them unanswerable."[11] Paul Weiss has written:

> What the future holds in store is beyond the power of God to know, granted even that he be omniscient, for God cannot contradict himself, do evil for the sake of evil, make himself impotent, ignorant or debased. His omnipotence is the power to do all that can be done, and his omniscience is the power to know all that can be known. He has not the power to do what cannot be done, the power to know what cannot be known. He cannot now know the future in its concreteness, for such a future is not, and thus is not knowable. Even if he thoroughly grasped the nature of things that now exist, their habits and the kind of power they exert, he could not tell in advance just what in detail their effects would be, for there are no such details before they actually occur. One might conceive of effects to be, but these effects and every feature of them would be general, abstract. The details of actual effects cannot be known in advance, for there are no such details to be known. Not even God can know just what will be.[12]

---

10   Lucas, *The Future*, p. 34.
11   Craig, *The Only Wise God*, p. 12; see also p. 15. He also said: "To suggest that these last predictions were not founded on foreknowledge, but were inferences based on the character of the disciples and the context of events soon to occur, is to evacuate the incidents of all theological significance whatever" (ibid., p. 36; see also pp. 55-60). I quote him, not as someone who denies foreknowledge, but as someone who reported that it was being denied.
12   Weiss, *Nature and Man* (1947) p. 13. My italics. Lucas says: "Where it is not due to an incapacity of the person but is in the nature of the case that

My position

I wish to maintain here, to put it briefly, that God does not know the future, or, if you want more technical terms, that God has no foreknowledge of free acts and random events, not because he is ignorant of things which are in themselves knowable, but because prior to their actuality they are, *as actual* as opposed to *as possible*, intrinsically unknowable.

It seems to me that the Banezians implicitly denied human free will. In their system, without ever willing anything unnatural, God pre-decides all human acts, so that he is, and we are not, free. Also, a hypothetically-existing human being cannot make a decision, and therefore God cannot bring a human being into existence, knowing exactly what he or she will do. God is like a father who brings children into the world, not knowing what they are +going to do. He is not like the author of a play, who knows, before the play is performed, everything that will happen when it is performed.

The idea that God is "outside time"

For us on the earth, if we disregard east and west, everything is either north of us, on our latitude, or south of us. If we are looking towards something which is north of us, we are looking in only one direction and not looking at what is south of us. If we want to look at something which is south of us, we have to turn our backs on what is to the north and look in the opposite direction. If, however, we had gone to the moon and were looking at the earth from there, we would not have a latitude on the earth and hence nothing would be north or south of us, or on our latitude. We would see that New York is north of Sydney, but neither city would be north or south of *us*, or on our latitude. In a similar way, it was said, God, looking down on the universe, simultaneously sees all that happens as it happens. He knows that Napoleon lived before Churchill, but neither of them is past, contemporaneous or future *to him*. So God, to whom we pray, knows what *to us* is the future.

One can make an analogy between the author of a play and God as our creator. When a man writes a play, he forms the idea of each event, and decides to put it in, a few seconds before he writes the words for

---

something cannot be done or known, then it is no derogation from God that He cannot do it or know it" (*The Future* [1989], p. 226).

it. When it is finished and he is discussing it with a director, the two of them are outside the time-frame of the play, so that they can discuss the ending then something at the beginning, and they can put things into early scenes because of what is going to happen later. If they want to, they can put into Act One a fortune teller who makes a prophecy which in Act Three is realised. In a similar way, it was sometimes said, God is outside the time-frame of the existing universe and can put things into the past because of other things that are going to happen in the future, and he can cause prophets to reveal the future.

The obvious trouble with this is that when there is talk of divine foreknowledge, the "fore" is a matter not always of time but always of causality and by "foreknowledge" we do not mean earlier in time but causally prior. Also, actual men and women are persons, who make decisions, and whereas the author of a play decides what the characters say and do, God does not decide our acts.

Probability of particular events

Whereas free will is incompatible with *certain* foreknowledge of particular events, it is possible to believe in divine foreknowledge provided that one understands by this not certain but probable knowledge.[13] That is my thesis here. The certain knowledge of every event in every possible universe is not included in what scholastic philosophers called *scientia simplicis intelligentiae*, or God's detailed knowledge of all possible universes, which is prior to the decree of creation and hence to the actual existence of any creatures. I maintain that a particular existing person determines his or her free acts, and so makes them knowable, which means that prior to actual existence there is nothing to know. If, then, a child is born deformed or if a child dies, and people ask, "Did God want this to happen?", instead of telling them that, as Caussade said, they should abandon themselves to God's will and be happy about it, I believe that a correct answer would be: "No – and not only did he did not will it, he didn't even know for a fact that it was going to happen".

The predictions in the scriptures can be interpreted as statements about what was probably, even almost certainly, going to happen. For instance, instead of explaining Jesus' prediction of his passion as an eye-witness report of future events, which he saw happening, it is

---

13   See my *Free Will*, pp. 64-66, 132, 138-142.

surely reasonable to say that when Jesus saw how fixed the Jewish authorities had become in their opposition to him, he realised that it was only a matter of time before (probably, even almost certainly) they brought about his death. They were free beings so that it was possible that they would relent, but it was highly unlikely. The apostles, who at the time had not known what was coming, realised that he had known it and they did not make the fine distinction between high probability and certainty.

Necessity in large numbers

I said earlier than when there are many free acts or chance events, there can be a certain necessity in what I might call the mass when there is indeterminacy in particular events. Thus there can be divine foreknowledge not of particular free acts and chance events but of general movements, one of which is evolution and another is the survival of the Church.

The divine sensitivity

In ancient Greece, the state religion was belief in gods, of whom there were many. They were passionate beings, they had their favourites and they were emotionally very human in a wild way. I suspect that thoughtful men like Aristotle, while they did not openly dismiss the gods, did not believe in them and evolved the idea of a supreme being who had no passions or feelings and was "unaffectable". Needless to say, he had no contact with Jews, who believed in one God and who was said to experience various feelings: for instance, in the Old Testament God says: "My compassion grows warm and tender" (Hos 11:8). In the early years of the Christian era, some thinkers appeared in the Jewish and Christian communities who, it seems to me, were influenced by Greek philosophy and wanted to interpret their beliefs in ways which made them academically respectable or less human and more Aristotelian. Philo (ca. 20 BC – 40 AD) was a Jew (not a Christian) who interpreted the Scriptures in this way and his writings, including *On the Unchangeableness of God*,[14] later influenced Christian thinkers. I pass over a couple of centuries. In the third century a profession of faith, which expressed the general belief, began: "I believe

---

14 Weinandy devoted eight pages to Philo in *Does God Suffer?*, pp. 74-82. "Unchangeable" is "atrepton", a word which Aristotle had used for past events (Aristotle, *De Mundo*, 7 401 b 20).

in God the Father, omnipotent, invisible and impassible".[15] This was taken to mean that God does not suffer when creatures suffer, which is to say that he does not sympathise with them. In the Middle Ages the scholastic philosopher-theologians deduced impassibility from the idea that God is pure act, and during the Reformation it was not challenged, so that for centuries Catholic and Protestant theologians agreed about it.

In the nineteenth century impassibility began to be denied. In Germany, Isaak August Dorner denied it in the eighteen-fifties[16] and in 1893 in England A. M. Fairbairn said: "Theology has no falser idea than the impassibility of God".[17] In 1928 B. R. Brasnett said: "Men feel, and perhaps will feel increasingly, that a God who is not passible, who is exempt from pain and suffering, is a God of little value to a suffering humanity".[18] In 1974 Jürgen Moltmann said: "Were God incapable of suffering in any respect, and therefore in an absolute sense, then he would also be incapable of love".[19] Writing in France in 1975, François Varillon said that he was afraid that "the image of an impassible God, looking down, with olympic serenity, on the evil and misery in the world remains and pursues its secret existence in the depths of mankind's unconscious",[20] though I doubt whether its existence was secret; he, as is clear, did not agree with it. In 1990 P. Fiddes said: "If God is not less than personal, and if the claim that 'God is love' is to have any recognisable continuity with our normal experience of love, the conclusion seems inescapable that a loving God must be a sympathetic

---

15 Sometimes Greek words were taken into Latin with slightly changed spelling, and with another change in spelling they passed into English (this is the case with "eucharist"). If *apatheia* had been taken into Latin with changed spelling and then into English, we would now be saying that God is "apathetic". At other times existing Latin words were used to translate Greek words and the English words were derived from these. This happened here: *apatheia* became *impassibilitas*, which became "impassibility". The profession of faith is from a commentary, written around 404 AD, on a profession of faith in Aquileia, which was an important city at the north end of the Adriatic (Denziger-Schönmetzer, *Enchiridion*, # 16).

16 See the bibliography.

17 Fairbairn, *The Place of Christ in Modern Theology*, p. 483.

18 Brasnett, *The Suffering of the Impassible God*, p. ix.

19 Moltmann , *The Crucified God*, p. 230.

20 Varillon, *The Humility and Suffering of God*, p. 129.

and therefore a suffering God".[21] In 1994 a group of Protestant theologians in Canada and the United States produced *The Openness of God. A Biblical Challenge to the Traditional Understanding of God*, which is an eloquent attack on impassibility. Thomas G. Weinandy said in 2000 that he had been teaching theology since 1975 and had been aware during that time that the majority of theologians (I presume that he meant both Catholics and Protestants) believed in a suffering God, and that in a huge number of books and articles they had argued for this belief.[22]

I believe that we need to distinguish between different ways of being affected. There are changes which consist in the gain or loss of perfection, that is, in being improved or damaged. Clearly, God cannot be affected in this way. But if, for example, a human father and mother see a son or daughter suffering and feel sorry for him or her, they are not damaged in their own natures and yet they feel deep sorrow and may weep for their suffering son or daughter. In a similar way, when God sees human beings suffering he is not damaged in his own nature, which would be impossible, but he suffers in sympathy with his creatures.[23] I shall return to this question of the divine impassibility later, when I discuss moral evil.[24]

---

21 Fiddes, *The Creative Suffering of God*, p. 17.
22 Weinandy, *Does God Suffer?*, p. vii. Weinandy himself believes in impassibility and his book is a long, scholarly defence of it. He gives a long and detailed account of the authors who have attacked it (chap. 1, pp. 1-26), and most of the quotations above have come from there.
23 "Sym" means "with" and "pathy" is from the Greek word for suffering, so that "sympathy" means "suffering with".
24 See below, ch. 11.

Part Three

The Second of My Two Theories: Moral Evil, Its Nature & Cause

8 Moral Evil

As I said, this Part will be about moral evil and its physical and psychological consequences – that is, about precisely those things which the theory which I have just expounded does not explain, and I shall be expressing my own beliefs. I shall begin by working at the level of philosophy, not theology, which is why I shall not, except in quotations, use the word "sin", which I take to be a religious term. Also, I shall not in this Part say anything about the remedies for moral evil. If anyone reading it gets the impression that I believe that the harm done by moral evil is irreparable, I can only ask him or her not to throw the book away but to read on.

What moral evil is

Free ought not to be defined as the ability to choose between right and wrong, but sometimes one alternative is immoral and then we need to distinguish clearly between two kinds of discussion. One is about whether *in general* an action is immoral or not. In these discussions, what is in a particular agent's mind is not considered. The other kind of discussion is about whether a man or woman who has done something wrong is a bad person or not, and for this his or her beliefs, which may be mistaken, are of critical importance. It is perfectly reasonable to say that in general a certain action is immoral and at the same time to say that because someone who performed an action of that kind did not believe that it was wrong, he or she was and is not a bad person. For instance, people in ancient Rome and the American Old South did not believe that it was immoral to own slaves. Virtuous slave-owners saw to it that their slaves were well housed, well fed and not cruelly overworked, but they owned them and they punished runaways. Also, they often separated slave children from their mothers, as farmers separate foals from mares, and sold them. Anyone directing a film like *Gone With the Wind* should instruct the actors, when they are acting, not to think of the characters they are playing as wicked. Moreover, in some countries women are treated in ways which we believe to be unjust, and marriages are arranged in ways which we (anyway, I) regard as morally wrong, but the people concerned do not believe that what they are doing is wrong. In our own societies there are groups which have their own subcultures, and it may be believed in these groups that theft, drug-trafficking or killing is right. Members of these groups may feel a properly moral obligation to provide for their children's education and they may comment on the bad moral character of others who do not do this, while they themselves rob and murder with no sense of doing wrong. Let me say again that by moral evil I mean here the doing of something which the agent himself or herself believes to be wrong.

Subjectivity

In ordinary conversation, "subjective" usually means peculiar to the speaker, not the general view or preference. For instance, if I say that a belief of mine or a preference for a particular wine is purely subjective, I mean that it is not the general view or preference. In a more technical context, however, "subjectivity" means the inner world of thoughts, ideas, beliefs, attitudes and feelings, some of which (not all) correspond to realities in the outside world, so that if a man has actually committed a murder I can say that his guilt is a subjective experience without implying that he did not do it. Likewise, if global warming is causing some of us to feel afraid, we can say that our fear is a subjective experience, meaning only that it is in our consciousness and not meaning that it is baseless. When I say, then, as I do now, that moral obligations and guilt are subjective experiences, I certainly do not mean that they are airy-fairy and imaginary.

Moral evil is real

It has often been said that no one does anything which he or she believes to be immoral. However, Vatican II said that morally evil acts have been committed "from the very dawn of history",[1] and it did not mean that people did things which we judge to be immoral, but which they thought were right. Peter Berger says that certain deeds committed in our time "seem to violate a fundamental awareness of the constitution of our humanity"; they are "not only evil, but monstrously evil". It is, he says, impossible to say that we think them evil because of the particular way in which we have been socialised; our condemnation is absolute and certain. It does not permit modification or doubt, and

---

1   Vatican II, *Gaudium et Spes*, # 13.

it is made in the conviction that it applies to all times and to all men and women as well as to the perpetrator or putative perpetrator of the particular deed.[2] In his old age, when he accepted free will, Karl Menninger said: "There is immorality; there is unethical behaviour; there is wrongdoing".[3]

When in 1945 allied soldiers arrived at the German concentration camps, saw the starving survivors there and learned what had been going on, they were appalled. These were men whose friends had been killed and who in many cases had themselves killed German soldiers; they had seen bombed cities and suffering civilians; but this was different. It was *evil* and most of them never got over it. It was like a mystical experience in reverse. Perhaps for some of the people who had been involved in the Holocaust as agents, for instance people who had worked in the railways, what they had done had been just a somewhat unpleasant job, but that no one at any level had seen that what was being done was extremely evil and nevertheless had taken part in it – that was unbelievable. Also, it seems to me that possibly some of the agents in the drug trade which is going on now believe that what they are doing is not wrong, but I feel sure that not all believe that. This is the kind of thing that Berdyaev had in mind when he said: "Every serious conception of life implies the vision of evil and the admission of its existence. To ignore it or not to see it makes a man irresponsible and superficial".[4]

The old fairy stories were fantastic and every child knew that. They told of wicked witches, cruel stepmothers and older sisters who humiliated and inflicted pain on the heroines. Then it came to be regarded as wrong to tell frightening stories to children, and evil disappeared from their reading matter. Speaking for myself, who read Grimm's stories when I was a child (I also had a stepmother, by the way), I believe that it is good for children, when then or later they encounter mysterious evil forces, to have been led by their fairy stories not to be completely surprised by them. It seems to me that one of the merits of the Harry Potter books is that they have not only people like Harry's uncle, aunt and cousin, in whom Harry encounters what I might call everyday nastiness, which is neither evil nor mysterious, but

---

2   Berger, *A Rumour of Angels* (1971), pp. 85-86.
3   Menninger, *Whatever Became of Sin?* (1977), p. 46.
4   Berdyaev, *Freedom and the Spirit*, pp. 160-161.

also Lord Voldemort, who is powerful, mysterious and *evil*. I am sure that Berdyaev would congratulate J.K. Rowling on preparing children for real evils, which most of them will later encounter and which some of them are encountering now.

Kinds of immoral act

There are different kinds of acts of the will and hence different kinds of immoral act.

AN IMMORAL ACTION

The easiest kind of immoral act to understand is the deliberate decision to perform a physical action which, as the agent knows, is immoral. For instance, Macbeth conceives the idea of hastening his predicted ascent to the throne by killing Duncan, reflects on how unnatural and foul a deed that would be, but makes up his mind to do it ("I am settled", he says) and does it.

IMMORAL ATTITUDES

There are other kinds of volition since we are capable of making choices not only about our physical actions but also about our attitudes towards things which are not in our control. A person who is growing old can accept the disadvantages of old age, gratefully accepting help when it is offered, or else he or she can be deliberately unhappy and belligerently refuse all offers of assistance. Let us be clear about this: one can put the full force of one's will into the choice of an attitude and there are immoral acts besides decisions to perform physical actions. Also, though this is less obvious, if a man decides to perform an immoral action and then for a purely practical reason, such as that it would cost too much money, changes his mind, the original decision was immoral.

OTHER PEOPLE'S ACTIONS

It is also possible to commit a purely interior immoral act about someone else's immoral action, whether it happened in the past or is going on in the present, even if one has no control whatever over it. It would, for instance, be wrong for a person seriously to say to himself or herself: "I know that the Holocaust was immoral but I don't like Jews so I'm glad it happened". Also, the end does not justify the means for spectators any more than for agents, so that it would be immoral seriously to say: "I believe that it was morally wrong to drop the atomic bombs on Hiroshima and Nagasaki, but I am glad that it was done, as it shortened the war". I will call this "spectator immorality". Thus it is not morally critical whether one does something oneself or it is done by someone else.

When one has a connection of some kind with the agent, the situation is more difficult. Consider these two different cases:

> A man and his wife learn that their unmarried adult daughter is having an affair with a married man and they say to themselves, "If this goes on she may become pregnant and we would love to have a grandchild", and *for this reason* they do nothing to stop the affair.

This is the second case:

> A man's wife tells him that she is about to leave him and go to live with another man. The husband believes that this will be disastrous in its consequences for himself, for their children and ultimately for her as well, and he tries to persuade her to stay. He fails. When he sees that she is not going to change her mind, it might be physically possible for him to hold her in the house indefinitely as a prisoner, but he does not attempt to do that. In the end he says, "If you are going to go, go now", and he does not physically intervene when his wife goes upstairs, packs a suitcase, carries it downstairs and out to her car, then gets in and drives away.

The first case is one of immorality because the end does not justify the means for interested spectators any more than for agents. In the second case, the husband knows that it is wrong to assume total control of the life of a sane adult person against his or her will, that while we should help each other as far as we can and this includes saving each other from making mistakes, there is a point beyond which one may not go to help someone else, and that when that point is reached one must draw back and let the other act, rightly disclaiming responsibility for what he or she does. In the example which I gave, the husband does not stop the action but he does not in any way will it. If he were to be asked why he let his wife leave him, he would say, "Because after I had said all I could say, she was still determined to go".

Serious and unserious immoral acts

Certain decisions are serious and others are of small moment. At one extreme are the choice of a career, the decision about whether or not to propose marriage or to accept a proposal and the decision about whether to become a priest or to cease to be one. At the other extreme are such decisions as which toothbrush to buy. When making a serious decision we have to consider almost every area of our lives: for instance, a man wondering whether or not to enter politics thinks about his religion, his family, his friends, his work, his finances and his interests, because they all affect his decision or will be affected by it. But when making a small decision one does not do this – one's religion, family, friends and work are not involved in a decision about a toothbrush. Also, by serious decisions persons structure their lives and make themselves the kinds of human being they are going to be, whereas trivial decisions do not affect our lives in any significant way. All this is a matter of observation but it may also be remarked that life would be unbearable if at almost every moment we were obliged to make decisions that affected our entire lives.

In the light of this we may distinguish between morally good acts which are important or serious, and others which are of little moment. If, for instance, a man intercedes for a victim of injustice, thereby endangering his own career and his standing in society, he performs a great morally good action, whereas someone who repays a debt of a dollar performs a morally good act of small moment. We may also distinguish between serious morally evil acts and morally bad acts of small moment, or between mortal and venial sins. At one extreme are deep hatred of another person, injustice on a large scale, and acts like Macbeth's; at the other extreme are knocking off work five minutes early, being impatient with an old man who cannot make up his mind quickly, or stopping to look at something in a shop window when one is running late for an appointment. On the one hand, these lesser acts are bad and one ought not to do such things. Also, they are signs of irresolution in one's intention to be a good person and they can make serious wrong actions in the future less unlikely. On the other hand, by them a person does not introduce evil into the structure of his or her life and make himself or herself a morally evil person. As Bonhoeffer says, "One sin, then, is not like another. They do not all have the same weight. There are heavier sins and lighter sins."[5] Also, there are degrees of guilt. Simon Wiesenthal says: "A man who, as a member of an ad-hoc execution squad, shot dead ten Jews is less guilty than one who,

---

5   Bonhoeffer, *Ethics* (Fontana edn.), p. 65. *Works*, vol. 6, p. 77.

without any order or under any pressure, broke a detainee's limbs by beating".⁶ In all that follows I shall be considering serious morally evil acts.

The personal choice

A person commits a morally evil act when he has before him two or more alternatives, one of which he believes to be wrong for him here and now, and he deliberately opts for it. Nothing inside or outside him antecedent to the choice itself – not his nature, the objects under consideration nor the circumstances – *makes* him choose as he does, and hence nothing outside his own self at the moment of choosing provides a complete causal explanation of the choice: one can only say, of this as of any other free choice, that the person is responsible for his choice. Augustine said: "Nothing else can make the mind the companion of evil desire except its own will and free choice";⁷ "we do evil from the free choice of the will".⁸ He went on to say that when we say that a person does evil because he or she chooses to do so we have arrived at the root of evil or have given the ultimate explanation. "A perverse will," he said, "is the cause of all evil. ... But if you are looking for the cause of this root, how will it be the root of all evil?"⁹ "The will itself is ultimately the cause of sin";¹⁰ "sin must be imputed to the will alone and we need look no further for the cause of sin".¹¹ Kant insisted on the same point. Speaking of moral evil, he said: "Man himself is its author";¹² "'moral evil' is possible only as a determination of the free will";¹³

> man himself must make or have made himself into whatever, in a moral sense, whether good or evil, he is or is to become. Either condition must be an effect of his free choice (*Willkur*); for otherwise

---

6 Wiesenthal, *Justice not Vengeance*, p. 4.
7 Augustine, *On Free Will*, book 1, ch. 11, # 21. This was an early work, much of which he later "retracted".
8 Ibid., 1 16 #34
9 Ibid., 3 17 #48
10 Ibid., 3 17 # 49.
11 Ibid., 3 22 # 63.
12 Kant, *Religion Within the Limits of Reason Alone*, p. 17.
13 Ibid., p. 24. I would say, "the person" rather than "man himself".

he could not be held responsible for it and could therefore be morally neither good nor evil.[14]

Speaking of sin, Barth said:

> For the knowledge of sin it is formally decisive that it should be recognised as man's personal act and guilt, that man should be and be made responsible for it, and this in such a way that he can neither renounce his liability nor impute it to others nor to an inexorable fate. ... This is indeed the only serious knowledge of nothingness.[15]

I would say: of evil.

The abiding intention

At times a person decides to embark on a series of actions which stretches into the foreseeable future: for instance, someone decides to get married, to become a doctor, or to have a serious affair. In the outer world, this involves intermittent actions, which may be either frequent or rare. In the person's inner world, however, the decision fixes an intention which is in the person all the time. If it is immoral, the person is immoral all the time and not only when he or she is performing immoral actions.

At other times a person performs a single serious action. Suppose, for instance, that a woman who is a nurse comes upon the scene of a car accident and, making a quick decision, springs into action, giving first aid, calling for an ambulance and looking after the victims while waiting for the ambulance to come. The will to do all this becomes the will to have done it, and it remains in her memory and in her will for the rest of her life. In a similar way, if a person decides to do some single morally wrong thing, which is serious, there can remain in him or her, as an abiding intention, the will to have done it, and in later years, if it remains, this renders him or her immoral.

The moral quality of a person at any moment is determined by his volitions at that moment. If he is continually doing good and has no intention of doing any wrong, and if he has no will to have done anything evil in the past, then he is a morally good person. If he has been doing wrong and intends to go on doing it, if he has the intention of doing something evil in the future, or if he has done wrong at some

---

14 Ibid., p. 40.
15 Barth, *Church Dogmatics*, III/3, # 50, p. 306. Concerning "nothingness", see below, p. 108.

time in the past and now wills to have done it, then he is morally bad. I will say later that if, on the other hand, he wills not to have done it, he is (at least as far as it is concerned) morally good.

The evil moment

While it is sometimes possible to pinpoint the moment when a morally evil decision is made, it is often impossible. This should not lead us to conclude that no decision was made. If one person hates another, it hardly matters when precisely he or she decided to do so; if a man forms the intention of doing something wrong, it does not very much matter when exactly he formed it: what matters about any person at any moment is what his or her freely held attitudes and intentions are *at that moment*.

Laws

Human beings form not only communities but societies, by which I mean groups which have at least some organisation and rules. Even something as free and seemingly unorganised as a group of friends has unwritten rules and expectations, some of which they invent (such as that they will meet once a month, taking it in turn to be the host) and others which they accept. If a man and a woman love one another they form a couple and, even if they do not get married, they live by certain rules. If they have children, more rules are made. Small societies such as families are banded together and form larger societies, which make rules concerning many things, including marriage and the bringing up of children. That is, the larger societies may make marriage a social institution as well as a personal arrangement between two people. At times societies become over-organised and demand strict observance of rules which once had a reason but which have become meaningless. We should not, however, dismiss all laws and we should see that the Roman legal system and the British common law system were or are great cultural achievements, like our literature, and with all their imperfections the various forms of democracy in countries today – I pass over other countries because I know little about them – deserve not merely the reluctant acceptance which we might give to a disagreeable necessity but our respect.

There is a prima facie moral obligation to observe laws. At exceptional times we may consider ourselves morally free or even morally obliged to act illegally, but as a general rule laws are for the common good and a certain moral obligation exists to behave in a legally correct way.

Moreover, the making of laws is to some extent subject to the demands of morality. For one thing, many civil laws make illegal what is immoral. This is obviously the case with laws against theft, murder and rape, and laws requiring parents to provide for their children. On the one hand, the authority of the government is restricted to certain areas of behaviour and therefore we do not make illegal everything which we believe to be immoral, but on the other hand these laws are not based on purely pragmatic considerations.[16] Breaches of our laws, then, are dealt with not in a chemically pure legal way but with a measure of moral outrage.

However, laws can be immoral. For instance, laws against interracial marriage are immoral because, other things being in order, interracial couples have a right to get married; and many eugenic laws, in accordance with which during the nineteen-thirties thousands of people were sterilised without their consents, were immoral. In many countries which were dominated by Nazis, it was illegal to protect Jews but many people, believing that what they were doing was morally obligatory, at great risk acted illegally and hid them.

Sometimes governments ask courts to decide whether or not something is illegal, and if it is not illegal they do it, even when the situation had not arisen when the laws were made. Also, if people in Australia (say) have certain legal rights, the government sometimes prevents people from setting foot here and, instead, puts them on islands which are outside Australian territory, so that they cannot claim these rights. In an extreme case, they may even take them to countries where torture is not illegal. The *morality* of the action is not considered and a result is that certain governments, claiming that what they are doing is legal, behave immorally. It is not enough to ask of an action, "Is it legal?"

Moral and legal obligations

It is important to be clear about the differences between moral and legal obligations.

---

16 Paton says of the law: "Its rules cannot, of course, be determined without reference to moral values" and "it is not suggested that criminal laws can or should be entirely divorced from the moral views of a particular community" (*Textbook of Jurisprudence*, pp. 320-321).

1. Moral obligations are inherent in human nature and not created by legislators. On the other hand, in every country there are purely legal obligations which are created by whoever has authority to make laws: for instance, in Australia we are obliged by law to vote in elections. When Paul talked about freedom from the law, he meant purely legal regulations; he did not mean the ten commandments. (At an even lower level are good and bad manners.)

2. Persons have moral rights. They also have legal rights: for instance, in Melbourne a pensioner has the right to free use of public transport on Saturdays and Sundays, because that is the law.

3. It would be wrong to say that morality is purely subjective whereas legality is objective. However, subjective and objective factors are differently involved in the two spheres. First, the law is concerned only with outward actions and not with purely inner acts like wishes, whereas purely inner acts can be immoral. Second, for someone to be condemned for a legal offence there must be a minimum of knowledge and free will, that is, of responsibility, but attention is mainly fixed on whether as a matter of objective fact a law was broken. In the moral sphere there are objectively immoral actions but, if a person's moral quality is to be judged, attention is mainly fixed on what he or she believed at the time about the morality of the action and how free he or she was, that is, on subjective factors.

4. What is legal or illegal varies from place to place. For instance, at one time it was legal to sell beer after 6 pm in Jingellic, New South Wales, illegal three kilometres away in Walwa, Victoria; during World War II it was against Catholic Church law to eat meat on Fridays in Walwa, but not in Jingellic; and Victorians broke no law if they crossed the Murray River to have a beer after 6 pm or, if they were Catholics, to eat meat on a Friday during World War II. Morality, however, is independent of place. There have been and still are countries where slavery and polygamy are legal, but these things are as immoral there as they are anywhere else.

5. Finding out whether an action is legal is usually easy. Most laws are clearly promulgated and when we are in doubt we ask lawyers, who if necessary consult books. In rare cases matters are referred to the highest court in the land, and almost always it is possible to obtain a definite, authoritative judgement. Finding out whether an action is immoral or not is quite different from this, not nearly so clear-cut, and

whether we are moral or immoral persons depends in the end on our moral beliefs.

6. The difference between morality and the law also becomes apparent in cases of actions which are immoral but not illegal, or even immoral but legally obligatory. For instance, adultery is immoral but in most countries it is not illegal, and in Nazi-occupied Europe it was legally obligatory but immoral to reveal the hiding places of Jews; also, if late on a cold night when there is no traffic at all, a pedestrian crosses a street against a red light rather than waiting miserably for it to change, the action is not morally wrong, even if the law does not allow exceptions and the action is as illegal then as it would be in the middle of the day.

7. The division between morality and the law becomes apparent when someone does something illegal, believing that it is morally obligatory. As I said, whether a person is morally good or bad depends on whether or not he believes that all his actions are morally good, so that if someone is accused of behaving immorally he can defend himself as a moral person by saying, "I didn't think it was wrong" or more strongly by saying, "I believed that I was morally obliged to do it"; but, as Paton says, *legally* "it is no defence that the accused considered it his moral duty to perform the act".[17] During the Cold War, Klaus Fuchs and others revealed secrets to Russia, because they believed that they were obliged to do that; when they were found out, this belief did not constitute a legal defence and they were found guilty of crimes. An extreme case occurred around 1964 in Perth, West Australia, when a philosophy lecturer came to the conclusion that for the sake of his wife he was morally obliged to kill their retarded child. He did that, then reported his action to the police. In due course he was found guilty of murder and sentenced to a term in gaol. That is, legally he was guilty of a crime; his action, however, had not been subjectively immoral. In this respect, the legal system seems to work as though moral considerations are not its business.[18]

---

17 Paton, *Textbook of Jurisprudence*, p. 320n.
18 I find myself here in disagreement with Pakenham, who says: "It hardly squares with ordinary thought or practice to find no room at all for a *minimum* quantity of guilt, legal and moral, as a normal condition of punishment" (*The Idea of Punishment*, p. 33, my emphasis).

8. Another difference between morality and the law is that our attitude towards an immoral person is different from our attitude towards a mere law-breaker. If someone has stolen some money from another person, we regard that as immoral and we treat the thief with some disdain, but if someone has not put money in a parking-meter we may regard that as a purely legal offence and feel no disdain for him – we may, indeed, envy his luck if he has not been given a ticket. And whereas the West Australian lecturer whom I mentioned was found guilty of the crime of murder and placed in gaol, he was (I hope) treated with respect and not in the way that immoral murderers are treated.

Legal and moral order

A society has economic order when there is little unemployment and the exchange of goods and services proceeds smoothly, and a society might be said to have legal order when its laws are sensible and, generally speaking, observed. Also, a country can be said to have medical order if most people are healthy and those who become sick are well treated. Similarly, what I might call primary moral order exists in a society where most people are morally good. If one arrives in a small town and finds that theft is virtually unknown, so that people do not need to lock their houses or their cars; that there is practically no adultery; and that, generally speaking, the people of the town are charitable in their speech and in their deeds; one may say that moral order exists there.

Legal and moral order are not exactly the same. A group of people could be completely law-abiding and nevertheless immoral, either because they were sexually promiscuous (which is not against the law) or because they were selfish and proud. On the other hand, a group of people could be to some extent habitual law-breakers in non-serious matters, by which I mean occasionally guilty of traffic offences, but in all serious matters be morally good people.

Legal positivism and the connection between law and morality

For legal positivists, the law has nothing to do with morality, which they say is a meaningless term. They maintain that laws should be made on purely pragmatic grounds, and that they should be enforced for purely practical reasons. They also recognise no rights other than legal rights, so that if (for instance) there is a law against killing retarded children, they have a right to live, but if there is not, they do not. They disagree with what I have said here.

9 The Content & Effects of a Morally Evil Act

THE CONTENT

The explicit and implicit content of decisions

All decisions which one makes are concerned with objects that are expressly mentioned in one's interior monologue. Serious decisions, however, are also concerned with things which one knows about but does not expressly mention to oneself. For instance, if a man in Melbourne says to himself, "I will fly to Sydney", he decides quite expressly about Sydney and an aeroplane, and without saying so, he decides to pay his fare, go to the Melbourne airport, walk into an aeroplane and spend some time in an enclosed space with other people. Also, in deciding to post a cheque to pay a bill, a woman – usually without saying any of this to herself – accepts, at least provisionally, private property, the monetary system, banks, the postal service and the government. Moreover, she accepts her own existence as a person, identified by her signature, and also the existence of other people and the world. That is, our decisions have both explicit and implicit content. Of course, to be the object of a decision, the person making the decision must know about it: if, for instance, if I decide to drive a car which has a loose axle that I do not know about, the axle and the trouble which it will cause are not in my decision, even implicitly.

In this chapter I shall be concerned not only with express or formulated intentions but also with those which are known though not expressed. Here begins, then, a journey into darkness as we explore the implications of a morally evil act and unravel the intentions which persons have when they make seriously wrong decisions.

The destruction of the self

It might seem that in most morally evil acts people seek to do themselves good, and often at the expense of others. Thinking along these lines, some writers say that moral evil springs from excessive self-love.¹ However, persons who commit morally evil acts render themselves in their own judgement evil. Paul Weiss says:

> Wickedness is self-defeating. It destroys value and thereby injures him who was finally to benefit. ... It would be wrong to say that they [the wicked] really prosper, since they defeat themselves, forcing themselves further and further away from the status of beings who are perfect, complete men.²

Simone de Beauvoir says: "Evil is not at one with itself; self-laceration is its very essence".³ Karl Barth says that sin is "at one and the same time a denial of God, a hatred of one's fellow and" – to come to what concerns us now – "self-destruction".⁴ A sinner, A. C. Bradley says of Macbeth, knowingly makes mortal war on his own soul;⁵ in the extreme case he or she is "dominated by the lust of self-demolition".⁶ Thomas Aquinas said that self-hatred is absolutely impossible,⁷ but he was wrong. As Georges Bernanos said, "How easy it is to hate oneself!"⁸ There can even be pleasure in it, as appears in this passage from D. H. Lawrence:

> He [Birkin] knew that his spirituality was concomitant of a process of depravity, a sort of pleasure in self-destruction. There really was a certain stimulant in self-destruction, for him – especially when it was translated spiritually.⁹

Erich Fromm shrewdly observes: "The selfish person does not love himself too much but too little: in fact he hates himself",¹⁰ and self-

---

1 De Finance, for instance, says: "Hatred for others or for God is only the expression ... of a love of self, of one's own excellence, of one's own freedom, etc. This love is in itself good, for it is directed towards real values. Only, it is not ruled by reason." (*Connaissance de l'être*, p. 192.)
2 Weiss, *Man's Freedom*, p. 250.
3 De Beauvoir, "Must We Burn Sade?" in Beauvoir, *Sade*, p. 70.
4 Barth, *Church Dogmatics*, IV/1, #60, p. 399.
5 Bradley, *Shakespearean Tragedy*, p. 301.
6 Eliot, *Murder in the Cathedral*, chorus in part 2; *Collected Plays*, p. 43.
7 Thomas Aquinas, *Summa theologiae*, 1-2 29 34.
8 Bernanos, *Diary of a Country Priest*, p. 314.
9 Lawrence, *Women in Love*, chap. 23, p. 301.
10 Fromm, *The Art of Loving*, p. 60.

destruction is in all moral evil. It is usually implicit, so that it is not mentioned even in the person's interior monologue. Explicitly, the person usually acts in order to gain some advantage, but he or she knows that the act is destructive.

The rejection of love

It takes two to make a friendship but one person can break it by cancelling his or her commitment to the relationship. If, then, two people have been friends and one seriously hurts the other, the friendship is broken. More generally, any personal human relationship is held together by mutual respect and by the common acceptance of certain values. Often by evil actions people break away from groups to which they have belonged, or they deliberately reject the values in which these groups believe, and either leave or, remaining in the group, they are estranged from the other members. A person who commits serious moral evil opts for alienation from his or her fellow human beings.

This is extremely clear in the Marquis de Sade, whose system "is based upon the primary fact of absolute solitude",[11] achieved by total negation of others: "For the Unique Person, all men are equal in their nothingness, and the Unique One, by reducing them to nothing, simply clarifies and demonstrates this nothingness".[12] Byron expresses it, too, when his hero sets out

> to separate
> Himself from all who shared his mortal state.[13]

For such a one, "hell is alone"[14] or "hell is other people"[15] – other people are absent, or if present are enemies – and he or she has chosen it. Camus is speaking of murder in the following passage but it holds true of any serious wrong done to another:

---

11 Blanchot, "Sade" in Sade, *Justine etc.*, p. 140.
12 Ibid., p. 55.
13 Byron, *Lara*, canto I, lines 347-348.
14 Eliot, *The Cocktail Party*, act 1, scene 3; *Collected Plays*, p. 169.
15 Sartre, *No Exit*, near the end of the play.

It suffices for a man to remove one single human being from the society of the living to automatically exclude himself from it. When Cain kills Abel, he flees to the desert.[16]

Hurting other persons

At times, when a person acts immorally, no other person is hurt. People sometimes say, of a bad action, that no other person was hurt, as though that made it all right. While whether other persons are hurt is not the only criterion of morality, very often other persons are immorally hurt. Sometimes the hurting of others is willed indirectly – often the direct object of a robber's will is not the hurt which is inflicted on the person who is robbed – but morally evil acts often contain the will to hurt particular persons. This can be explicit, as happens when burglars not only steal from a house but vandalise it. At times it reaches an extreme. Lady Chatterley experienced it in her adultery:

> She realised for the first time what a queer subtle thing hate is. For the first time, she had consciously and definitely hated Clifford [her husband], with vivid hate: as if he ought to be obliterated from the face of the earth. And it was strange, how free and full of life it made her feel, to hate him and to admit this fully to herself.[17]

The will to destroy another person is quite explicit in Valmont's peculiarly heartless seduction of the virtuous lady in *Les liaisons dangereuses* (1782). He wants to possess her but he declares, first, that he wants her to continue to believe in God and in virtue and to be terrified of sin and damnation:

> Far be it from me to destroy the prejudices which sway her mind! They will add to my happiness and my triumph. Let her believe in virtue, and sacrifice it to me; let the idea of falling terrify her, without preventing her fall; and may she, shaken by a thousand terrors, forget them, vanquish them only in my arms. Then, I agree, let her say to me: "I adore thee". … I shall be truly the God whom she has preferred.[18]

---

16 Camus, *The Rebel*. Camus says that this is so "if the world has no higher meaning, if man is only responsible to man", but this condition is unnecessary.
17 Lawrence, *Lady Chatterley's Lover*, chap. 13, p. 200.
18 Choderlos de Laclos, *Les liaisons dangereuses*, 6th letter.

He wants her, he says, "to let her virtue expire in a slow agony".[19] Second, he has made up his mind that he will not ask her to become his mistress; instead, he will woo her until she asks him to become her lover, thereby making her fall from virtue all the greater. Third, from the beginning he intends subsequently to reject her and to let the world know that he has had an affair with her and then rejected her; this will hurt her feelings, ruin her reputation and publicly humiliate her. The intention of hurting another person, which is rarely as explicit as in these cases, is implicit in many immoral actions.

At a less exotic level, the infliction of pain on human beings by persons who seem to enjoy doing precisely that seems to be fairly common. A small boy may find that it gives him pleasure to inflict pain on animals or on his smaller brother or sister. When he is larger, he may become a playground bully, who bashes or tortures weaker boys, or solitary boys, whom others do not defend. He does this not to get money from his victims, nor to make them leave the school, but simply because he enjoys it. When he is an adult, he may for no advantage inflict domestic violence on his wife or children, who will be afraid to report him. He may obtain employment in a military prison, or in a police station where people are interrogated, and there humiliate and torture people for the sheer pleasure which he gets from it. There have been cases of people letting themselves be photographed inflicting humiliation and pain on prisoners, so that they can enjoy looking at the photographs later, and showing them to others who are similarly inclined.

The will to destroy

Acceptance is an act of the will in which persons are not creative, but give assent to what they find; and good persons accept reality. I do not mean that they accept everything that exists, just as it is, any more than we mean, when we say that we love a city, that we love everything in it. I mean that they see that the world is there, and they accept it in general; they willingly accept the fact that other persons besides themselves exist and that these others have value in themselves; they accept themselves, too; and they recognise certain values which are in some sense outside them. This acceptance might seem at first to be servile acquiescence rooted in powerlessness, but good persons often accept

---

19 Ibid., 70th letter.

reality because they see it as good, not because while they would like to change it they cannot. They may – indeed, should – refuse to accept some particular real beings, but this does not cancel their acceptance of reality; indeed, their refusal derives from their more basic acceptance.[20] The acceptance of reality may never be expressed, but it is present in every serious good act.[21] When persons refuse to respect the value of other persons, or refuse some elements of human institutions that are not merely conventional but (as they themselves believe) necessary, or when they refuse to act in accord with their own essential nature, they implicitly say no to reality.

This no is not a simple turning of the mind away from reality, choosing to ignore it but wishing it no harm. On the contrary, whoever performs an immoral act takes a positively hostile attitude towards reality: he or she wills it away, wills the void, which brings us to destruction. Small boys throw stones, break windows, scratch cars, or make dignified men slip and fall, and they do this "for fun". According to Camus, Bakunin vehemently proclaimed a pleasure in destruction[22] and Macbeth does not simply decide to ignore the moral order but wills it to be torn to pieces. Milton's Satan says:

> *For only in destroying I find ease*
> *To my relentless thoughts.*[23]

Goethe's Mephistopheles says:

> *I am the Spirit that always denies!*
> *And rightly so, for everything that comes into being*
> *Deserves to be destroyed.*[24]

One of Sade's characters says:

---

20   In *The Rebel* Camus emphasises that noble revolt stems from a prior acceptance (p. 16 and elsewhere).

21   Lavelle says: "At the heart of freedom there is an act of acceptance, a yes which we say to being and to life. ... This yes is always present deep within us, even when we refuse to formulate it." (*Les puissances du moi* [1948], pp. 151-152.)

22   Camus, *The Rebel*, p. 158. Bakunin (1814-76) was a Russian anarchist.

23   Milton, *Paradise Lost*, book 9, lines 129-130.

24   Goethe, *Faust*, part I, in the study.

> Oh, what a pleasure it is to destroy! ... I know of nothing more deliciously enjoyable. There is no ecstasy like that which one enjoys when one gives oneself up to this divinely infamous action.[25]

All of Sade's writing, indeed, is expressive of a will to destroy which reaches not only other people but Nature or being itself:

> It is she [Nature] I should like to outrage. I should like to upset her plans, thwart her progress, arrest the wheeling courses of the stars, throw the spheres floating in space into nightly confusion, destroy what serves nature and protect what is harmful to her: in a word, insult her in her works.[26]

In Paul Claudel's *Partage de midi* (1906), Mesa says, "There is no tomorrow" and his mistress, Ysé, replies:

> *You are right, there is no tomorrow ...*
>
> *There is no more past, no more future, no more husband, no children, no, no, no.*
>
> *Our desire is not to create but to destroy.*
>
> *Let there be nothing in existence but you and me, and in you only me, and in me only your possession and rage and tenderness and the desire to destroy you. ...*
>
> *Ah, it is not your happiness I bring you, but your death and mine with it.*[27]

John Glenn Gray says that some soldiers find that they enjoy killing and become killers-for-pleasure, after which, unlike other delights, killing "becomes, relatively soon in most men, a consuming lust which swallows up other pleasures".[28] This what Karl Barth has in mind when he says that moral evil involves the will for the void, and F. A. Staudenmaier says that sin negates being, truth, order and law, but is not satisfied with mere negation – "it wants to liquidate, to destroy, what it negates".[29] This manifested itself in Nazism: as Ulrich Simon says in *The Theology of Auschwitz*, "The victims of Auschwitz died

---

25   Sade, *Juliette*, quoted in Praz, *The Romantic Agony*, chap. 3, p. 107.
26   Ibid.
27   Claudel, *Partage de midi*, in Claudel, *Théâtre*, I, p. 1116. For more about Claudel, see below, p. 111.
28   Gray, *The Warriors*, p. 57 (see also pp. 51-58).
29   Staudenmaier, quoted in Küng, *Justification*, p. 147.

because pagan madness wished to extirpate the light and to rule the world in dark, ecstatic nihilism".[30] Finally, I quote a psychologist, Erich Fromm, who says that people are at times malignantly aggressive, cruel and destructive not in order to achieve useful purposes but for the sheer lustful pleasure of destroying. He talks of

> that form of aggression which is characteristic of man and which he does not share with other mammals: his propensity to kill and to torture without any "reason", but as a goal in itself, a goal not pursued for the sake of defending life, but as desirable and pleasureful in itself,[31]

and of "the wish to destroy for the sake of destruction".[32]

This implies that badness is secondary to goodness for, as Paul Ricoeur says, "however radical evil may be, it cannot be as primordial as goodness"[33] or, as G. C. Berkouwer says, "Evil has no thesis in itself but only antithesis".[34]

The will to evil

Some authors define the good as that which is willed, or the will as the faculty whose object is good, and then say that a direct will to evil is a contradiction in terms. They say that what we call moral evil choosing a lesser good now rather than a greater good which will come later, sensual satisfaction (which is a good) rather than the peace of a good conscience, or one's own good rather than the general good. They say that what makes moral evil psychologically possible is the ability which we have to concentrate our attention on the first member of any of these pairs. In an immoral act, however, a person chooses not a lesser good but an evil, and not his own good but his own destruction. It therefore remains a mystery how it is psychologically possible for people to commit morally evil acts. However, sad to say, we have now reached what is in every serious immoral act: the will to evil. The will should be described as the faculty of striving towards or withdrawing from, accepting or rejecting, desiring or abhorring, and choosing between objects that are known and actions that are thought of; and

---

30 Simon, *The Theology of Auschwitz*, p. 88.
31 Fromm, *The Anatomy of Human Destructiveness*, p. 100.
32 Ibid., p. 186.
33 Ricoeur, *The Symbolism of Evil*, p. 156. .
34 Berkouwer, *Sin*, p. 238.

the good should be said to be that which has what its nature requires it to have, or that which suits some other being's nature. A will to evil is not excluded by these descriptions and to this we have now come. Biblical authors were well aware of it; they said that sinners call evil good, good evil, they put darkness for light and light for darkness (Isa 5:20) and they deliberately become absurd in their thinking (see Rom 1:21). In their own minds, and wherever their influence reaches, they destroy good sense. These authors saw that it is possible to "love evil more than good, and lying more than speaking the truth" (Ps 52:3); they knew that we can "love all words that devour" (Ps 52:4) and yield to "the fascination of wickedness" (Wis 4:12); they knew about the fierce will to evil and when they exhorted their hearers to 'seek good, and not evil" (Amos 5:14) and "hate what is evil, hold fast to what is good" (Rom 12:9), they knew that the opposite is possible. Paul Ricoeur remarks that for them hubris was "something like a deliberate will, distinct from being led astray by desire and from being carried away by anger – an intelligent will to evil for the sake of evil".[35] Shakespeare, too, clearly believed that a person can will what he or she knows to be evil. Macbeth is fully conscious of the fact that what he is doing is evil:

> *Let not night see my black and deep desires,*[36]

he says, but he himself sees them and how black they are – in his "If it were done when 'tis done" speech he goes over in his mind the reasons why the deed he is going to commit is evil. Lady Macbeth expresses a fierce will to be unwomanly, inhuman, and unnatural – she wants, she says, to be filled with direst cruelty, she wants nothing to shake her fell purpose, she wants murdering ministers, nature's mischief and thick night,[37] all of which clearly means that she fully intends to be evil. In *Titus Andronicus*, Aaron's only regret is that he has not done more evil in his life:

> *Even now I curse the day – and yet, I think,*
> *Few come within the compass of my curse -*
> *Wherein I did not some notorious ill,*
> *As kill a man, or else devise his death,*

---

35   Ricoeur, *The Symbolism of Evil*, p. 156.
36   Shakespeare, *Macbeth*, 1 4 51.
37   Ibid., 1 5 40-54.

> Ravish a maid, or plot the way to do it,
> Accuse some innocent and forswear myself,
> Set deadly enmity between two friends,[38]

and so on for another ten lines. As Helen Gardner says, there is in Shakespeare's plays absolute or sheer ill-will, "implacable malevolence, a hardness of heart that appals".[39] Milton's Satan could hardly be more explicit: "Evil, be thou my good," he says.[40] Sade's character, Madame de Clairwil, required of Juliette that she cease doing evil things in order to obtain sexual pleasure; she told her to purify her motives and do evil "solely for the pleasure of doing it". Dostoyevsky, too, saw the possibility of the will to evil and the strange attraction that the will to evil can have. Dmitry Karamazov says: "I loved vice and I loved the feeling of shame that vice gave me. I loved cruelty."[41] And Lisa Khokhkakov says: "I simply don't want to do good. I want to do evil".[42] In one of Edgar Allan Poe's stories the narrator says:

> And then came, as if to my final and irrevocable overthrow, the spirit of perverseness. Of this spirit, philosophy takes no account. Yet I am not more sure that my soul lives, than I am that perverseness is one of the primitive impulses of the human heart – one of the indivisible primary faculties, or sentiments, which give direction to the character of man. Who has not, a hundred times, found himself committing a vile or a silly action, for no other reason than because he knows he should not? Have we not a perpetual inclination, in the teeth of our best judgement, to violate that which is Law, merely because we understand it to be such? This spirit of perverseness, I say, came to my final overthrow. It was this unfathomable longing of the soul to vex itself – to offer violence to its own nature – to do wrong for the wrong's sake only – that urged me to continue.[43]

Lautréamont's creation Maldoror "sinks down into the vertiginous abysses of evil" and says: "When I commit a crime I know what I am

---

38 Shakespeare, *Titus Andronicus*, 5 1 125-131.
39 Gardner, *Religion and Literature* (1971), p. 49.
40 Milton, *Paradise Lost*, book 4, line 110.
41 Dostoyevsky, *The Brothers Karamazov* (1880), book 3, ch. 4, p. 124.
42 Ibid., book 11, ch. 3, p. 682.
43 Edgar Allan Poe (1809-49), "The Black Cat" in *Tales of Mystery and Imagination*.

9 ⁑ The Content & Effects of a Morally Evil Act

doing. I would not wish it otherwise!"[44] So much for Mercier's statement that evil as such is never willed. So much, too, for William Temple's statement, "That any man ever chose evil, knowing it to be evil for him, is to me quite incredible". So much, indeed, for the cheerful thought that no one ever intends evil, itself.

THE EFFECTS OF MORAL EVIL

Immorality often has some pleasant results, such as money, power, prestige or pleasure, but in deliberately doing wrong a person at least implicitly wills destruction, and it follows. The extent of the damage can be learned from life or from the Bible and great literature, including Shakespeare's tragedies, in almost all of which moral evil is the main source of the disturbed state of affairs which exists at the beginning or which comes into existence as the play proceeds, and of the suffering and deaths which occur. In this chapter I shall discuss the moral wrongdoing of an individual.

The after-effects of immorality in the consciousness or subjectivity of the agent

THE EXPERIENCE OF GUILT

Guilt is the experience of a person who has done something which he or she believed to be immoral, and who, therefore, is or at any rate was in his or her own judgement evil. There are therapists who, if such persons come to them, set about trying to convince them that they ought not to feel guilty, for instance because they could not help doing what they did.[45] One such person went to a number of therapists before he found one who believed in his guilt, and to this person he said: "You are the first person who has not tried to explain away my culpability and hence the guilt I now feel; I'm glad I've found you". Martin Buber tells of a conference which he attended in 1948 at which "the genesis of guilt" was discussed and the psychologists who were present all offered explanations of the origin of *guilt feelings*, which they classed as pathological: it did not occur to them that some people might have

---

44   Lautréamont's *Maldoror*, pp. 66, 75. Lautréamont published *Les chants de Maldoror* in 1868.
45   Concerning responsibility, see my *Free Will*, pp. 168-170, 206.

deliberately committed evil deeds and that these deeds might be the origin not precisely of their *guilt feelings* but of their *guilt*. He says:

> There exists real guilt, fundamentally different from all the anxiety-induced bugbears that are generated in the cavern of the unconscious. Personal guilt, whose reality some schools of psychoanalysis contest and others ignore, does not permit itself to be reduced to the trespass against a powerful taboo.[46]

Guilt can be a horrible experience. I talked earlier of how authors have said that wicked men oppose and defeat themselves and, like Macbeth, make mortal war on their own souls. A person derives his identity from his past, his specific qualities and his aims; if he has done evil and still wills to have done it, or if he intends to do evil, then in his own eyes he is detestable. His anguish of conscience is guilt. "The worm of conscience still be-gnaw thy soul" is Queen Margaret's curse on Gloucester in *Richard III* and on the night before his death it does. He says:

> *Alack! I love myself. Wherefore? for any good*
> *That I myself have done unto myself?*
> *O! no: alas! I rather hate myself*
> *For hateful deeds committed by myself. ...*
> *My conscience hath a thousand several tongues,*
> *And every tongue brings in a several tale,*
> *And every tale condemns me for a villain.*
> *All several sins, all us'd in each degree,*
> *Throng to the bar, crying all, "Guilty! guilty!"*
> *I shall despair.*[47]

THE SENSE OF MEANINGLESSNESS, VANITY, ABSURDITY

A morally evil person denies reason and so destroys meaning for himself or herself. The feelings then grows in him or her that

> *There's nothing serious in mortality,*
> *All is but toys,*[48]

---

46 Buber, "Guilt and Guilt Feelings" in *The Knowledge of Man*, p. 132.
47 Shakespeare, *Richard III*, 5 5 141-153.
48 Shakespeare, *Macbeth*, 2 3 92-93.

or that everything in life is inane and meaningless. The biblical word for this is "vanity". The corresponding modern word is "absurdity" and the feeling that life is absurd is powerfully expressed by Macbeth:

> *Life's but a walking shadow, a poor player*
> *That struts and frets his hour upon the stage*
> *And then is heard no more. It is a tale*
> *Told by an idiot, full of sound and fury,*
> *Signifying nothing.*[49]

SADNESS

With all this comes ennui, *taedium vitae*, the loss of the will to live, and sadness. Brunner says that "if we had eyes to see, even in feeling we would discover the effect of sin as a fundamental joylessness, which always lies concealed under all other feelings",[50] and again I quote *Macbeth*. There is immense sadness in these lines:

> *I have lived long enough; my way of life*
> *Is fallen into the sere, the yellow leaf;*
> *And all that which should accompany old age,*
> *As honour, love, obedience, troops of friends,*
> *I must not look to have.*[51]

John Glenn Gray, whom I quoted earlier, said of killing::

> It tends to turn men inward upon themselves and make them inaccessible to more normal satisfactions. Because they rarely can feel remorse, they experience no purgation and cannot grow. The utter absence of love in this inverted kind of creation makes the delight utterly sterile. Though there may be a fierce pride in the numbers destroyed and in their reputation for proficiency, soldier-killers usually experience an ineffable sameness and boredom in their lives. The restlessness of such men in rest areas behind the front is notorious.[52]

I quote, also, from Georges Bernanos. A character in *Joy* says:

> I too can be sad ... with a sadness that is as cold as hell! Now that I have experienced it I shall never forget it, never! There is an

---

49 Ibid., 5 5 23-27.
50 Brunner, *Man in Revolt*, p. 255.
51 Shakespeare, *Macbeth*, 5 3 24-28.
52 Gray, *The Warriors*, p. 57. Gray was writing about what he had observed.

intoxication in sadness, a vile intoxication! It is like foam on the lips. I have eaten of the forbidden fruit. Oh, it is horrible! ... Sadness came into the world with Satan – that world our Saviour never prayed for, the world you say I do not know. Oh, it is not so difficult to recognise: it is the world that prefers cold to warmth! What can God find to say to those who, of their own free will, of their weight incline towards sadness and turn instinctively towards the night?[53]

In this sadness there is trouble and fear or, to use Kierkegaard's term, dread.

OUTSIDERHOOD

Outsiderhood often turns out to be greater and more painful than the wrongdoer expected. It might seem that in sexual immorality a person finds another person or persons, but men of experience have thought otherwise. Camus says that when Cain kills Abel, he flees into the desert, and he continues: "If murderers are legion, then this legion lives in the desert and in the other kind of solitude called promiscuity".[54] Saint-Exupéry's sage says: "I ... got nothing of my sensual pleasure but the morose and futile satisfaction of a miser's greed. Seeking, I found but myself."[55] One might think that there is honour among thieves, but in *The Thief's Journal* Jean Genet says that evil never unites persons at a deep level. He tells of a theft which he himself committed and he says: "I had, in achieving it, destroyed once again ... the dear bonds of brotherhood".[56]

THE FEAR OF PUNISHMENT

Gaylin says that "true guilt does not stand or fall on impending punishment".[57] Also, fear of punishment can be an obstacle to true repentance, which, as we shall see, ends guilt. However, in many cases wrongdoers, besides feeling guilty, are afraid of being found out and punished, so I include fear in this list.

---

53   Bernanos, *Joy*, chap. 3, p. 85. The reference is to Jesus' words, "I am not praying for the world" (John 17:9 NJB).
54   Camus, *The Rebel*, p. 245.
55   Saint-Exupéry, *The Wisdom of the Sands*, ch. 113, p. 311.
56   Genet, *The Thief's Journal*, p. 66.
57   Gaylin, *Caring*, p. 121. Also, see below, p. 142.

The effects of immorality in the outside world

I come now to the harm which immorality does to human communities and to the whole world.

SOME PEOPLE ARE HURT, IN MANY CASES SERIOUSLY

Besides hurting themselves, people who do wrong often directly hurt others. They swindle them, they cause them physical pain and even death, and they hurt them emotionally. In recent times it has become evident that sexual abuse of children and young persons harms them terribly. Old Testament writers insisted that innocent persons do not suffer for long, and certainly not to the ends of their lives, at the hands of the wicked, but we have discovered, as one of Faulkner's characters did, "that God either would not or could not – anyway, did not – save innocence just because it was innocent",[58] and the sufferings and death of the innocent Christ, which were caused by evil men, prove this beyond all doubt.

THERE IS DESTRUCTION OF MORAL ORDER

Imagine that about twenty people who belong to a club of some sort are in a house which belongs to the club and that at first people trust each other in the matter of money, so that they leave cash in their rooms, which they do not bother to lock. After ten days someone finds that a large sum of money is missing from his or her room. It is certain that it was stolen and that it was an inside job. At once everyone is suspicious of everyone else, and from then on people take care to keep their money on their persons or in locked suitcases. The old moral order has gone. Imagine, also, a group of married people who are all firmly committed to fidelity and who mix freely in a friendly way. If a man sees his wife deeply engaged in conversation with another man, he does not suspect them of being lovers or fear that they may become lovers. Then one day it becomes known that a man and a woman who belong to this group have been having an affair. At once, all is changed. Now, no one feels safe. If a man and a woman who are married, not to each other, begin to have an interesting conversation, they wonder if it is dangerous; their spouses, if they can see what is happening, wonder if what they are seeing is a moment of an affair. The old moral order has been disturbed and now there is anxiety. If things go from bad

---

58   Faulkner, *Requiem for a Nun*, act 2, scene 1, p. 145.

to worse so that a situation is arrived at where theft and adultery are commonplace and honesty and fidelity are exceptional, grave moral disorder reigns.

More generally, various institutions – private ownership and the rules which have been worked out to protect and limit it, marriage and the code of sexual ethics, or the state – are important human achievements which have taken centuries to develop to their present state and they are necessary for the physical, intellectual and moral well-being of people. By immoral actions they are harmed. For example, the system which has been worked out to facilitate the exchange of goods and services is damaged, if only by virtue of the fact that the trust between people which is necessary for it to work smoothly is undermined. Similarly, those who deliberately disobey a legitimate authority, knowing that they are in the wrong, undermine that authority and implicitly will the destruction of the system to which it is essential.

THE EVOLUTION OF MORALITY IS SET BACK

Through centuries of experience human beings have come to see what respect for persons demands of us and so to agree on moral laws governing human behaviour. For instance, we have come to see what respect for persons demands of us in the context of sexual relationships, and so to agree on certain moral laws governing sexual behaviour. If someone is immoral, he or she wants to "cancel and tear to pieces that great bond"[59] which is the moral law, and take us backwards towards the lawlessness and unhappiness which we are trying to leave further and further behind.

It is one thing for a person to believe that some human institution is bad and endeavour to destroy it. Of that I am not talking here, since it is not immoral and it may even be heroic. A morally evil decision is quite different and in it a person sets himself or herself against the development of the institutions which he or she knows that we need and which have been developed in the course of time.

Moral evil and nature

Nature, too, is ruined by the wrongdoing of human beings. In *Paradise Lost*, when Eve succumbed to temptation,

---

59 Shakespeare, *Macbeth*, 3 2 50.

> Forth reaching to the fruit, she plucked, she ate.
> Earth felt the wound, and Nature from her seat,
> Sighing through all her works, gave signs of woe,
> That all was lost,

and when Adam ate,

> Earth trembled in her entrails, as again
> In pangs, and Nature gave a second groan,[60]

and if some pollution of earth, air and water is an unavoidable side-effect of industrial progress, which further developments in technology will enable us to rectify, much of it has been and is being caused by sheer greed and in full awareness of the avoidable damage that is being done. Earth had good reason to tremble when human beings began to do wrong.

Evil leads to more evil

A frightful consequence of moral evil is – more moral evil. It is almost a rule that wrongdoing leads the person who commits it to commit more wrongs. "The sinner," says Ecclesiasticus, "heaps sin on sin" [Sir 3:27]. Macbeth, having murdered Duncan, goes on to murder Banquo, saying:

> Things bad begun make strong themselves by ill.[61]

Later he says:

> I am in blood
> Stepped in so far, that, should I wade no more
> Returning were as tedious as go o'er.[62]

Richard III says:

> I am in
> So far in blood that sin will pluck on sin[63]

---

60 Milton, *Paradise Lost*, book 9, lines 781-784, 1000-1001
61 Shakespeare, *Macbeth*, 3 2 56. The sense of the line is that once a person has embarked on a course of evil, by doing evil things he or she becomes more committed to evil.
62 Ibid., 3 4 135-137.
63 Shakespeare, *Richard III*, 4 2 64-65/

Moral evil in a person's consciousness is like a defect in a machine, which, if it is not removed, causes undue strain to be placed on other parts of the machine so that they, too, become defective. For one thing, a decision to do wrong is rarely a commitment to one isolated act. More often, a series of acts is involved, and with each act a person makes himself more deeply committed to evil. Also, it often happens that by his morally evil acts a person puts himself into such a position that a tremendous effort of will would be needed for him not to go on: if, for example, a man obtains a good deal of money dishonestly and uses it to buy a beautiful house, live expensively and send his children to exclusive schools, it would almost seem to be asking too much of him to require that he impoverish himself by returning the money to its rightful owners; again, if a man has a sexual liaison which he himself believes to be immoral, it may require a tremendous effort on his part to break it off; if a man is dishonest or commits adultery, he thereby commits himself to telling lies to cover what he has done, and when he tells these lies he commits himself to telling more lies later on. In such cases as these a person by doing what he believes to be wrong binds himself to further wrongdoing. Again, after a person has done wrong he is often strongly inclined to alleviate his sense of guilt by trying to persuade himself that what he did was not wrong after all; when he thinks he has just succeeded in doing this he will experience a strong drive to do whatever it was again, to show himself that he can do it now without compunction.

Moreover, moral evil in one person often leads to moral evil in others:

> *The act of evil*
> *breeds others to follow,*
> *young sins in its own likeness,*[64]

says Aeschylus in a trilogy in which adultery leads to war and another adultery leads to the killing of a husband, which in turns leads to the killing of a mother by her son. Violence breeds violence; sexual vice poisons a milieu so that more sexual vice follows it; if in politics or in business people start to use "dirty tricks", their competitors are (or claim to be) put under pressure to do the same.

---

64 Aeschylus, *Agamemnon*, translated by Richard Lattimore, lines 758-760.

The evil in the world

The immorality of human beings has caused our world to be corrupt or fallen. For years we lived with the threat of a nuclear war between superpowers, now terrorism is a threat to us all. Hostility between human beings is constant, whether between people of different classes, of different races, of different religions or of different political views; and I do not mean simple opposition but contempt and hatred stoked by repeated telling-over of atrocities. This always simmers dangerously and at times breaks out in violence. Theft and dishonesty are so rife that it seems perfectly natural to us to lock our homes and cars whenever we leave them. Almost wherever we look a perverse eroticism, in which there is a strong element of sadism, invades our senses through our eyes, poisons our imaginations and feelings, and works against happy relationships between men and women. There is also a perverse delight in the violent destruction of human beings and things, so that "violent sorrow seems a modern ecstasy". Our world in some measure resembles Scotland under Macbeth's rule,

> *where to do harm*
> *Is often laudable, to do good sometimes*
> *Accounted dangerous folly.*[65]

Also, it is in some measure a world which has no morals ("right and wrong lose their names"), so that in the end it is sheer power that counts. We recognise its description in Ulysses' speech in *Troilus and Cressida*, where he says that when people disregard "degree",

> *Force should be right – or rather, right and wrong,*
> *Between whose endless jar justice resides,*
> *Should lose their names, and so should justice too.*
> *Then every thing includes itself in power,*
> *Power into will, will into appetite;*
> *And appetite, an universal wolf,*
> *So doubly seconded with will and power,*
> *Must make perforce an universal prey,*
> *And last eat up himself. Great Agamemnon,*
> *This chaos, when degree is suffocate,*
> *Follows the choking.*[66]

---

65 Shakespeare, *Macbeth*, 4 2 74-75.
66 Shakespeare, *Troilus and Cressida*, 1 3 116-126.

And we have all felt at some time that

> *It is not we alone, it is not the house, it is not the city which is defiled,*
> *But the world that is wholly foul,*[67]

or we feel like the man who said that he was all right

> *so long as I could think*
> *Even of my life as an isolated ruin,*
> *A casual bit of waste in an orderly universe.*
> *But it begins to seem just part of some huge disaster,*
> *Some monstrous mistake and aberration*
> *Of all men, of the world, which I cannot put in order.*[68]

Even if there is no danger of more immoral actions, a gravely immoral action creates a moral disorder which endures. In 1977 a certain Richard Herrin, who had been a student at Yale, killed Bonnie Garland, who had been his girl-friend, by going to where she was sleeping and battering her head with a hammer. He was arrested and was going to be tried. A nun associated with the Catholic centre at Yale took the view that since, as she said, "the girl is dead", there was no point in thinking about her and she proceeded to work for defence of Richard Herrin. Willard Gaylin, a psychiatrist who studied this case, found her attitude shocking. He meant, I think, that it was wrong to act as if a murder was like a disturbance of water in a pool, which creates ripples that die away and then all is as it was before. The horror of it remains, it continues to poison the moral atmosphere, and the disorder which it created does not disappear of its own accord.[69] As Georges Bernanos says,

> every crime creates around it a sort of whirlpool which inexorably draws both the innocent and guilty towards its vortex. It is impossible to determine in advance its strength or how long it will last. ... An act that scarcely seems to be more important than a flick lets loose a mysterious power that rolls the criminal and the judge

---

67   Eliot, *Murder in the Cathedral,* chorus during the murder; *Collected Plays,* p. 48.
68   Eliot, *The Family Reunion,* part 2, scene 1; *Collected Plays,* p. 98.
69   For more, see below, p. 191.

pell-mell in the same swirl, for as long as it has not exhausted its violence, and we do not know the laws which govern it.[70]

Finally, it was in Nazi Germany that Dietrich Bonhoeffer wrote the following, but it has not become utterly irrelevant:

> The void towards which the west is drifting is not the natural end, the dying away and decline of a once flourishing history of nations. It is a rebellious and outrageous void, and one which is the enemy of both God and man. ... It is the supreme manifestation of all the powers which are opposed to God. It is the void made god. No one knows its goal or its measure. Its dominion is absolute. It is a creative void, which blows its anti-god's breath into the nostrils of all that is established and awakens it to a false semblance of new life while sucking out from it its proper essence, until at last it falls in ruin a lifeless husk and is cast away. The void engulfs life, history, family, nation, language, faith. The list can be prolonged indefinitely, for the void spares nothing.[71]

Again, this disorder is not comparable to that of natural disasters, distressing though these sometimes are.

---

70 Bernanos, *Un crime*, near the end of Part I.
71 Bonhoeffer, *Ethics* (Fontana edn.), pp. 105-106. See *Works*, vol. 6, p. 128. See also Bach on *das Nichtige*, p. 64.

10 The Mystery of Evil

Moral evil is not non-being

The theory that badness is non-being, or lack of being, and so is neither willed nor caused as such has been applied to moral evil, which is or was explained as lack, failure, or absence of perfection. For instance, Dom Mark Pontifex said:

> When the creature sins, this is ultimately due, not to any positive act initiated by the creature … but to a failure on the creature's part to do all that he has the power to do. So far as the creature fails and acts less perfectly than he could act, this is due to a mere lack of causality, and is the responsibility of the creature.[1]

In several places Maritain has expounded what he says is Thomas Aquinas's explanation of how people make morally wrong decisions.[2] He says that immediately before making an immoral decision, a person does not think about the rule which he or she is about to break. This non-thinking is an absence of thought, not a positive reality. It is voluntary and free, but it is not in itself culpable because we are not obliged to be thinking of all moral rules all the time and because it is a mere absence. It is the root of immorality, but it is not itself immoral. If, then, we ask how persons can do morally wrong things, we have here an explanation: immediately beforehand they were not thinking of the moral rules which they were about to break. Maritain says that it is a fundamental thesis of Thomas Aquinas that "the cause of moral evil or of sin is a failure of the will, to wit, the voluntary and free nonconsideration of the rule, which is not yet culpable, because it is a mere negation, not a privation".[3] There may be more in this than meets the eye but it looks like a desperate attempt to reconcile the existence of evil with the scholastic belief that only what is good can be willed.

---

1 Pontifex, *Freedom and Providence* (1960), p. 69. See below, p. 106.
2 Maritain, *St Thomas and the Problem of Evil* (1942), pp. 22-36; *God and the Permission of Evil* (1960), pp. 21, 41-46.
3 Maritain, *God and the Permission of Evil*, p. 21.

10 ❧ The Mystery of Evil

The difficulties with it are, first, that as a matter of fact some people do think about the moral law at the very moment of deciding to break it. Other people decide to do something immoral and subsequently say to themselves that what they have decided to is wrong, but that they will nevertheless do it, so that there is a time when the immoral decision and the moral law are both in their minds. Second, according to Maritain a person who does wrong does not think about the law which he or she is on the point of breaking and this non-thinking is not culpable. However, while no one is obliged to think of all moral laws all the time, a person is obliged to think of any moral laws that concern a serious act which he or she is thinking of performing, and therefore this voluntary non-thinking about the relevant moral law is culpable, and we are no nearer an explanation of how it is psychologically possible for a person to commit moral evil. Third, what one habitually knows enters into one's acts even if one does not expressly think about it at moments of decision.

A similar idea is that evil is a sign of lack of development. If a man went into a remote jungle, met natives who saw him as an invader and killed him, his death was due to the natives' primitiveness and if all people could be educated such deaths would cease. The trouble with this, of course, is that while it fits many non-moral causes of distress, which I dealt with earlier, it does not begin to explain moral evil. If natives killed an intruder, their primitiveness may explain it, but if an educated person cruelly and unjustly reduces other people to poverty, knowing perfectly well that the action is wrong, that is totally different. Also, moral evil is not our primitive ancestry coming out in people today. Our most primitive ancestors were incapable of moral evil, properly so called, as were the primates before them. It made its appearance with rationality, and as we grew in mental ability and moral awareness, our capacity to be evil increased. Austin Farrer said:

> It is quite unrealistic to describe the damaging part of our inheritance as the brute or the savage clinging to us, and not yet shaken off. There are vices of which the primitive, not to say the animal, is incapable. Progress in sophistication is not all progress in virtue; the corruption of the best is the worst, and the villainies of the civilised are the blackest.[4]

---

4   Farrer, *Love Almighty and Ills Unlimited*, p. 151. See also Fromm, *The Anatomy of Human Destructiveness*, p. 4.

Moreover, deliberate murderous violence is not mere lack of gentleness, gross selfishness is more than a lack of consideration for others, hatred is not lack of love (to be hated means far more than not to be loved, even by someone by whom one should be loved) and pride is not a name we have for an absence, a nothingness, that exists when someone has no humility. If, exercising a good deal of forethought, a man sexually abuses a child, it is absurd to say, with Pontifex, that he fails to do all the good that he has the power to do and that he acts less perfectly than he could act. In general, a vice is not the mere absence of the corresponding virtue but a driving force; it is not merely non-constructive but positively destructive; it is not the non-assertion of some value or the non-willing of some good; it is "active positive negation".[5] If it is symbolised by darkness, this is not the darkness which most of us want to have when we put out the light to go to sleep, or the darkness which comes over a peaceful countryside when the sun goes down; it is the horrible darkness which one might find in a fairy-tale or remember from one's childhood – no mere absence of light but an almost tangible reality charged with menace and about to devour us. Hick says: "To describe, for example, the dynamic malevolence behind the Nazi attempt to exterminate the European Jews as merely the absence of some good, is utterly insufficient". He goes on: "The evil will as an experienced and experiencing reality is not negative. It can be a terrifying positive force in the world".[6] Possibly with the Holocaust in mind, Ricoeur says: "Evil is not nothing; it is not a simple lack, a simple absence of order; it is the power of darkness; it is posited".[7]

How is moral evil possible?
Incomplete explanations which have been offered

One of the most puzzling of questions is: how is it psychologically possible for human beings to do what they believe is wrong?

---

5   Brunner, *Man in Revolt*, p. 130.
6   Hick, *Evil and the God of Love*, pp. 62-63.
7   Ricoeur, *The Symbolism of Evil*, p. 155. See also Jung, *Aion*, in *Collected Works*, vol. 9, part 2, most of ch. 5, especially pp. 41-62.

FLAWS IN THE PERSON'S NATURE

Determinists explain bad behaviour by saying that it is caused by inherited flaws in the natures of certain people. According to them, some people are criminals by nature and commit crimes as necessarily as water flows downhill. Many of them also believe that people's natures cannot be changed and they draw the conclusion that for the protection of the population at large people who have committed crimes should be executed, put in gaol or deported. As this involves a denial of morality, properly so called, I shall not discuss it here.

Other authors, without professing determinism, explain bad actions by saying that wrongdoers have flawed natures, for which they are not responsible. John Hick, for instance, says that

> the idea of an unqualifiedly good creature committing sin is self-contradictory and unintelligible. If the angels are finitely perfect, then even though they are in some important sense free to sin they will never in fact do so. If they do so we can only infer that they were not flawless.[8]

He insists that "to say that an unqualifiedly good (though finite) being gratuitously sins is to say that he was not unqualifiedly good in the first place",[9] and he says that the idea that God made angels and men free

> and that they themselves inexplicably and inexcusably rebelled against him ... amounts to sheer self-contradiction. It is impossible to conceive of wholly good beings in a wholly good world becoming sinful. To say that they do is to postulate the self-creation of evil ex nihilo! There must have been some moral flaw in the creature or in his situation.[10]

Anatomise Regan, Hick says in effect, and you will find that she is naturally hard-hearted, which is why she is cruel; Macbeth is over-ambitious *and therefore* murders Duncan; and any evil deed that has ever been committed can be similarly explained. John Kekes says that "given the characters of Lear and Oedipus, they could not have acted differently" and people with character defects "may know what they

---

8   Hick, *Evil and the God of Love*, pp. 68-69.
9   Ibid., p 180.
10   Ibid., pp. 285-286.

ought to do; nevertheless they cannot do it".[11] As we shall see, quite the opposite view was expressed by various Fathers of the Church. Hannah Arendt attended the trial of Eichmann expecting to see an obviously evil monster such as one might see in a horror film, the mere sight of whom would frighten everyone in the court, but what she saw was a very ordinary-looking man. She coined the phrase "the banality of evil".

The Fathers whom I mentioned above were guilty of overstatements. Some people have tendencies or antecedent dispositions which amount to flaws in their natures, so that not all of us have quite the same natures, and some people have, for instance, strong aggressive tendencies which make it more probable that they will hurt people than that others will. However, as Kant remarked, in principle a person who has no bad tendencies can commit moral evil;[12] and Hick must face the dilemma: if a man with a tendency to violence (for example) is provoked, is it possible for him to restrain himself? If not, his violent behaviour is perfectly explained by his natural tendency, but it is not morally evil and hence it is irrelevant to the present discussion. If, on the other hand, he can restrain himself, but becomes violent, his behaviour is morally evil and the question arises: "Why did he give free rein to his violent tendency though he knew it was wrong to do so?"

FLAWS IN THE ENVIRONMENT

Other authors who profess determinism explain anti-social behaviour by saying that it is the result of defects in the environment. Erich Fromm maintains that if people are aggressive it is not because of any innate tendency but because the conditions under which they live make it impossible for them to develop properly.[13] This is especially offered as the explanation of the violence, dishonesty and sexual misbehaviour which is common when huge numbers of people are crowded into insect-infected unhygienic slums where children cannot obtain an education, and crime offers almost the only way for an enterprising person to make some money. These authors, unlike those whom I mentioned above, usually maintain that the way to deal with the problem is to remedy the environments in which many people live.

---

11 Kekes, *Facing Evil*, pp. 38, 73.
12 Kant, *Religion Within the Limits of Reason Alone*, p. 36.
13 Fromm, *The Anatomy of Human Destructiveness*, pp. 226-227.

10 ❦ The Mystery of Evil

There can be no doubt that bad environments partly explain a great deal of the violence which occurs in certain places, and we ought to do all we can to remedy their defects, but they cannot be offered as a total explanation of immorality, which also occurs in good environments. Also, anyone who thinks that fixing environments will lead to universal good behaviour is being over-optimistic.

INFLUENCE OF PARTICULAR OTHER PEOPLE

Sometimes morally evil acts are explained by saying that they were committed under the evil influence of some other person: Adam disobeyed God under the influence of Eve, who was influenced by the serpent; in the middle ages it was thought that if some people committed fornication it was because of the influence of the spirit of fornication; and commits murder under the influence of the witches. Clearly, the influence of other people partly explains much immorality but there are two difficulties in it as a complete explanation. First, for an act to be immoral the agent must be capable of withstanding the influence of the tempter; therefore, if he yields to influence and commits wrong, the question arises, "Why did he yield to the other person's influence even though he knew that he ought not to do so?" That is, the essence of the morally evil act – the person's choice of moral evil on his or her own responsibility – is not explained by pointing to an outside influence. This is clear in the case of Adam, and also of Macbeth, who never suggests that either his wife or the witches made him act as he did. Second, the question arises: "This other person – how is his or her moral evil to be explained?" The tendency has been to reach back beyond the tempter to yet another person: thus Eve was influenced by the serpent, the spirit of fornication was thought to be driven by Lucifer and the witches in Macbeth seem to be subject to Hecate. One cannot go on like this indefinitely and therefore there must be a being who commits moral evil without being influenced by another person to do so.

I have mentioned the devil and his angels, including the spirit of fornication, who according to a great tradition are constantly influencing human beings and, without depriving us of free will, making us act immorally. While I realise that a book on evil, by a priest, should have more to say about the devil and his agents, I will not have a chapter on them.

How can moral evil have a place in the scheme of things?

Another puzzle is: how can evil have a place in human life and in the scheme of things which is our universe and its history?

It has been suggested that it has a place in human life because it does men and women good to experience moral evil: it opens their eyes to the dark side of reality, of which they might otherwise be unaware; it makes them feel their need for forgiveness; it cures them of any inclination they might have to arrogance; and it makes them understanding and sympathetic towards others who do wrong. However, the normal effect of wrongdoing is not to make a person aware of moral evil so much as to dull that awareness – as Louis Monden says, "every sin makes us blind to that awareness of sin".[14] Also, for every person who commits a moral fault, repents like Peter and is perhaps the better for the whole experience, there are others who after their moral falls despair and never recover their moral goodness, who commit suicide or who tell themselves (without really believing it) that what they have done is perfectly all right and go on in bad faith to do it again. Moreover, it is by no means certain that behaving immorally makes a person sympathetic towards wrongdoers: moral people can be sympathetic and reformed wrongdoers can be harsh. Finally, no one who has even half understood the terrific force of moral evil could suggest that a dose of it might do anyone good.

The idea that many bad actions have good rather than bad effects in the long run, has already been dealt with. It has also been shown that moral evil does not find its explanation in Teilhard's evolutionary world-view. Whether in individual persons or in the human race as a whole, moral evil is not, like ignorance, a deficiency which is remedied by growth and effort; rather, the more persons develop, the greater becomes their capacity for moral evil. Also, whereas some suffering may be the price of progress, moral evil tends to destroy whatever progress has been made.

I said earlier that when particular events involve free will or chance, and hence are unpredictable, there is often statistical necessity and at least approximate predictability in large numbers of events. Some authors have explained moral evil in the same way, saying that it would be statistically impossible for a multitude of human beings to exist

---

14   Monden, *Sin, Liberty and Law*, p. 150.

without some of them committing immoral actions sometimes. Joseph Rickaby (1845-1932) said:

> If it be asked how there can be a necessity [of sin occurring] which is not a necessity in any individual, let it be observed that where there is a real trial of free will there is a real likelihood of sin: but a multitude of such likelihoods means a necessity of sin somewhere.[15]

Maritain said: "If it is in the nature of things that an event can happen, this event will actually happen sometimes";[16] human beings can do wrong, he said, and therefore they sometimes do. Sertillanges said the fact that glass is fragile means that inevitably some glass is broken; similarly, he said, the fact that human beings are morally fragile means that inevitably some commit sin. Teilhard said that in a system which is in process of organisation it is statistically inevitable that disorders appear, and that this implies that it is statistically inevitable that immoral acts were and are committed in an evolving universe with human beings in it.[17] The people whom I have quoted, and whom I respect, see an equivalence between the non-moral activity which goes on in nature and causes individual beings to suffer, and the immoral behaviour of some human beings. It seems more reasonable to me to say that the former can be understood as natural, whereas immoral behaviour is unnatural.

Moral evil is ultimately inexplicable

Some theologians, working as philosophers, have seen that moral evil is ultimately inexplicable In his two-volume study of sin first published around 1840, Julius Müller said that moral evil is "in its nature inconceivable, i.e. incomprehensible", and that it is

> the inscrutable mystery of the world; it even remains, in its inmost depth, impenetrable darkness. This inconceivableness holds true of every sinful act.[18]

---

15 Rickaby, "The Greek Doctrine of Necessity: a Speculation on the Origin of Evil", quoted in Hick, *Evil and the God of Love*, p. 268.
16 Maritain, *St Thomas and the Problem of Evil*, p. 6.
17 Teilhard, *Christianity and Evolution*, p. 195. See also the appendix to *The Phenomenon of Man*.
18 Müller, *The Christian Doctrine of Sin*, II, pp. 173-174.

Karl Barth has said that man as sinner is "an inexplicable but actual absurdity"; a person, he says, is a sinner "on grounds or lack of grounds which are quite irrational"; we can describe a sinner but not explain sin.[19] Emil Brunner says:

> All attempts to explain evil end in explaining it away; they end by denying the fact of evil altogether. It is of the nature of evil … that it should be inexplicable.[20]

Austin Farrer writes:

> Perversity is both utterly inexplicable, and perfectly simple. It is inexplicable, because it is perverse; how can you rationalise sheer unreason? It is the one irreducible surd in the arithmetic of existence. Non-rational acts, like those of blind passion, can be explained by natural causes, as can the actions of beasts. Sensible decisions are explained from the reasonable grounds which motivate them. Innocent mistakes may be explained by a mixture of the two: there are the reasonable grounds on which the mistaken man proceeds, and there is the interfering natural cause, the fatigue or the prepossession, leaving him to misinterpret them. But nothing can explain wicked perversity; nothing can explain why reason, supplied with rational grounds, should wilfully falsify her own procedure in relation to them.[21]

Among philosophers, Kant said that the origin in us of moral evil is inscrutable, and that there is "no conceivable ground from which the moral evil in us could originally have come".[22] Berdyaev says:

> Evil being absolutely irrational, it is therefore incapable of being grasped by reason and remains inexplicable. … Evil represents the absolute limit of irrationality.[23]

Vladimir Jankélévitch says that when one comes against moral evil,

> one cannot understand it. There is nothing there to understand. For the depths of pure wickedness are incomprehensible.[24]

---

19   Barth, *Church Dogmatics*, IV/1, # 60, p. 433.
20   Brunner, *The Mediator*, p. 124.
21   Farrer, *Love Almighty and Ills Unlimited*, p. 140. See also "The Riddle of Sin", ch. 5 of Berhouwer, *Sin*.
22   Kant, *Religion Within the Limits of Reason Alone*, p. 38.
23   Berdyaev, *Freedom and the Spirit*, p. 163.
24   Jankélévitch, *Le pardon* (1967), p. 92.

Pardon, he says, personifying it,

> has not understood wicked freedom (for no one understands the incomprehensible), but it understands that there exists a wicked freedom. ... It understands that there exists what cannot be understood.[25]

Bernard Lonergan says:

> All that intelligence can grasp with respect to basic sin is that there is no intelligibility to be grasped. What is basic sin? It is the irrational. Why does it occur? If there were a reason, it would not be sin.[26]

Shakespeare, if I may include him among the philosophers, saw this. As Helen Gardner says, some of his characters have "monstrous and inexplicable wickedness", which "cannot be reduced or explained. ... It terrifies because it is inexplicable".[27] Finally, in England a certain Dr Harold Shipman, married with four grown-up children, was charged with having murdered eight elderly women, none of whom was sick and in pain, and the police inquired into a hundred and fifty deaths. Someone said: "This is the first time in my life I have met real evil. Real evil that you can't explain away".

Because a free act is not determined by its antecedents, every free act is unpredictable and therefore in a sense inexplicable. An immoral choice is inexplicable in a more profound way, because it is a choice of something which is irrational and bad.

It is true that a partial explanation of moral evil is often possible. For instance, if two men work in an office and one of them steals some money and the other does not, one may partly explain their different behaviour by saying that one desperately needed money and the other did not or that one was brought up by a father who regularly stole things from his workplace and bought stolen goods in pubs whereas the other's father was strictly honest. This perhaps made it probable that the second man would steal and the first man would not, but neither his need of money nor his upbringing forced the first man to steal and there is a gap between the antecedents of the act and the act itself, which gap is inexplicable.

---

25   Ibid., p. 207.
26   Lonergan, *Insight*, p. 667.
27   Gardner, *Religion and Literature*, pp. 48-49.

Explaining Hitler

I quoted Beaudelaire, who said that discussions of evil always come to the Marquis de Sade.[28] If he had been writing late in the nineteen-forties Baudelaire would probably have said "Hitler", and Ron Rosenbaum has written *Explaining Hitler*, which is not so much about Hitler himself as about attempts which have been made to explain him.[29]

Some authors explain the Holocaust by saying that it sprang from a mistake: Hitler thought that it was right. Rosenbaum says that H.R. Trevor-Roper could not bear to think that conscious evil of the magnitude of the Holocaust is possible, and he maintained that "Hitler was convinced of his own rectitude".[30] However, Alan Bullock finds "damning evidence for the degree to which Hitler was consciously, knowingly evil"[31] and Berel Lang insists that Hitler was consciously evil and responsible.[32]

Others, usually assuming determinism, have explained the Holocaust in psychological terms. Some Freudians, for instance, have started out with the idea that all strange behaviour can be explained by subconscious, almost always sexual, forces which exist because of problems in the agent's infancy, and they have deduced Hitler's behaviour, some from how he was treated by his father, others from how he was treated by his mother, when he was a child. Other authors have looked for a social explanation of the Holocaust. They have said that it was caused by the anti-semitism which was traditional in Central and Eastern Europe, and that if Hitler had not brought it about, someone else would have. All these theories imply that Hitler was the victim of his own subconscious or that he was the involuntary instrument of cultural forces, and hence, as Rosenbaum says, "Hitler disappears from these explanations" and something other than him is said to be

---

28   See above, p. 36.
29   Rosenbaum has also written a long essay, "Explaining Hitler", in *The Secret Parts of Fortune*, pp. 711-740.
30   Rosenbaum, *Explaining Hitler*, p. 69 and *The Secret Parts of Fortune*, p. 726.
31   Rosenbaum, *Explaining Hitler*, p. 96.
32   Ibid., chap. 11. Rosenbaum says that Lang "jumps from saying that the perpetrators of the Final Solution did evil despite knowing that it was wrong, to the suggestion that they did it *because* it was wrong" (p. 214).

the cause of his actions.³³ Understandably, this led the Jewish theologian Emil Fackenheim to say that to explain the Holocaust "can verge on ameliorating, excusing, even colluding with evil" and Claude Lanzmann, the maker of the documentary film, *Shoah* (France, 1985), which has been shown on television in many countries, goes into a blind rage when anyone attempts to explain the Holocaust, alleging that he or she is pro-Hitler. Rosenbaum himself, near the end of his book, says of Hitler: "I don't think he has been explained but, on the other hand, I'm not convinced he is, categorically, inexplicable".³⁴ To which I would, in all humility, say that I am convinced that what Hitler did is inexplicable. I agree with Hannah Arendt, who said that what the Nazis did was "absolute evil which could no longer be understood and explained by the evil motives of self-interest, greed, covetousness, resentment, thirst for power, and cowardice".³⁵ At Auschwitz, an inmate asked a guard "*Warum?*", which means "Why?", and the guard said: "*Hier ist kein Warum*", "Here there is no why", and commentators have said that the guard, probably unthinkingly, uttered a deep truth when he uttered those words: there was no reason why.

The horror of moral evil

To say that moral evil is inexplicable is to use far too gentle a word. It is absurd, horrible, a violent attack on reason and goodness. It is as it were nothingness become real, the impossible become actual, darkness visible. It is a force – the force of nothingness devouring being. As Hick says, when we think of Belsen and Auschwitz we are compelled to take seriously the idea of the demonic, in the sense of a force willing evil for the sake of evil, and then we have to see that in all moral evil this same force is at work.³⁶ T.H. Huxley, who was a rationalist, said that "ethical nature may count upon having to reckon with a tenacious and powerful enemy as long as the world lasts".³⁷

---

33 Ibid., p. 292.
34 Rosenbaum, *Explaining Hitler*, p. 394.
35 Arendt, *The Origins of Totalitarianism* (1951), pp. 458-459.
36 Hick, *Evil and the God of Love*, pp. 324-325.
37 T. H. Huxley, quoted in Vereker, *Eighteenth-Century Optimism*, p. 296.

Moral evil is inexcusable

I said above that where there is no fault we should not blame either ourselves or others, and that where others are concerned we should accept their valid excuses. Where there has been fault, the situation is different because, since there can be no explanation, there can be no excuse. Paul was not being unduly harsh when he said, "They are without excuse" (Rom 1:20). It is of immense importance here to note that inexcusable is not synonymous with unforgivable – indeed, as shall be said later, it is precisely the inexcusable which is the object of forgiveness.

11 God & Sin

The idea that sin is non-being

As I said, it is or was maintained that all being is good, so that badness in any form is non-being and hence cannot be willed by God. This gave scholastic philosophers and theologians what seemed to be a solution to a problem which they could not otherwise solve. Unfortunately, as we have seen, evil is not non-being and it is sometimes willed, though not by God. I quoted Pontifex earlier, with elisions, and here is the full quotation:

> When the creature sins, this is ultimately due, not to any positive act initiated by the creature without God's causality, but to a failure on the creature's part to do all that he has the power to do. So far as the creature fails and acts less perfectly than he could act, this is due to a mere lack of causality, and is the responsibility of the creature and not of God.[1]

Bernard Lonergan says something similar:

> By basic sin I shall mean the failure of free will to choose a morally obligatory course of action or its failure to reject a morally reprehensible course of action. ... If he [a person] wills, he does what he ought; if he wills, he diverts his attention from proposals to do what he ought not; but if he fails to will, his attention remains on illicit proposals; the incompleteness of their intelligibility and the incoherence of their apparent reasonableness are disregarded; and in this contraction of consciousness, which is the basic sin, there occurs the wrong action.[2]

This, of course, is another attempt to make moral evil fit the definition of evil as non-being and to reconcile it with the idea that only what is good can be willed. Also, if there is a basic sin it is not a "contraction of consciousness" but hate. In a conversation about Hitler, Alan Bullock

---

1   Pontifex, *Freedom and Providence* (1960), p. 69. See above, p. 96.
2   Lonergan, *Insight*, p. 666.

said to Ron Rosenbaum: "If you ask me what I think evil is, it's the Incomplete".[3] He also said that it is

> a less highly evolved form of humanness. Lower, far lower on the Great Chain of Being but still part of the same continuum of creation that gave birth to us and emanates from or evolves toward God. Thus, even the most consciously evil figure in the New Testament can be embraced as part of creation, albeit the most singularly incomplete element of it.[4]

It would be pointless to discuss this idea here.

Our relationships with the divine persons

In Old Testament times, God was one being, the creator of the universe, who created human beings and had a very personal relationship with the Jewish people. Then he sent his Son to live among us, and he said that we have two fundamental obligations, to love God and to love each other. In the Catholic Church, and in others churches, not much was said in theology about the divine persons, about human beings as persons, or about love; but in spirituality there has been much talk of the personal relationship which ideally exists between the divine persons, especially the Father and the Son, and human persons – I am told that many contemplative nuns have intense personal love-relationships with Christ – and the love which we should have for other human beings. This has come into theology, which has become less metaphysical and more "psychological".

There has also been a significant development in our theological picture of our relationship with God. When it was said that God is our Father, our mental picture used to be one of God as an adult and us as young children. There was great emphasis then on God's commandments and on our obligation to *obey* him. It was personal, but in that way. Now, it seems to me, the relationship is thought to be analogous to that which, if all goes well, exists between parents and their grown-up sons and daughters. With this goes a strong belief in our free will and independence. Instead of being minimised in theoretical discussions, to "save" the divine omnipotence, the importance of free will is being stressed or (more often) simply assumed. To understand serious

---

3   Rosenbaum, *Explaining Hitler*, p. 78. Alan Bullock may have read Teilhard.

4   Ibid., p. 93.

sin, then, we should think of it as not primarily the violation of an unpersonal order but as the breach of a love relationship between persons, and the primary effect of sin is an estrangement between a divine person or persons and a human person or persons.

Some writers define sin as turning away from God towards a creature. If commitment to God were irreconcilable with commitments to oneself, to other people or to human causes, this statement would make sense: a good person would then have turned away from himself or herself and other creatures, towards God, and a bad person would have taken exactly the opposite direction. However, a good person is turned towards God and also towards creatures; and moral evil is a turning away from God and also a turning away from – or even a will to destroy – the self and other creatures. Moral evil is also often directed against others and indeed against creation. As Piet Schoonenberg says, "when sin is defined as 'a turning away from God towards the creature' (*aversio a Deo, conversio ad creaturam*), that formula ... is, by itself, incorrect, and a source of harmful misunderstandings".[5] I said earlier that moral evil is an attack on the human community and its institutions. When it is sin, it is also an attack on the Christian community, which involves a life and institutions of its own. It is an attack on the moral order and on being and when the sinner knows that God is the ground of being, it is an attack on God. As Karl Heim says, "if we are God's enemies then we want to dethrone God. ... We wish God were not there".[6] Karl Barth says that in sin "man does want to pass his limits, to be as god"; it is a vain wish, of course, but "the impotence of the enterprise does not alter the fact that for all its perversion it does take place".[7] Pride is a very feeble word to describe this," he says. "The correct word is perhaps megalomania".[8] Moreover, the sinner hates God, like the men of whom Jesus said: "They have seen and hated both me and my Father" (John 15:24). In certain evil cults this comes into the open, and in Sade's writings it is expressed frequently and violently, for Sade was obsessed by God and on page after page he shows his hatred for him. Also, in so far as the sinner wills the destruction of being, his or her will is to destroy God. As Heim says, rebellion against

---

5   Schoonenberg, *Man and Sin*, p. 20.
6   Heim, *Jesus the World's Perfecter*, p. 60.
7   Barth, *Church Dogmatics*, IV/1, # 60, p. 419.
8   Ibid., p. 437.

God "assumes superhuman proportions and a demoniacal character and aims at the destruction of God".⁹ As Vergote says, "Christ makes sin say what at first it did not quite say: that in the end it is murder of the Father"; Christ manifested sin "by letting evil accomplish, on his person, the murder [of God] that it signified already in the half-dark of impulsive desires".¹⁰ Karl Barth says eloquently:

> We have called sin the concrete form of nothingness [*das Nichtige*] because in sin it becomes man's own act, achievement and guilt. ... Sin as such is not only an offence to God; it also disturbs, injures and destroys the creature and its nature. ... [It is followed by] the suffering of evil as something wholly anomalous which threatens and imperils this existence and is no less inconsistent with it than sin itself. ... Nor is it a mere matter of dying as the natural termination of life, but of death itself as the life-destroying thing to which all suffering hastens as its goal, as the ultimate irruption and triumph of that alien power which annihilates creaturely existence and thus discredits and disclaims the Creator. There is real evil and real death as well as real sin. ... That nothingness has the form of evil and death as well as sin shows us that it is what it is not only morally but physically and totally. It is the comprehensive negation of the creature and its nature.¹¹

Sin has other effects, one of which is sadness, which is the opposite of the peace of which Christ speaks. Another is, at least sometimes, enslavement. It might seem that sinners enjoy unlimited freedom as they refuse to accept and be bound by anything, even their own natures. The Bible, however, constantly says that a consequence of sin is servitude. Jesus says: "Everyone who commits sin is a slave to sin" (John 8:34) and Peter says that false teachers promise freedom "but they themselves are slaves of corruption; for people are slaves to whatever masters them" (2 Pet 2:19). Our ideas of salvation and redemption are based on the insight that the sinner is not free but rather enslaved. This is shown with force in Marlowe's *The Tragical History of Dr Faustus*, where Faustus expects to be "on earth as Jove is in the sky", to be "great

---

9   Heim, *Jesus the Lord*, p. 106.
10 Vergote, "La peine dans la dialectique de l'innocence, de la transgression et de la réconciliation", *Le mythe de la peine*, p. 398.
11 Barth, *Church Dogmatics*, III/3, #50, p. 310. See Bonhoeffer on "the void" (above, p. 95). See also Brunner, *Man in Revolt*, p. 115 and Buttrick, *God, Pain and Evil*, pp. 32-33.

emp'ror of the world", to have Mephistopheles always obedient to his will and to have unlimited mastery and freedom. However, once he has signed his agreement with Lucifer his first request, for a wife, is refused, he is denied an answer to his question, "Who made the world?", he is reprimanded for talking of Christ and he is told that, if he does not revolt against God, Mephistopheles will in piecemeal tear his flesh and in the end drag him screaming to hell. His soul is now not his own for he has become the slave of tyrannical evil. To quote Camus, the truth is that "real freedom is an inner submission to a value", and "the negation of everything is in itself a form of servitude".[12] The concept of enslavement is particularly important for an understanding of the Christian idea of redemption, of setting free.

The explicit and implicit rejection of God

God respects all real values and because of this he cannot accept us if we kowingly reject any of them, which means that he demands moral goodness of us. Sometimes, I imagine rarely, a person quite directly offends God. In most cases, however, when someone who believes in God does something which he himself believes is morally wrong, he is conscious of the fact that he is offending God or doing something which will break the positive relationship which he has had with God, or deepen that break if it already exists, so that he *implicitly* offends him.

One can see what this means by thinking of human situations, like this one:

> Marcel and Henry became friends as law students and on graduation got jobs in the same law firm. At about the same time they fell in love with different girls, they became friends of each other's girlfriends, who also became friends of each other, they got married and they and their wives became a foursome of close friends.
>
> In the firm, one of the partners retired and the remaining partners decided to invite someone else to take his place. They began to interview prospective partners, who included Marcel and Henry. During this time, Henry, who very much wanted the position, said to someone else in the hearing of one of the partners: ' I know Marcel wants to be a partner but I'll be worried about him if he gets it. His father was unstable and he himself had a breakdown while he was at university". None of this was true. As Henry intended, the

---

12 Camus, *The Rebel*, p. 155.

partner reported what he had overheard to the other partners, who, assuming that what Henry had said about Marcel was true, decided that Marcel would be too much of a risk and offered the partnership to Henry, who accepted it.

Some time later, the person to whom Henry had spoken said something to Marcel about his father or his breakdown, Marcel asked him, "What do you mean?", and the person reported what Henry had said. When Marcel and Henry next met, Marcel told Henry what he had heard and asked: "Did you actually say those things about me?" Henry said that he had and offered no apology. Marcel then made it clear to Henry that he could no longer regard him as a friend. Henry, who expected now to move at a higher social level than before, accepted this in a matter-of-fact way, and all that remained of the foursome was that the two wives sometimes met for lunch without telling their husbands.[13]

If, when they meet, James shows that he no longer regards Thomas as his good friend, this is not punishment. He does not break their friendship by not talking to Thomas as he used to do. Rather, he sees that by his unjust act Thomas has deliberately broken their friendship and he refuses to pretend that nothing has happened to disturb it. It is true that Thomas did not directly or explicitly hurt James, but he implicitly (which does not mean unknowingly) hurt him in a serious and unjust way. In a similar way, if someone who has a happy love-relationship with God does something very wrong, especially if by a deliberate wrong action he immorally hurts a human person whom God loves, he implicitly breaks the relationship which he has had with God. He commits a sin.

The idea that immoral acts are willed by God

Many authors say that God causes sins to be committed. This was fairly directly stated in a few passages in the Old Testament. In Genesis, Joseph says to his brothers, who had sold him to slave-traders: "God sent me before you to preserve life" (Gen 45:5), and in Exodus God is said to make Pharaoh's heart stubborn. In 1 Samuel, after we are told that "the sons of Eli were scoundrels" (2:12) and that "the sin of the young men was very great in the sight of the Lord" (2:17), we are told that Eli remonstrated with them but "they would not listen to the voice of their father; for it was the will of the Lord to kill them" (2:25).

---

13   This story is continued below..

The writer's idea may have been that God was so offended by the sins of these men that he wanted to punish them, and therefore prevented the reform which would have obliged him to pardon them. In the New Testament John says that the Jews could not believe because God had blinded their eyes and hardened their hearts (John 12:39-40); and 2 Thessalonians (which, by the way, is of doubtful authenticity) says:

> God sends them a powerful delusion, *leading them to believe what is false*, so that all who have not believed the truth but took pleasure in unrighteousness will be condemned (2 Thess 2:11-12).

In all these cases God seems to be making people sin in order to achieve some purpose of his own.

Surprising as it may seem, many of the optimists whose world-view I am presenting here maintained that immoral actions, which one thinks of as *against God's will* are as much his will as natural mishaps. I earlier quoted Rodriguez to this effect, and in 1732, in England, Alexander Pope said:

> *Respecting Man, whatever wrong we call,*
> *May, must be right, as relative to all,*[14]

and also

> *If plagues and earthquakes break not Heav'n's design,*
>
> *Why then a Borgia, or a Cataline?*[15]

In 1759 Soames Jenyns said that some people think that while God's designs are benevolent, human beings obstruct them by morally evil acts, and he said:

> But to suppose in this manner, that God intended all things to be good and happy, and at the same time gave being to creatures able and willing to obstruct his benevolent designs, is a notion so inconsistent with his wisdom, goodness, omniscience, and omnipotence, that it seems equally unphilosophical, and more evidently absurd, than the other ,[16]

---

14   Pope, *An Essay on Man*, Epistle I, section II.

15   Ibid., section V.

16   Jenyns, *A Free Enquiry into the Nature and Origin of Evil*, p. 13. Jenyns was a man of renown in his time but he seems to be virtually unknown now.

He gave some curious examples of how wrongdoing can have good results:

> Robbery may disperse useless hoards to the benefit of the public; adultery may bring heirs, and good humour too, into many families, where they would otherwise be wanting; and murder free the world from tyrants and oppressors.[17]

This implies that a believer, encountering even moral evil, should conclude that it must be a necessary occasion of greater good, since otherwise God would not have willed it. For example, as we look back on the slave trade, instead of blaming God we might say that it was his way of moving some people from Africa to America, where their descendants now enjoy greater freedom and prosperity than they would be having in Africa. Also, as we look back on the mistreatment of the Australian aboriginals, especially during the early years of European settlement, we might say that it was God's plan that the continent should be settled by Europeans, *and in that way*.

Paul Claudel

Paul Claudel (1868-1955) was a Catholic in the French foreign service in China who in 1900 on a visit to France discovered that he did not have a religious vocation. He sailed back to China and on the ship fell in love with a married woman, usually called Rosalie Vetch, who was travelling with her husband and children. In China she and Claudel became lovers and in 1904 she became pregnant by him. She set sail for Europe, having agreed that she would have the child there, get a divorce and in due course marry him. However, on the way to Europe she decided in Canada to leave both her husband and Claudel, who in 1905 together tried without success to find her. Claudel wrote a highly autobiographical play, *Partage de midi*, and Rosalie gave birth to a daughter, Louise. Claudel married another woman early in the following year. In 1917, probably when Louise made her first communion or *communion solennelle*, Rosalie wrote a letter to Claudel. Deeply moved, he replied. They did not arrange to meet but from then on they wrote to one another. Claudel now wrote a second play, *Le soulier de satin*, in which he expressed his belief that *God had deliberately sent Rosalie to him* to smash his self-centredness and make him a better human being. In it Claudel and Rosalie are represented by Rodrigue

---

17   Ibid., p. 85.

and Prouhèze and the following dialogue occurs between Rodrigue's guardian angel and Prouhèze. I will quote it in French and then in a free translation:

> Prouhèze: *Rodrigue, c'est avec moi que tu veux le capturer?*
>
> L'ange: *Cet orgueilleux, il n'y avait pas d'autre moyen de lui faire comprendre le*
>
> *prochain, de le lui entrer dans la chair;*
>
> *Il n'y avait pas d'autre moyen de lui faire comprendre la dépendance, la nécessité*
>
> *et le besoin, un autre sur lui,*
>
> *La loi sur lui de cet être différent pour aucune autre raison si ce n'est qu'il existe.*
>
> Prouhèze: *Eh quoi! Ainsi c'était permis? cet amour des créatures l'une pour l'autre, il est donc vrai que Dieu n'en est pas jaloux? l'homme entre les bras de la femme?*
>
> L'ange: *Comment serait-Il jaloux de ce qu'Il a fait? et comment aurait-Il rien fait qui ne Lui serve?* ...
>
> Prouhèze: *L'amour hors du sacrament n'est-il pas le péché?*
>
> L'ange: *Même le péché! Le péché aussi sert.*
>
> Prouhèze: Is it with me that you will catch Rodrigue?
>
> Angel: There was no other way to make that proud man understand the neighbour, to make him experience dependence, need, another person, the demands of another being who simply exists, who is there.
>
> Prouhèze: What! It was then permitted? Our love for one another, God was not jealous of it? A man in the arms of a woman?
>
> Angel: Why would he be jealous of what he himself created? And why would he create something that did not serve him?
>
> Prouhèze: Is love outside the sacrament not a sin?
>
> Angel: Sin, too, has a purpose.[18]

In the published play, under the title, Claudel quoted what he said was a Portugese proverb, which means "God writes straight with crooked lines" and from St Augustine (he says) he quotes *"Etiam peccata"*, which means "Sins, too". In 1920 he met Rosalie again and, for the first time,

---

18   Claudel, *Le soulier de satin*, 3rd day, scene 8; *Théâtre*, II, 804-805.

his daughter Louise. They were destitute and he gave them enough money to live on. He and Rosalie did not become lovers again but he seems to have told her that he and she would be united for ever in heaven. In this way he justified treasuring the memory of his sinful affair, and maintaining a sort of spiritual marriage with one woman while married to another. Claudel never wrote a work of this kind again. Indeed, about ten years later he began to write almost only religious works, so that he came to be recognised as a Great Catholic Author.

Sin mysticism

Some Catholics have taken this idea even further and and presented what is variously called *Le mystique du péché* and *Sündenmystik*. I will call it "sin mysticism". They often begin by quoting passages in the gospels in which Jesus at least seems to say that he came precisely for sinners and loves sinners. They go on to say that for a full *Christian* life, and to understand what Christianity means, a person must be a sinner. If sin involves darkness, they say in effect, it is like the dark night of the soul of which the mystic, John of the Cross, spoke. They may go further and say that sin is not, like the dark night of the soul, an experience through which a soul passes on its way to perfection. It should be our permanent state. Indeed, if we cease to be sinners, Christ will no longer love us. Francis Scarfe says:

> Baudelaire presents the first case (to be followed by Bloy, Mauriac, Jouhandeau, and Graham Greene) of the modern Catholic adventure towards and beyond the boundaries of orthodoxy, the search for God in the nature of evil itself, and for salvation even by our sins.[19]

Charles Péguy was probably echoing Baudelaire and others when he said that the habit of good behaviour is like a suit of armour which protects a person from temptation but also makes it impossible for grace to get through:

> This explains the astonishing victories of grace in the souls of great sinners and the impotence of grace in the souls of decent people, the most decent people, those who have no cracks in their armour. Those who are never wounded, whose moral skin is intact and

---

19 Scarfe, introduction to Baudelaire, *Baudelaire*, p. xl.

makes a faultless leather jerkin. At no point do they offer grace the opening of an appalling wound. ... They do not offer grace that door of entry which sin leaves open.[20]

A recent Catholic author, who has had a great influence, has said: "Be grateful for your sins. They are carriers of grace".

Two defences which implicitly deny foreknowledge

THE IDEA THAT GOD *PERMITS* SIN

I said earlier, when I was not dealing with immorality, that many authors say that all events are either caused by God or, if they are unpleasant, are, prior to their occurrence, *permitted* by him, so that nothing happens which he does not at least permit. They apply this to sin and say, with Augustine, "nor would he who is good permit evil to be done unless in his omniscience he could turn evil into good".[21] In this way they put distance between God and sin while retaining their belief in the divine control and the optimism which that implies. What I said earlier about permission of disasters applies to this. For instance, John Clarke said in 1720 that "as God himself is the supreme governor of the world, nothing can be done but by his permission and consent".[22] He went so far as to say that "it is all one, whether they [troubles] come to pass by the natural course of things, or by the interposition of any wicked agent" – either way, they are for the best.

It seems to me that if God knows beforehand that a disaster is going to occur or that someone is going to commit a sin, and if he somehow can choose between stopping it and permitting it, he cannot be excused if he deliberately permits it, and we would not say that Macbeth was merely permitted by Shakespeare to kill Duncan. The only way to deny God's responsibility is to deny foreknowledge, as I am going to do later in this chapter.

---

20 Villiers, *Charles Péguy*, p. 356. The above is a translation by Marjorie Villiers of a passage from *Note sur M. Bergson et la Philosophie Bergsonienne*, which was published in April 1914 (Péguy was killed at the front in September of that year).
21 Augustine, *Enchiridion*, ch. 26, # 100.
22 Clarke, *A Defence of Natural and Revealed Religion*, vol 3, p. 267.

THE FREE-WILL DEFENCE

Many Christians point out that, generally speaking, if human beings behave badly, their parents should not be held responsible for this. Similarly, they say, God has created free beings and should not be held responsible for any evil they do. The similarity exists only if, prior to the actual immoral actions, God does not know what the person is going to do.

THIS DEFENCE AND SOME MODERN PHILOSOPHERS

Some anti-Christian authors assume that, according to Christians, a sinless universe is inherently possible and they go on to say that, since God is omnipotent, he could have created such a universe. This means, they say, that according to Christians God had a choice between sinless universes and universes with sin in them, and chose one of the latter group. Therefore, they say, according to Christians, God is responsible for sin. Thus they use the Free-Will Defence to prove that Christianity is irrational.

As I said earlier, some analytical philosophers think that logical impossibility is the only kind of inherent impossibility and they maintain that there is a logical contradiction between the statement that God exists and the statement that sins are committed. For instance, J. L. Mackie, implicitly rejecting my view concerning the difference between particular cases and large numbers, argues against theism as follows:

> If there is no logical impossibility in a man's freely choosing the good on one, or on several, occasions, there cannot be a logical impossibility in his freely choosing the good on every occasion. God was not, then, faced with a choice between making innocent automata and making beings who, in acting freely, would sometimes go wrong; there was open to him the obviously better possibility of making beings who would act freely but always go right.[23]

He goes on to talk of God's "failure to avail himself of this possibility". In a similar way, Anthony Flew says that the fundamental or key position of the Free-Will Defence is "that there is a contradiction in

---

23 Mackie, "Evil and Omnipotence", p. 209. In the first sentence it is established that something is not logically possible, and then in the second sentence it is regarded as a practial impossibility, as if logical impossibility were the only kind of inherent impossibility.

the suggestion that God could create a world in which men are able to do what is right or what is wrong, but in fact always choose to do what is right".[24] That, however, is not my position. I deny that God was (as Mackie would say) faced with a choice between creating a universe in which people sin and creating another in which they do not. I maintain that he decided to create a universe, not knowing in advance whether it was going to include sin or not, and certainly not knowing that any particular sin was going to be committed.

The rejection of all this

The clear teaching of Genesis is different from that of the few texts I have quoted above. In Genesis, God tells Adam not to eat the fruit of the tree, then leaves him and *in God's absence* Adam sins. His sin is partly explained by the fact that Eve tempted him, her sin is likewise partly explained by the fact that the serpent tempted her, and there the search for an explanation stops. There is no suggestion that God was behind the serpent or that in any other way he had a hand in bringing about the sin. He was against it.[25] In Deuteronomy, Moses says to the Israelites, "At Horeb you provoked the Lord to wrath, and the Lord was so angry with you that he was ready to destroy you" (Deut 9:8). Isaiah says that "the name of the Lord comes from far away, burning with his anger" and that the Lord will cause his majestic voice to be heard "in furious anger" (Is 30:27-30). There must be a hundred passages like this in the Old Testament. However one explains this wrath and anger, the passages mean that God is totally opposed to sin. This is also clearly the teaching of Sirach:

> *Do not say, "The Lord was responsible for my sinning",*
> *For he does not do what he hates. (Sir 15:11 NJB)*

In the New Testament we have Jesus' teaching in the parable of the wheat and the darnel, where the owner of a field sows good wheat in it. When his servants later report to him that there is darnel among

---

24 Flew, "Compatibilism, Free Will and God", p. 233.
25 Ricoeur says: "The etiological myth of Adam is the most extreme attempt to separate the origin of evil from the origin of the good; its intention is to set up a radical origin of evil distinct from the more primordial origin of the goodness of things. ... [It] makes man a beginning of evil in the bosom of a creation which has already had its absolute beginning in the creative act of God." (*The Symbolism of Evil*, p. 233.)

the wheat, he says, "Some enemy has done this". The whole point of the parable would be ruined if the owner had made the enemy sow darnel in his field, therefore its sense is that God is not responsible for evil. There is also the parable of the owner of the vineyard, the tenants, the messengers whom he sent to them and how they were treated: there is no suggestion that everything went according to the owner's plan. In their Passion narratives, both Luke and John say that Satan entered into Judas and he went to the priests: whatever this means, it implies that God had no part in his action. After his mind was made up and his decision had been sealed by an arrangement with the priests, Jesus said to him: "Do quickly what you are going to do" (John 13:27). At the risk of seeming to be irreverent, I will say that Jesus was like the husband whose story I told earlier, whose wife had made up her mind to leave him, and who said to her: "If you are going to go, go now." No approval whatever is implied, only a desire to be finished as soon as possible with an unpleasant business. Finally, in Acts Paul and Barnabas say that God in the past "allowed all the nations to follow their own ways" (Acts 14:16) and in Romans Paul says that God "gave them up in the lusts of their hearts to impurity" (Rom 1:24). This dissociates God from sin, though he does not stop it. John says: "God is light and in him there is no darkness at all" (1 John 1:5); there is no connection between God and sin.[26] But why quote such passages when from beginning to end the Bible tells of God's commandments not to sin, his warnings to human beings not to commit sins, his anger at them when they do, his severe judgements on sinners and the punishments he inflicts on them? This constant teaching of the Bible makes it necessary to exclude from God any will for sin or responsibility for it.

I come now to the Greek Fathers of the Church. Surrounded by people who believed that human life is governed by fate or necessity, the Greek Fathers did not reply: "No, it is governed by God" but "No, man governs himself".[27] Justin said: "It is not by destiny's law that what man does or what happens to him occurs; each freely does good or evil.

---

26 I am told that in *Aion* Jung objected to the idea that God is purely good, with no darkness or evil in him. He said that to be complete God must combine light and dark or good and evil. This is not the Christian idea.

27 They used the words "free" (*eleutheros*) and "self-governing" (*autexousios*).

11 ⸱ God & Sin

... God made men and angels masters of themselves".[28] Theophilus of Alexandria said that "God made man free and autonomous, and man chose the way of death and so became the cause of his own death".[29] Irenaeus said that "man has been created rational, and in that way like God; he has been created free in his decisions and autonomous".[30] He also said:

> If it was by nature that some are bad and others good, the latter would not be praiseworthy by virtue of being good, since they would have been created such, and the former would not be blameworthy, because they would have been made such. But in fact all are of the same nature, capable of holding and doing good, capable also of refusing it and not doing it.[31]

Gregory of Nyssa wrote: "As the proper character of free will is to choose freely the desired object, the responsibility for the ills you suffer today does not fall on God, who made us independent and free, but on your imprudence, which chose the worst instead of the best".[32] Methodius of Olympia wrote a *Dialogue on Free-Will (De autexousio)*, in which the representative of Christianity says: "I maintain that the first man was created autonomous, that is, free, and his descendants have inherited this freedom".[33] The sky, he says, just does God's will, but human beings obey whom they choose. He also says: "We have received an autonomous reason subject to no necessity, so that we would choose by our own determination what we please, far from being slaves of Destiny and the vicissitudes of chance."[34] Cyril of Jerusalem, for instance, said: "There is not one class of souls [persons] who sin by nature, another who are just by nature; all souls do good or evil by their free-will; they all have the same nature".[35] John Chrysostom said in effect that the entire explanation of Judas's betrayal of Christ

---

28   Justin, *Apologia secunda*, # 7; PG, 6, 456.
29   Theophilus of Antioch, *Ad Autolycum*, II, 27; PG, 6, 1096.
30   Irenaeus, *Adversus Haereses*, IV 4 3; PG, 7, 984.
31   Ibid., IV 37 2; PG, 7, 1100.
32   Gregory of Nyssa, *Oratio catechetica magna*, ch 5 at the end; PG, 45, 25.
33   Methodius of Olympia, *De Libero Arbitrio*, xvi.
34   Methodius of Olympia, *Convivium Decem Virginum*, VIII. 13; PG, 18, 162.
35   Cyril of Jerusalem, *Catechesis IV*, # 20; PG, 7, 1100.

is in Judas.[36] John of Damascus, in his summary of Christian doctrine called *The Orthodox Faith*, says that we ought to be filled with wonder when we see the works of divine providence, and adds that by "works of divine providence" he means things which are not the work of human beings, for "those things that are in our power are not providential, but belong to our free will".[37] In general, the Greek Fathers unambiguously and with great emphasis affirmed human free will and independence – the above quotations are not isolated examples untypical of their thought – and so denied that God had any responsibility for sin.

What the proposers of sin mysticism have said may seem plausible where some actions which are regarded as sinful, but which are not really sins, are concerned. However, one cannot apply them to wife-beating, child abuse, torture, the use of gas chambers in concentration camps, or the exploitation of poor people by rich men. Speaking for myself, I will say that if a man were to tell me, in confession, that in 1941 he had killed hundreds of Jews in the Ukraine, knowing that it was wrong, or that as a priest he had sexually abused many boys, I would not tell him to be grateful for his sins because they were carriers of grace or that, because he was a sinner, he was precisely the kind of person whom Jesus loves. In response to Charles Péguy I will add that really good people are not encased in an armour through which neither temptations nor the motions of grace can penetrate. Moreover, to write straight with crooked lines is a contradiction in terms.

Moreover, it cannot be said that God merely permits sins to be committed when he could prevent them, and not only that, when the consent of his power is necessary. For instance, if a drunk man wants to borrow my car, I ought not to lend it to him and if I do and he causes great harm I will be partly responsible. In the example which I gave of the driver and the fire in the church, the driver was partly responsible for what he saw happening and to continue. Therefore when people say that God "permits" unpleasant events, they do not take away from him his responsibility for them.

This idea has a certain plausibility when it is applied to sins of people other than ourselves and unknown to us. I said earlier that when Christian optimists see past evils such as slavery, they maintain that in the end good came of them which justified God's permission of

---

36   John Chrysostom, *Homilia I de proditione Judae*, # 3; PG, 49, 377.
37   John of Damascus, *De Fide Orthodoxa*, II, 29; PG, 94, 964.

them. This is often hard to believe but not entirely shocking. When, however, there is question of recent or present evil, optimism becomes less acceptable. When they see oppression, total optimists have to say: "This is the situation, *it is*, therefore *it is right*". If they are rich people in Brazil, they can say: "We are extremely rich and many others are extremely poor; whatever is, is right; this is, therefore it is right and we must accept the situation as God's will. So must the poor. And the priests should instruct them to accept it." In past times priests have, indeed, instructed people along these lines, telling them to accept wealth or poverty as God's will; but such situations must be changed, by human beings, whose starting-point should be a judgement that certain existing states of affairs are unjust, destructive of human beings, or in a word evil and not wanted by God.

The idea has very strange implications when a person applies it to himself or herself. Milton saw that if the idea of the Fortunate Fall is correct, and if Adam had known about it, he would not have felt sorry for his disobedience but, on the contrary, would have felt glad about what he had done. In *Paradise Lost* he says:

> *Full of doubt I stand*
> *Whether I should repent me now of sin*
> *By me done or occasioned, or rejoice*
> *Much more, that much more good thereof shall spring -*
> *To God more glory, more good will to men*
> *From God.*[38]

If every event is God's will, Adam should have had no doubt, he should not have repented of sins done or occasioned by himself; he should have rejoiced much more in the great good that was going to spring from them. This has been said to have been true for Judas, and indeed for all sinners. "Whatever I did," the sinner should say to himself or herself, "it was precisely what God intended, it was a necessary element of his eternal plan and it will turn out to have been for the best." Even if by an immoral action I caused someone's death, I should say to myself what the priest possibly said to his or her relatives, namely that everyone dies at the time and in the way that has been appointed by God and it is always the right time and way. Perhaps I should feel privileged to have been used by God in such an important way.

---

38   Milton, *Paradise Lost*, book 12, lines 473-478.

According to total optimism, then, repentance can spring only from a lack of theological understanding. This cannot be right.

Moreover, if God permits sins to be committed when he sees that more good than harm will come of them, when I am tempted to act immorally I can say to myself: "It may be wrong, and at a superficial level an offence against God; but if I do it I will know that God is permitting me to do it because he sees that good will come of it, so that at a deeper level I will be pleasing him by carrying out his design". Like an actor playing Iago, I can say to myself that if God wants me to be wicked, the more wicked I will be, the better.

I earlier quoted Ernesto Cardenal, who said: "We should gladly accept everything that happens because everything that happens, however unpleasant it appears, is for our good". In fairness to him I should point out that he drew the line at sin:

> Only sin is not providential, because it is the one thing that is not made by God but by man, even though the effects and consequences of sin which do not depend on man but on God are providential.[39]

The divine foreknowledge of sins

I said earlier that God does not know the future, or, if you want more technical terms, that God has no foreknowledge of free acts and random events, not because he is ignorant of things which are in themselves knowable, but because prior to their actuality they are, *as actual*, intrinsically unknowable. God, I said is not like the author of a play, who knows, before the play is performed, everything that will happen. He is like a father who brings children into the world, not knowing what they are going to do. I will add here that this applies to immoral acts.

This has serious implications, at least most of which are acceptable. For instance, it implies that when Jesus chose Judas as an apostle and when he later put him in charge of the group's finances (as he seems to have done), he did not know, even as a divine person, that Judas was going to betray him. He knew that it was probable that he would be put to death but he did not know that that was certain to happen. When he preached, he did not know whether he was going to be accepted by the leading Jews or not. As time went on he saw what was

---

39 Cardenal, *Love*, pp. 111-112.

happening and where it was probably going to lead, but he did not know for a fact that what happened was going to happen.

Also, suppose that a married man knows for a fact that in ten years time his wife will leave him and go to live with someone else, who is a friend of his. Is it possible for him, knowing this, to love his friend and his wife now? I doubt it, and believe that God is not refraining from telling him what is going to happen: he does not know. I also do not see how God can love any human being if he knows that at some future time he or she will commit a serious sin.

That the divine persons are hurt by sin: the divine sensitivity

As I said earlier, from an early time there was in the Church a tendency at the academic level to have an idea of God which in some ways was more like Aristotle's idea of a supreme being than the idea of God which is in the Bible. Aristotle had a great influence on scholastic thinkers, especially Thomas Aquinas and the Thomists who followed him, and it came to be generally believed that God is "impassible". This became the standard teaching of both Catholics and Protestants. It meant not only, as I said before, that God does not sympathise with us when we are hurt by natural causes, but (to come to what concerns us here) it also meant that God is not hurt when human beings sin. Peter de Rosa was repeating this teaching, not presenting a novel idea, when he said:

> When we sin against God the change and the loss are entirely in us. … The loss is all on our side: we suffer the injury and not he. This is what it means to offend or injure God: to be responsible for a situation in which we suffer dreadfully.[40]

The idea that God is hurt by sin, which was current in "popular" circles and in pious literature, was usually dismissed by theologians as "popular" and metaphoric.

However, I venture to think that in Biblical times it was assumed that if God is offended, he feels it in one way or another, and in the fourth century Lactantius said: "What beatitude could there be in God, if he was always quiet and unmoved (*immobilis*), if he was deaf to our prayers and blind to those who worship him"?[41] He also said that there would be no point in honouring God if he felt nothing

---

40 Peter de Rosa, *God Our Saviour*, p. 96.
41 Lactantius, *De ira Dei*, ch. 4.

(*si nihil praestat colenti*) when he was not honoured.. Preachers and writers of works of spirituality (as distinct from theology) usually assumed that sinners not only choose against their own happiness: they offend, which is to say that they hurt, God. The devotion to the Sacred Heart, in its Paray-le-Monial form, emphasised Jesus' sadness as a result of human neglect and promoted devout prayer as a means of lessening his sadness and so making "reparation" for it. Most Christian theologians now believe, first, that by our free choices we determine the divine knowledge, second, that God suffers in sympathy with suffering beings and, third, to come to what concerns us here, that he is hurt by sin. Theodore J. Kondoleon says:

> Contrary to his [Thomas Aquinas's] teaching that God gains absolutely nothing by creating or by what transpires in the world and that He is not in the least affected by how His creatures act, they [recent authors, especially J. Norris Clarke] maintain that God is actually affected by what goes on in the world as He in some way receives joy and knowledge from His creatures' [good] actions.[42]

The following two stories, the beginnings of which I shall tell together, may shed light on this question.[43]

> There were two men in Australia, each of whom was intelligent, morally good, married and with a daughter aged seventeen. In each case, a multi-millionaire, on a visit to Australia, seduced the wife and asked her to fly to America with him, to live with him there, and eventually to marry him. The woman was attracted both by the man and by the prospect of luxury, glamour, servants and unlimited money, but she was reluctant to leave her daughter. The rich man said, "She can come with us", and each wife invited her daughter to go with her and enjoy winters in Aspen, the company of glamorous people, including film stars, and unlimited money for clothes and anything else a young girl might desire. In each case the daughter was tempted by this prospect and went off with the rich man and her mother. A year passed, during which neither man heard from his daughter. Then both the girls returned to their fathers and said: "It was terribly wrong of Mother to leave you, and it was wrong of me to go with her. At first the high life was so exciting that I managed not to think about you, but before long I could not get you

---

[42] Kondoleon, "The Immutability of God: Some Recent Challenges" (1984), p. 293.
[43] I have told these stories in *Personalism and Scholasticism*, pp. 185-186.

out of my mind and now I have come back, to say I am sorry and ask you to forgive me". In each case, the father accepted his daughter and she moved back into her old room.

The two fathers were very different and their stories from now on must be told separately.

> The first father was an emotionally self-sufficient man who, when his wife and daughter left him, judged intellectually that they had made bad choices and would suffer for them in the end, but he experienced no sadness, felt no pain, was not hurt. People who had regular dealings with him in the city saw no difference in him and when someone offered him sympathy he said that there was no reason for anyone to feel sorry for him. When his daughter returned he took her back into the house. It did not make him happier, he did not celebrate, and no one in the city saw any change in him.

> The second father was deeply hurt when his wife told him that she was going to leave him, and hurt in a different but intense way when he learned that his daughter was going to go with her: and it hurt that he did not hear from his daughter. He was a man of strong character and so did not drink to excess or tell everyone he knew, at length, how badly he had been treated, demanding bucketfuls of sympathy almost every day; and he did his job as well as before; but his friends (who, by the way, were a great help to him) could see that the joy had gone out of his life. When, a year later, his daughter returned, with a flood of emotion he hugged her and told her that he forgave her, completely. Overwhelmed by joy, they both wept. Then they celebrated, laughing uproariously and crying. In the weeks that followed, his friends commented to one another on how joyful he had suddenly become, how often he laughed. He was, they said, more like his old self, though the hurt inflicted by his wife remained.

On metaphysical principles the first man, with his "apathy" or "impassibility", was great whereas the second man was lacking in perfection; but surely the first man was an insensitive monster. It is no wonder that his wife left him, and when his daughter found that he was quite unmoved by her return, she probably wondered why she had bothered. The second man in my story was not at all weak or lacking in greatness: in fact, he showed strength in not going to pieces, he showed greatness in generously forgiving his daughter, and in experiencing pain and then joy he showed that he had the great virtue of sensitivity.

This shows that the capacity to be hurt by others is not always rooted in limitation of any kind; it also shows that impassivity is an imperfection, whereas sensitivity is a perfection. The highest being is not totally "immanent" or self-centred. To be affected by persons whom one loves is not to be improved or damaged, and so it is not incompatible with the divine infinity. Let us therefore feel free to say that the divine persons are infinitely sensitive, that they can be moved to joy or sorrow by us when we exercise our free will, and that they are deeply pleased if we love them and hurt if we commit sin. The idea of divine impassiibility was a temporary victory of metaphysics over Christianity.

Risk

At times, one takes risks because of ignorance, which is not knowing something which is intrinsically knowable. God knows everything that is knowable. Consequently, he never takes a risk of this kind. The free acts of a person, however, cannot be known beforehand with certainty, and this not-knowing is not ignorance. If, then, one trusts someone to do a job, one cannot be *certain* that he or she will do it, and to that extent one often takes risks. Also, if a man and a woman marry, they both risk their future lives, and if people have a child, this is a risk. In most cases, it is perfectly rational to take a risk. In my theory, creation was a risk for God, including a risk of moral evil. Such a risk is not morally evil, for otherwise it would be immoral for any couple to have a child.

Incidentally, according to the Molinist theory God knows with absolute certainty what any free being would choose to do in any situation which he or she could possibly be in, and so brought human beings into existence, knowing in detail what they were going to do. If this is true, then God bears responsibility for the morally evil acts of his creatures. I will not admit more than that God took a risk and I claim that it involves no responsibility for the sins which have been committed.

Teilhard de Chardin

I criticised Teilhard on philosophical grounds earlier and will add here that he was open to the theological criticism that he failed to come to grips with sin and redemption. "Redemption," he said in effect, was another name for evolution. His opponents in the Catholic Church objected to this, with reason. This became apparent when Teilhard's writings were published and books *about* them began to appear. Christopher Mooney (who was on his side but not uncritical) said that at an early stage of his life Teilhard wanted to show that Christ came firstly to create and secondarily to redeem from moral guilt, but in the end "reparation for sin does not in fact have such a secondary place in his Christology; in spite of his good intentions he can find no place for it at all."[44] Redemption in this system is not a gratuitous gift but the natural process by which a material universe necessarily evolves out of its initial primitive state. Piet Smulders (who also was not an anti-Teilhardian) said: "Here, in our opinion, lies the weakest point in Teilhard's design, a real danger of failure to do justice to the doctrine of the Catholic faith".[45]

---

44 Mooney, *Teilhard de Chardin and the Mystery of Christ*, p. 106.
45 Smulders, *The Design of Teilhard de Chardin*, p. 141.

12 Corporate Guilt & Original Sin[1]

Solidarity

There are groups to which we choose to belong and which we are free to leave. For instance, a man or a woman can join a political or other club. I shall not be talking of such groups here. Instead, I will write about the solidarity of groups to which we belong by birth, not by choice, and I want first to describe four ways in which this solidarity is experienced.

GOOD THINGS DONE BY MEMBERS OF A GROUP TO WHICH ONE BELONGS

A young woman cellist, let us suppose, gives her first concert in her home city, playing a concerto. When the last movement ends there is silence, and then deafening applause. Everyone feels, "This concert will be talked about for years to come – the girl is going to be, she already is, the greatest woman cellist since Jacqueline du Pré", and claps like mad. In the audience are some of the girl's family. They are as it were in two places at once: as individual persons they are in the audience clapping the performer, but as her blood relatives they are on the stage with her, drinking in the applause. They will later tell the girl that they are proud of her – not just that she has a right to be proud, but that *they* are proud. Other people will congratulate them on the cellist's success, and they will accept these congratulations. At times like these a family is like a body: if the hands do something good the credit goes to the whole person, and when one member of a family does something great the whole family gets credit for it and every family member shares the credit.

This works at times for the entire human race. When in 1969 a man set foot on the surface of the moon, people all over the world felt that this was an accomplishment not merely of the scientists and others at NASA or of the people of the United States, but of all human beings or, as was said then, "man". We felt that we were no longer confined to our earth, and we all felt a sense of achievement.

---

1 In this chapter I shall re-state a theory which I presented in my essay in Scullion and others, *Original Sin* (1995).

12 ❦ Corporate Guilt & Original Sin

The experience reaches back into the past. Members of certain families are proud of the achievements of their ancestors, Greeks are proud of the ancient Greeks, English people are proud of what great Englishmen did in the past and I remember a guide in a church in Tyrol pointing to a medieval carved door and saying, "Look at what we could do before America was even discovered!"

GOOD THINGS DONE TO MEMBERS OF A GROUP

There can be solidarity in gratitude. Suppose, for instance, that when my grandparents emigrated to Australia, a certain man not only gave my grandfather a job but also gave him a great deal of helpful advice and lent him some money, which of course he needed. Suppose that I am now a doctor and someone comes to me who has the same surname as my grandfather's employer, about whom my grandfather had talked to me. I ask him if he is related to that man and he replies that he is his great-grandson. I at once say: "Your great-grandfather was very generous to my grandfather, who worked for him, and I shall be delighted to help you if I possibly can". In this case the individual man in front of me did nothing for me or my forbears, and helping him will not benefit his great-grandfather, who is dead, but I think of the great-grandfather not as an individual but as a member of a family, and I think of how as a member of my family I will now in gratitude do all I can for the other family, which is represented by the man who has come to me.

BAD THINGS DONE TO MEMBERS OF A GROUP

If someone is treated unjustly, his or her entire family feels wronged. The appalling things done to Jews in Nazi Europe were and are felt by Jews everywhere as things that were done to *them*. Black people in the United States felt hurt by the wrongs inflicted on blacks elsewhere. Women, in the solidarity of sisterhood, feel in their own hearts the unjust treatment of women in their own countries and women in other countries, where women are systematically oppressed. And in the solidarity of the whole human race we all feel that wrongs inflicted on any human beings are inflicted on humanity, and hence on us, and we protest.

This reaches back into the past. Present-day Jews still feel wronged by the persecutions of Jews by Christians in earlier centuries; Irish people identify with the Irish people who were in Ireland at the time of the Famine, which began in 1846, and for the appalling effects of which Britain was responsible; some American blacks feel that (as they say) *we* were brought to America in slave-ships, sold, kept in bondage and hideously mistreated; Australian aborigines feel that *we* were driven off *our* land and in many cases killed, and that until the 1960s some of *our* children were stolen from *us*.

BAD THINGS DONE BY MEMBERS OF A GROUP

Let me begin with a simple case, which is hardly moral. You, an Australian (let us suppose), are with some people who are not Australians, watching an international tennis match, and an Australian competitor has tantrums, abuses the umpire, sulks, makes rude signs and throws away some points. You hang your head in shame. More seriously, you are a white southern American and you have discovered what slavery and the racial discrimination which followed it involved. It weighs on you, it makes you feel dirty. Or you are a German, who in 1945 were not yet born. You learn what happened in your country in 1933-45 and you say to yourself, "How could we Germans have done that?" Finally, and most generally, we ought all to feel that we share in the guilt of all the evil things that human beings have done and are doing. Many people happily appropriate successes, debts of gratitude and grievances, but they draw the line at appropriating guilt. This is to act like supporters of a football team who when it wins say "We won", but when it loses say "They lost".

The analysis of guilt by solidarity

It would be possible to take an extremely individualistic line and dismiss as irrational all the feelings which I have described. If I were to take this line I would say that if someone in my family were to do something wonderful, that would have nothing to do with me and if anyone were to offer congratulations to me I should refuse to accept them; if anyone were to help a member of my family, this would put no obligation of any kind on me; if someone were to persecute a relative or associate of mine, that should make no difference to his or her relationship with me, if there is one; and, finally, if a member of my family or a fellow-countryman or another member of the human race were to have done something bad, I would share his or her guilt in no way whatever. In this individualistic world-view, there are only personal credit and guilt.

It is, however, more reasonable to say that the feelings which I described above are not irrational. Human solidarity, in its various forms, is a reality and because of it each of us really does share the credit, indebtedness, hurt and guilt of at least some other persons. There exists, then, guilt-by-solidarity which I will now analyse. It is distinct from personal guilt.

NOT PERSONAL COMPLICITY

Our sense of involvement in other persons' actions may sometimes spring from the fact that we were in some way, however indirect, the cause of them. For instance, an American might say to himself that the taxes he paid had gone into killing civilians in Vietnam, and so feel remotely but nevertheless in some way responsible for it. This is not the kind of guilt that I am talking about here, as is clear from the fact that people cannot in any way have been the causes of things that happened before they were born or be responsible for actions of which they knew absolutely nothing.

NOT "WE WOULD HAVE DONE THE SAME"

Our sense of accomplishment, gratitude, grievance or guilt does not come from the thought that if we had been in the same situation as someone else who has done something, we would have done the same. When a cellist plays brilliantly and her parents share the glory, this is not because they say to themselves, "If we had been on the stage we would have played like that"; and when someone does something wrong and his or her relatives feel ashamed, this is not because they say to themselves, "We are genetically like him, in the circumstances we would have done the same". First, one does not feel guilt because of what one might or even would have done. Second, in cases like that of the cellist's family, one feels glory even though one knows that one would not have done the same, and in cases of evil deeds one may be entitled to say to oneself, "I would not have done that", and nevertheless feel guilty.

NOT "WE MIGHT DO THE SAME IN THE FUTURE"

The being-ashamed or feeling-guilty does not come from the thought that we ourselves are likely at some future time to do something similar. If my sister gives a great performance on the cello and everyone claps, I feel proud, but not because she has shown me that I may at some future time enjoy similar acclaim; and if Germans of a previous generation did appalling things, present-day Germans need not deduce from this that they themselves are likely to do similar things and *for that reason* feel ashamed. The guilt feelings, like the pride, come from actual events, not from things which might happen.

NOT A FEELING WHICH COMES FROM OUR OWN SIMILAR EXPERIENCES

When a man first landed on the moon I did not say to myself, "This reminds me of the time I climbed a mountain" and feel elated or proud because of my memory of that. When Jews who have lived all their lives in Australia think of Auschwitz and feel angry, it is what happened *there* that angers them, not hurts which they themselves have experienced in Australia. Similarly, when I feel guilt because of the stolen children of Australian aborigines, I am ashamed of that; it is not as though when I hear about those children I remember misdeeds of my own and *they* make me feel guilty.

WHAT SOLIDARITY-GUILT IS

The conclusion of this analysis is that there is personal credit or glory, which I get by my own actions; there is a personal debt of gratitude, which I get when someone does a favour to me; and there is personal guilt, which I acquire by acting immorally myself. As well as this, there is a quite different credit, debt of gratitude, hurt and guilt which is not, even indirectly, derived from my own actions or from things done to me, personally; it comes from things done by or to other people with whom I am joined in solidarity.

One difference between personal guilt and solidarity-guilt is this: one must repent of one's own bad actions but one cannot repent of things done by others – one can regret them, but that is not the same. Also, one can in some cases be punished for one's own bad actions but it would be wrong to punish people for the actions of others.

The Fall and original sin

THE DOCTRINE

It has been the teaching of the Catholic Church that while not all human beings commit personal sins, all are born "in the state of original sin".

First, the doctrine and the story of Adam, which is connected with it, contain a solution to the classical problem of evil. We do not now believe that in one short week God brought into existence the world with all its planets, animals, plants and other creatures. Instead, we believe that over billions of years the material universe evolved, and it is still evolving. Similarly, it seems to me, we should assume that, like creation, the Fall should not be understood as something that happened in an instant, when Adam took a bite of the apple. Rather, it is an ongoing phenomenon, and just as present-day human beings continue creation when they make things, they continue the Fall when they sin. We do not inherit the guilt of one man, Adam, but the guilt of all the evil men and women who have ever lived or are alive now.

Second, original sin was used to explain the existence in us of certain natural instincts which seem to take human beings away from the life of grace, and, in one of the most-read of Catholic books, led Thomas A Kempis to talk of "the contrary motions of nature and grace". There was a time when Catholic clerics were very "strict" in their attitudes to anything connected with sex, and they complained of what they called the "naturalism" of younger clerics who encouraged dances for young people and were in other ways "permissive". A common criticism, which I heard, was: "They don't believe in original sin".

Third, and more theologically, it was believed that all human beings without exception, including those who die as babies, mentally disabled adults who never reach moral maturity, and those who live as adults without ever committing serious sin, are sinners by solidarity and Christ is their Redeemer.

At different times, one or other of these ideas has been stressed. When people were puzzled by earthquakes, floods and diseases in this world which God created, they found the explanation in the Fall. The "strict" clerics whom I mentioned above stressed the second idea. For theologians, the third idea was the essential one.

Many Christians have found the whole idea of inherited guilt hard to accept. Pascal, for instance, said: "Undoubtedly, nothing is more shocking to our reason than the statement that the first man's sin made people who were so far removed from it and had no part in it, guilty".[2] Also, what we have learned in the past century about the early

---

2   Pascal, *Pensées*, Lafuma numbering, # 131.

human beings has made it impossible to accept the story of Adam and Eve as literally true. Teilhard said:

> It is so impossible to include Adam and the earthly paradise (taken literally) in our scientific outlook, that I wonder whether a single person today can at the same time focus his mind on the geological world presented by science, and on the world commonly described by sacred history. We cannot retain both pictures without moving alternately from one to the other. Their association clashes, it rings false.[3]

Understandably, because original sin was presented to them as coming from Adam and Eve, many Christians who ceased to believe in Adam and Eve also ceased to believe in original sin. Others have proposed various ideas of what original sin might be, without Adam and Eve. Let us look at some of them.

A PROPOSED MODERN THEORY: MORAL IMMATURITY

For millions of years human beings were incapable of rational thought and, like infants now, they had no morality. Like all animals, they fought with others of their species who did not belong to their own group or tribe, and in general their behaviour was crude or brutish. It has been suggested that "sin" in the phrase "original sin" means, first, this early brutishness; it means, second, the remnant of brutishness which remained in human beings even as they became more rational, civilised and moral, and which still remains in us today, so that to say that we are all born in the state of original sin means, according to this theory, that we still have tendencies in us which have come down to us from our primitive ancestors, who inherited them from the brute beasts from which they came. If, then, a present-day alpha male, who attains a position of leadership and power, feels in some deep-seated way that it is right for him to mate with many attractive young women, and if many young women are strongly attracted to him, this is because of instincts which remain in spite of civilisation and which cause these men and women at least to feel inclined to behave like the earliest human beings and the primates before them.

---

3   Teilhard, *Christianity and Evolution*, p. 47.

This, in essence, was Teilhard's view, which got him into serious trouble.[4] In this view, Christ is the redeemer in so far as he inspires evolution and Teilhard went into some detail about how Christ is at the heart of evolution. An objection to it is that sin always implies a turning away from God, indeed a turning against him. Whatever form it takes, it is always in some way in disaccord with nature and hateful to God. But there was nothing wrong with early human beings being primitive, indeed brutish. As Teilhard insisted, that was in the nature of things: they were as God expected them to be; they could not have acted differently; there was nothing for them or us to be ashamed of in how they were. Therefore their state cannot be called sinful and the mere existence of primitive tendencies in us does not make us sinners.

A SECOND PROPOSED MODERN THEORY: "ALL HUMAN BEINGS SIN"

Another theory of original sin does away with the distinction between original sin and personal sin and says that the doctrine means that all human beings sin, sooner or later. This fits the Genesis story if Adam is taken not as the historically first man but as like the character Everyman in the medieval play, who represents each and every human being.

To assess this theory we must ask: do all people sin? Babies and infants do not, but we talk about them being washed clean of original sin and so redeemed by Christ. Does every adult sin gravely, sooner or later in his or her life? After World War II Karl Jaspers, in Switzerland, was shocked at how Germans, including people whom he knew, denied all responsibility for the Nazi crimes and how also the Swiss, though they had profited from the war, felt clean. He took an extreme view, generalised it and declared that each of us should say:

> I am responsible for all the evil that is perpetrated in the world, unless I have done what I could to prevent it, even to the extent of sacrificing my life. I am guilty, because I am alive and can continue

---

4 Teilhard's essays on original sin are in *Christianity and Evolution*. They are "Fall, Redemption and Geocentrism" (July 1920); "Note on Some Possible Historical Interpretations of Original Sin" (March-April 1922), and "Reflections on Original Sin" (November 1947, pp. 187-198). They were intended as suggestions as to how original sin might be understood in an evolutionary world-view.

to live while this is happening. Thus criminal complicity takes hold of everyone for everything that happens.[5]

I for one believe that this was too severe. Many theologians today go to the other extreme and say that mortal sins are extremely rare. Whatever of that, this theory of original sin is incompatible with the doctrine that Jesus is the saviour of all human beings.

A THIRD PROPOSED MODERN THEORY: THE ENVIRONMENT

"Sin will pluck on sin" and it poisons a whole community or the world. Some theologians have seen in this insight a way to understand original sin: they have talked of "the sin of the world" and said that to be born in a state of original sin means to be born into a "world that is wholly foul."[6] They usually reject the idea that the world is completely outside us and insist that we are in and of it, so that if the world is foul, so are we.

This theory does preserve the distinction between original sin and personal sin: a person is foul in one way in being in this foul world, he or she becomes foul in another way if he or she commits serious sin. One problem with it is that it makes it hard to see how by baptism we can be said to be cleansed of original sin, since this does not take us out of the world.

WHAT I PROPOSE: SOLIDARITY-GUILT

We have seen that there is "corporate guilt" or guilt by solidarity, distinct from personal guilt. I have said that if a member of a group does something great, all members of the group share the credit and, similarly, if members of a group do something seriously bad, all members of the group should feel ashamed. That is, there is such a thing as corporate guilt or guilt by solidarity, which is quite different from personal guilt, and this is what original sin is. Max Scheler said:

> Considering that the very principle of solidarity lies at the roots of Christian doctrine, it is very superficial to say that one should rest content with "not judging" the guilt of others but rather be mindful of one's own individual guilt. Now this is the true meaning of the doctrine [of original sin]: that one should not only be mindful of one's own guilt but feel oneself genuinely implicated in the guilt

---

5 Jaspers, *Tragedy Is Not Enough* (1947), p. 53.
6 See, for instance, Schoonenberg, *Man and Sin*.

> of others and furthermore in the collective guilt of one's age; one should therefore regard such guilt as also one's "own".[7]

Original sin, understood in this way, is not the guilt which we have because of one sin of one man, our original father; it is the guilt which we have because of the many evil deeds of human beings, long past and recent. It is, then, independent of the story of Adam and Eve and quite reconcilable with what is now known about the earliest human beings. It is in us from the first moment of our existence, before we are even capable of committing sin, and it is distinct from any guilt that comes to us from any sins which we ourselves commit.

---

7   Scheler, *On the Eternal in Man* (1921), p. 58.

Part Four

The Remedy for Moral Evil

13 Judging & Excusing

Once a person has done wrong it remains for ever a fact that he or she has done it. Moreover, all that a person has done makes up his or her past, and if there are evil deeds in the past, unless something, to which I will come, is done, they poison the present and are waiting to poison the future as soon as it arrives, so that it seems as if once persons have done wrong they will always have to say, like Harry in *The Family Reunion*,

> I am the old house
> With the noxious smell and the sorrow before morning,
> In which all past is present, all degradation
> Is unredeemable,[1]

and many people feel that they will never be free of the burden that presses on them because of some wrong which they have done. From this it might seem that moral evil is irremediable but I am going to maintain that it is not. I will do this in stages: first I will talk about making judgements, or finding and telling the truth: this will be preliminary. Then I will talk about the healing of a person's guilt within himself or herself, after which I will talk about forgiveness and after that I will talk about the reconciliation of persons with each other after wrong has been done by one to the other, or by some to others. I shall then deal with the question of justice.

Excusing oneself and others where there has been no fault

Consider these cases:

> A man decided, when he was young, to devote his life to the cause of Esperanto as the world language and between the ages of twenty-five and fifty he did almost nothing but this. At the age of fifty he judges that he has been wasting his time.

> A woman is on a train which is delayed by an accident on the line and as a result some friends who have come to meet her are kept waiting for an hour.

---

1 Eliot, *The Family Reunion*, part 1 scene 1, *Collected Plays*, p. 66.

> Someone's parents honestly believed that to express emotion was sentimental and to spare the rod was to spoil the child, who is now an insecure adult who believes that they were misguided.
>
> A now-elderly religious sees that his or her early religious formation, which stressed abandonment to divine providence, was harmful but judges that the people responsible for it were acting as they believed they were obliged to do.

In all these cases there has been no fault and, while there may be regret, but no guilt should be experienced or attributed. There should therefore be no question of repentance and forgiveness. Instead, in the first case the man should excuse himself, in the second case the friends should excuse the woman, in the third case the person should excuse his or her parents, and in the fourth case the religious should excuse the people who caused the damage which was done. Here is another case:

> Before long-distance telephone calls were a simple matter, a man was far away from his home on business. His eighteen-year-old son was suddenly given an opportunity to go mountain-climbing in New Zealand and a decision had to be made at once. The mother, fearful of the risks involved but saying to herself that it would be unfair to say no to the boy because of her own womanly fears, reluctantly allowed him to go. Things went wrong and he was killed. The father returned for the funeral, blamed the mother because she had allowed the boy to attempt a climb which was beyond his powers, and told her that he would never forgive her.

It is perhaps understandable, up to a point, that the stricken father would react in this way, but it is horribly unfair. He should have allowed his wife to explain how she came to give the permission, accepted her explanation, assured her that he did not reproach her and that she should not reproach herself, and done all he could to help her sustain the loss which they had both suffered. If she had asked him to forgive her, he should have told her that there was nothing to forgive. Here is a different example:

> A childless married couple hardly ever spoke to each other and they thought that adopting a child would save their marriage. Presenting themselves as happy, they adopted a baby boy. Once they had done this, they remained together, but the estrangement between them remained. As a result the boy had a miserable childhood and at the age of twenty he understood both why he had been adopted and

why the adoption had turned out badly. Turning his mind to his birth mother, he judged that it was highly probable that she had agreed to the adoption in the belief that it would be best for him. He said to himself: "I wish my mother had kept me and if we ever meet and she asks me what my childhood was like, I'll tell her that it was unhappy, but I will tell her that I do not blame her for it". He also decided not to spend the rest of his life feeling sorry for himself: instead, he would have as good a life as he could.

As Jankélévitch says, in these cases "one simply grants him [the agent] what in justice is due to him".[2] That is, if a teacher punishes a child who has a valid excuse for what he or she has done, this is unjust. It is true that in Luke's gospel Jesus says of the soldiers who crucify him: "Father, forgive them; for they do not know what they are doing" (Luke 23:34). Dare one say that this is imprecise and that a more exactly worded prayer would have been: "Father, excuse them"?

Judging oneself where there has been fault: the admission of guilt
Sometimes people say that what they did was natural, that everyone does it, or that it is now perfectly normal. As they say this, they know in their hearts that what they did was bad, so that these are cases of "bad faith", which is pretending to believe what, deep down, one knows is not true.

At other times people offer elaborate theories according to which they are free of blame. Determinism is such a theory and in counselling situations concerning past bad actions therapists who are determinists do not try to get clients to accept responsibility for their actions and admit their guilt. Instead, they set out to enable them to understand why they acted as they did, implicitly assuming that they had not been able to help it and hence should not feel guilty. Frankl said that even criminals refuse to understand their own actions as predetermined:

> Criminals, at least once the judgement has been passed, do not wish to be regarded as mere victims of psychodynamic mechanisms or conditioning processes. As Scheler pointed out, a man has a right to be considered guilty. ... To explain his guilt away by looking at him as the victim of circumstances also means taking away his human dignity.[3]

---

2   Jankélévich, *Le pardon*, p. 90.
3   Frankl, *The Unheard Cry for Meaning*, p. 51, quoted in my *Free Will*, p. 214.

Utilitarianism is sometimes used to escape admission of guilt. If, for instance, a man left his faithful wife and went off with another woman, he sometimes says that "the greatest good of the greatest number" is the basis of morality and that the happiness of two (himself and the other woman) outweighs the unhappiness of one (the wife), and that he therefore did the morally right thing. As for social relativism, it is perhaps possible for people sincerely to believe that many accepted moral laws are like the rules of good manners, so that if one "misbehaves" it is like putting one's elbows on the table when one is not supposed to do that. It is, however, doubtful that people can sincerely think this about defamation or murder.

The reversal of guilt must begin with the intellectual act of admission of guilt. As Trudy Govier says, "we have to feel remorse and guilt; for a time we have to blame ourselves".[4] The wrongdoer must say: "I ruined such and such a person's reputation [or whatever the wrong action was]. I knew at the time that it was wrong but I freely chose to do it. I, who am speaking now, did an evil thing and I am responsible for its evil consequences. I am guilty." He may add, "through my fault, through my fault, through my most grievous fault". He must not act like the adulteress of whom Proverbs says:

> *This is the way of an adulteress:*
> *she eats, and wipes her mouth,*
> *and says, "I have done no wrong"* (Prov 30:20),

but like David, who said:

> *I acknowledged my sin to you,*
> *and I did not hide my iniquity;*
> *I said, "I will confess my*
> *transgressions to the Lord"* (Ps 32:5).

That is, he must face the fact, which I am here supposing is a fact, that when all the mitigating circumstances have been taken into consideration he himself freely chose to do what he knew at the time was wrong.

Albert Speer, who was one of the leading Nazis, is a fascinating case in this connection. In *Albert Speer, His Battle with Truth*, Gitta Sereny says that from soon after October 1943, if not before, Speer

---

4   Govier, *Forgiveness and Revenge*, p. 134.

knew about the long-planned and almost completed genocide of the Jews, including the women and children. And however far removed he himself was from these systematic murders, once he knew of them and yet continued to work for Hitler, he became an active participant in the crime.[5]

At Nuremburg, however, and later, while he freely admitted that certain deeds of the Nazi government had been crimes, he maintained that he had not known that Jews were being systematically killed. As a result, he was not hanged. Gitta Sereny says that for years Speer lived a lie.[6] In April 1977 Speer was asked to help some South African Jews in their effort to prevent the distribution in South Africa of a pamphlet which maintained that the Holocaust was a hoax. He said that it had happened and that he himself was guilty because of his "tacit approval of the persecution and murder of millions of Jews".[7] There it was: the admission of guilt.

Judging others where there has been fault

There are times when there can be no reasonable doubt about it: moral evil was committed. This can happen in a court of law, when a juror or magistrate hears the evidence according to which someone has been a swindler or abuser of children, and says to himself or herself: "This person was guilty, not merely legally but also morally – there is no way that swindling or child abuse could be thought to be morally right". It is true that Jesus said: "Do not judge" (Matt 7:1), but that text does not apply in cases like this. If the parable of the prodigal son has Jesus' teaching about how to deal with wrongdoers, we must note that in it the father does not welcome the son home with words like these:

> It is not easy to be a younger son. I suppose that being the younger son made it difficult for you to feel that you were growing up and you felt that in order to find yourself as a person in your own right you absolutely had to go far away from your brother and me. I should have seen this problem and paid more attention to you: it is all very understandable when I look back on it.

No, he judges that the son has done wrong and what follows supposes that.

---

5   Sereny, *Albert Speer, His Battle with Truth*, p. 704.
6   Ibid., p. 706.
7   Ibid., p. 708.

14 Repentance, Forgiveness & Reconciliation

REPENTANCE

The admission of guilt

A way of dealing with guilt is to turn the page and try to forget that anything happened. Lady Macbeth says:

Things without all remedy
Should be without regard; what's done is done.[1]

This, of course, means living as if something which happened had not happened. If a person has done wrong and is guilty, he or she should not live in an unreal world but needs at least to admit wrongdoing to himself or herself.

It is sometimes supposed that if a person has bad feelings because of something he did in the past, he can obtain relief by talking to someone about it and so "getting it out of his system". If, however, a criminal boasts to other criminals of goods which he has stolen or even of murders which he has committed, or if in a circle of tough men a man who has committed rape boasts proudly of what he has done, seeing in it an assertion of his masculinity, it is surely obvious that the narration (I do not call it the "admission") does nothing to remove guilt. Also, if a married man were to have sexual intercourse with a prostitute, then worry about infection, go to see a doctor and neither proudly nor remorsefully but in matter-of-fact terms tell him about it and obtain a test, this would not have the slightest effect on his guilt.

After World War II in France, Albert Camus attracted a great deal of public admiration for his integrity as a commentator while his private life was another story. He was unfaithful to his wife with a mistress, Maria Casarès, and he was unfaithful to both of them with an American woman, Patricia Blake, and other women. He wrote a novel, *The Fall*, which is in the form of a long monologue by a man in a bar in

---

1   Shakespeare, *Macbeth*, 3 2 13-14.

Amsterdam, which monologue, by universal consent (including that of Camus's wife), was his personal statement. The man in the bar makes no excuses for his behaviour: "No excuses ever, for anyone: that's my principle at the outset. I deny the good intention, the respectable mistake, the extenuating circumstance."[2] In opposition to the fashionable view that no one deliberately does wrong, he says that everyone does. He is, he says, a judge-penitent: he confesses his sins as a penitent, "indulging in public confession as often as possible. I accuse myself up hill and down dale".[3] He does this in order to be able to judge others and condemn them: "I pity without absolving, I understand without forgiving".[4] He calls this "practising my useful profession",[5] and he says of himself: "I am happy – I am happy, I tell you, I won't let you think I'm not happy, I am happy unto death!"[6] That is, Camus said that by telling the world of his wrongdoing he had become somehow liberated and was a happy man. It is one of the most unconvincing novels I have ever read.

Repentance: what it is

A distinction has to be made between the inner and outer worlds, or between objective reality and subjectivity, and guilt exists in subjectivity or consciousness When a man decides to do something immoral, the action has as yet no objective reality but there is guilt in his subjectivity because of his evil intention; after the action, it is an objective fact that it was done and cannot be undone and, as I said, "normally" what had been his intention becomes his will to have done whatever it was, and so the immorality continues to be a poison in his subjectivity. Repentance is the reversal of this will. If a person repents of an immoral action, he does not cause the action not to have happened but he changes his present attitude towards his own action: instead of willing to have done it and so being immoral, he wishes that he had not done it. Objectively, nothing changes, but in the person's subjectivity the attitude is reversed.

---

2   Camus, *The Fall*, p. 96.
3   Ibid., p. 105.
4   Ibid., p. 102.
5   Ibid.
6   Ibid., p. 105.

Repentance has a moral motive

If a person wishes that he had not done something, and the reason for this wish is that the action had unpleasant consequences for himself, this is regret, not repentance. If, for instance, a man were to commit financial fraud, be caught and sent to gaol, and *for this reason* wish that he had not committed the crime, this would not be repentance. Also, if a man were to leave his wife and go off with another woman, and if this other woman were to die, if he were to think how much better off he would be if he had stayed with his wife and *for this reason only* be sorry he left her, that would not be repentance, either.

Shame is largely a social phenomenon, which is experienced when something is known, either generally or by someone who matters to the person. For instance, when sons or daughters of relatively poor people become rich and move in a wealthy circle, they sometimes become ashamed of their parents, and have as little as possible to do with them. If a person commits immoral actions and this becomes known, with the result that he is rejected and despised by the people with whom he had previously mixed, this may cause him to feel ashamed of what he has done, but this is not precisely repentance.

Also, a person may regret a wrong action because he or she is afraid of being punished for it, but this is not of itself repentance, so that if parents punish a child saying, "This will make you sorry", they should realise that what they are doing is calculated to inspire regret, not repentance. Scheler went so far as to say that a person needs to be relatively free of fear in order to be able to repent of a deed because it was wrong. Moreover, he said, fear makes a person look forward, whereas in repentance one looks back; finally, a person repents from his or her inmost self, whereas fear comes over him or her from outside.[7]

That repentance ends moral guilt

A person's moral quality at a particular time is determined by what he or she wills at that time. If, then, at some time in the past a person deliberately did something immoral, he or she was then an immoral person; if he or she now repents of this, then he or she is now a good person. Scheler says:

> But what may Repentance accomplish in its attack upon guilt? Two things – of which it alone, and nothing else, is capable. It cannot

---

7 Scheler, *On the Eternal in Man*, p. 50.

drive out of the world the external natural [objective] reality of the deed and its causal consequences, nor the evil character which the deed acquires ipso facto. All that stays in the [objective] world. But it can totally kill and extinguish the reactive effect of the deed within the human soul [subjectivity], and with it the root of an eternity of renewed guilt and evil. Repentance, at least in its perfect form, genuinely annihilates the psychic [subjective] quality called 'guilt'.[8]

This is the first of the two things which, according to Scheler, repentance does; I will come later to the second. Jeffrie G. Murphy says the same:

Repentance. This is surely the clearest way in which a wrongdoer can sever himself from his past wrong. In having a sincere change of heart, he is withdrawing his endorsement from his own immoral past behaviour; he is saying, "I no longer stand behind the wrongdoing, and I want to be separated from it. I stand with you in condemning it.[9]

That repentance is not demeaning

Sade said, "Let's not cry over spilt milk; remorse is inefficacious, since it does not stay us from crime, futile since it does not repair it, therefore it is absurd to beat one's breast".[10] He also said that one should stand proudly by one's deeds and that remorse "merely denotes an easily subjugated spirit".[11] In the opera *Don Giovanni*, when the statue of the man whom he killed comes to Don Giovanni and in a deep voice sings, "Repent", Don Giovanni sings "No" eight times and goes to his doom; I feel sure that one is expected to admire him for this.[12] Spinoza said: "He who repents of his action is doubly unhappy and weak".[13] It seems that in some gangs anyone who has qualms about anything the gang has done is despised by all the others. It also seems that at

---

8   Ibid, p. 55.
9   Murphy, *Forgiveness and Mercy* (1988), p. 26.
10 Sade, "Dialogue Between a Priest and a Dying Man", p. 174.
11 Sade, *Justine*, p. 696.
12 It seems to me that the world of the opera *Don Giovanni*, which has much talk of vengeance and in which a murdered man returns for it, is not Christian and one should watch it more or less as one watches ancient Greek plays.
13 Spinoza, *Ethics*, part 4, proposition 54.

the trial after the war Goering proudly refused to repent and acted as leader of the accused Nazis. One can see the appeal of this but a wrongdoer who refuses to repent does not refuse to climb down; he refuses to climb up.

That repentance can be easy or difficult

Repentance is easy when a person, in a moment of weakness but still in the possession of his faculties and responsible for his actions, does something that is mean or spiteful, or out of cowardice betrays his own principles, then within a short time and quite spontaneously acknowledges his fault and repents of what he has done. At other times, however, repentance is difficult. Suppose, for instance, that a woman falls deeply in love with a married man, becomes his devoted mistress and for years lives only for him, though believing all the time that what they are doing is wrong. Suppose, then, that he dies. One might think that the way is now open to her to free herself from guilt by repentance, but it may be no easier to say, "I wish I had never made love with him" after his death than it would have been to break off the relationship with him before it. Told to repent of what she has done, the woman may reply: "But he was my life. For me to say, 'I wish that he and I had not become lovers' would be like destroying my life. I feel as though you are asking me to kill myself". Well, this is surely what "dying to one's old self" means: by repentance one disconnects oneself personally from a part of one's past life, or ends a life which one has been living with commitment; and if the wrongdoing has been a large part of one's life for a long time and if one was deeply committed to it, then this is not at all easy. It may, indeed, take a long time for a person to admit the evil of what he or she has done and repent.[14]

I mentioned Albert Speer, the leading Nazi who for many years refused to admit that he had known about the Holocaust but who later admitted his guilt. Markus Barth, the son of Karl Barth, said of Speer: "Meeting him, I was convinced that he had sincerely repented".[15] Undoubtedly, this repentance was difficult, and seems to have taken over thirty years.

---

14 In the example which I gave earlier, of daughters who left their fathers and later returned to them (p. 121), it took a year.

15 Sereny, *Albert Speer*, p. 698.

The "firm purpose of amendment"

Some authors think that all volitional activity is concerned with action in the future over which we have control. For them, the way for a wrongdoer to find moral goodness is to put the past behind him, since he cannot change it, and to resolve not to do the wrong again. However, it is possible for the doer of a wrong both to be glad that he did it and to have no intention of doing it again. For instance, if a man dishonestly obtains a large sum of money, and and sets out by using it shrewdly to become a rich man, he might at the same time approve of his dishonest action and, on the principle that honesty is the best policy, intend to be strictly honest from now on. Clearly, his "firm purpose of amendment" will not remove his guilt.

However, it is impossible to wish that one had not done something in the past, because it was wrong, and at the same time to intend to do it again at some future time. Therefore a "firm purpose of amendment" is an essential element of repentance, where repetition is possible. Thus, as Scheler says, repentance has, "together with, and even in consequence of, its negative, demolishing function, another which is positive, liberating and constructive";[16] repentance, he says, drives the deed with its root out of the living centre of the self, "and thereby enables life to begin ... a new course springing forth from the centre of the personality which, by virtue of the act of repentance, is no longer in bonds".[17]

> Well may the plain man say, "No regrets! – just resolve to do better in future". But what the plain man fails to tell us is where we may find strength to make these resolutions, still less the strength to carry them out, if Repentance has not first liberated the personal Self and empowered it to combat the determining force of the past.[18]

He says that repentance

> bursts the chain of evil's reproductive power which is transmitted through the growth in evil of men and times. This then is the way in which it enables men to embark on new and guiltless courses. Repentance is the mighty power of self-regeneration of the moral world, whose decay it is constantly working to avert. There lies the

---

16 Scheler, *On the Eternal in Man*, p. 36. This is the second of the two things which Scheler says repentance does.
17 Ibid., p. 42.
18 Ibid., pp. 42-43.

great paradox of Repentance, that it sorrowfully looks back to the past while working mightily and joyfully for the future, for renewal, for release from moral death.[19]

And so Ezekiel says: "If the wicked turn away from all their sins that they have committed and keep all my statutes and do what is lawful and right, they shall surely live; they shall not die" (Ezek 18:21).

I should note that if a person professes repentance and almost immediately does the same thing again, the sincerity of the profession of repentance is questionable. It is, however, possible for a person to be genuinely sorry for what he has done and at some later time, in disaccord with his present intention, to do it again.

Restitution

Repentance includes the will to repair any damage that was done, if that is possible. To take an obvious case, if someone has stolen something from another person and still has it, he or she must give it back. If someone told lies and damaged another's reputation, he or she must publicly make it known that what he or she said was untrue. I say "if possible" because the offender may be dying and in no fit state to take any action, or the offence may lie far back in the past and be irreparable, in which case the repentance can be genuine though it does not include the will to make restitution.

FORGIVENESS

Hannah Arendt seems to say that forgiveness is sometimes impossible. About the Nazi concentration camps she says:

> Here are crimes which men can neither punish nor forgive. When the impossible was made possible it became the unpunishable, unforgiveable absolute evil which could no longer be understood and explained by the evil motives of self-interest, greed, covetousness, resentment, thirst for power, and cowardice: and therefore which anger could not revenge, love could not endure, friendship could not forgive.[20]

However, forgiveness is never utterly impossible and to it I now come.[21]

---

19 Ibid., pp. 55-56.
20 Arendt, *The Origins of Totalitarianism* (1951), pp. 458-459
21 In the United States, since 1997 there has been a Campaign for Forgiveness Research, which received five million dollars from the John

What forgiveness is not

FORGIVING IS NOT EXCUSING

The object of forgiveness, says Jankélévich, is not that for which we can at the moment see no excuse, but for which we think an excuse might eventually be found: it may be something about which there can be no doubt. He also says that a forgiver does not look for extenuating circumstances, to make the offence appear less serious than it actually was, so that he can excuse it, at least partially. On the other hand, he does not try to persuade himself that the offence was worse than it really was: he is severe but not unfair. This, however, doenot mean that he cannot *forgive* the person who has hurt him. Indeed, Jankélévitch says: "The inexcusable is what forgiveness is concerned with, for the inexcusable is forgivable."[22] He says:

> When a crime can be neither justified nor explained nor understood; when, after all that is understandable in it has been understood, its atrociousness and the overwhelming evidence of responsibility are plain for all to see; when there are no attenuating circumstances of any kind ... then there is nothing to do but forgive.[23]

FORGIVING IS NOT FORGETTING

There exists the phrase, "forgive and forget", which seems to imply that if one forgives one also forgets. This idea has caused people to say: "I thought I had forgiven but I find that I have not forgotten, so apparently I have not forgiven after all".

However, our brains are not like computers in which it is possible, by pressing a button, to erase something in the memory, and if it ever becomes possible to erase things in our memories we will not have to do that whenever we forgive. As things now are, we are incapable of forgetting important events in our lives. But we can forgive.

Templeton Foundation and more money from other sources. It funds a number of scientific research projects into such things as neurochemical activity and muscular patterns associated with forgiveness. I know about it because a psychiatrist friend gave me a copy of an article in *Psychiatric News*. I do not intend to apply for a grant.

22 Jankélévich, *Le pardon*, p. 124.
23 Ibid., p. 139.

FORGIVING IS NOT CONDONING

To condone something bad which a person has done is to approve of what has been done. Suppose, for instance, that a woman were to discover that her husband had been unfaithful to her and that she were to say to a woman friend, "Modern science has shown that it is unnatural for alpha males to be physically faithful to one female; my husband is an alpha male if ever there was one, and I must accept his infidelity as natural *for him*"; or suppose that she says: "Before safe sex was invented, it was wrong for a married person to have sex with anyone other than his or her spouse because of the dangers of pregnancy and sexually transmitted disease; now all that is required is that the person have unsafe sex with no one except his or her spouse; since my husband obeyed this rule, I should accept what he did as in order by modern standards. I ought to demand of him that he live not by the old-fashioned rules which I was brought up to observe but by those of the liberal society to which we are proud to belong." This would not be forgiveness, which, Jankélévitch says, "does not require of us the sacrifice of our selfhood".[24]

IT DOES NOT SPRING FROM ADMISSION OF ONE'S OWN MORAL WEAKNESS

A certain hospital chaplain said in an address to a conference that forgiveness springs from

> the ability to recognise in one's victimiser one's own capacity to victimise and one's own need for forgiveness. Hence, the wayward spouse, the abusive partner, even the murderer, can be forgiven when an individual recognises his or her capacity for infidelity, abuse and murder.[25]

A Jewish author has said:

> I have learnt, for example, that forgiveness of sins is not just a mystical high. It also means understanding them in order not to repeat them, which means some hard spadework. It also means locating the sins of other people in yourself.[26]

---

24 "Le pardon, à vrai dire, ne nous demande pas de sacrifier le tout de notre être-propre" (ibid., p. 157).
25 Moran, "Forgiveness may be Divine but also Health-Giving" (2000), p. 33.
26 Lionel Blue, "On the Couch", p. 1482.

There are, however, many situations where offended persons in all honesty believe that they are extremely unlikely to commit a wrong comparable to the wrongs which have been done to them, and if this were the source of forgiveness, it would be utterly impossible for God to forgive.

FORGIVING IS NOT DEMEANING

I said earlier that repentance is not demeaning: it involves, I said, climbing up, not climbing down. In a similar way, forgiveness is not demeaning. A married woman who tolerates an unfaithful and unrepentant husband because she cannot afford not to do so may feel ashamed of herself; but to forgive a repentant offender is not like this at all. Indeed, forgiveness can be a sign of greatness.

What forgiveness is

Forgiveness starts from recognition of the fact that there has been wrongdoing. As John Paul II said, "Forgiveness, far from excluding the search for truth, demands it".[27] The forgiver then sees that the person has changed in his or her subjectivity: the will to do wrong has gone, and now he or she is no longer hostile to the forgiver but in favour of him or her. Having seen this, the forgiver accepts the other person. This can at times be difficult, even when the person is not present, because a person who has been hurt may have come almost to cherish the grievance and pain; having found himself cast against his will in the role of victim, he may have lived the part so intensely and for so long that he can be unwilling to relinquish it. What forgiveness offers is a way out of this state, a way which may demand a greatness of soul which is hard to achieve but which leads to healing and happiness.

I said a few pages ago that repentance has a moral reason, and so has forgiveness. As Jeffrie Murphy says, "My ceasing to resent will not constitute forgiveness unless it is done for a moral reason".[28] By "moral reason" he means, or I hope he means, a personal rather than a purely practical reason. If, for instance, a man discovers that his wife has been outrageously extravagant and throws her out of the house; and if he later lets her come back because she will probably inherit a great deal of money when her father, who is now in his nineties, dies, this is not

---

27 John Paul II, quoted in Stephen Pope, "The Convergence of Forgiveness and Justice", p. 826.

28 Murphy and Hampton, *Forgiveness and Mercy*, pp. 23-24.

forgiveness on his part. Forgiveness can be inspired only by love, of one kind or another.

In forgiveness a love-relationship of some kind is revived after having been broken, and the qualities of forgiveness are those of love. For instance, to love another person is to consent to him or her for his or her sake, not for one's own, and one forgives another for the other's sake. Also, love involves an acceptance of the present reality of the person, who is not regarded as the raw material out of which one hopes to make a being worthy of one's love. In a similar way, anyone who says, "If we let him off this time I'm sure he won't do it again, so let's do that" does not propose forgiveness properly so called.

Love is for ever, which is why though one can promise to help someone for a week it is a contradiction in terms to say, "I will love you for a week". Forgiveness, too, is for ever, so that one cannot forgive someone on the understanding that the forgiveness will cease after a certain time.

In certain kinds of love, two persons are on a footing of equality and their love is mutual. If, for instance, two men are friends, they are as friends equal, even if *as higher-up and lower-down in an institution in which they work* they are unequal. In forgiveness, two persons seem not to meet as equals, for one is in the wrong and the other is not. However, a person who forgives another does not lord it over him or her and savour a delicious sense of moral superiority: on the contrary, he or she removes the inequality which has existed and from then on regards the other as once more an equal.

The past and the future

A difference between accepting an excuse and forgiving a moral wrong is that when a person presents an excuse, the talk is all of the past: he explains what he knew and did not know when he did whatever it was, or what the circumstances were *then*. When a person asks forgiveness, however, he says that he is sorry *now*, and the person who was hurt attends not so much to the past as to the other's *present* state of mind and heart.

The idea that repentance is not necessary for forgiveness

Some people say that forgiveness involves only the offended person. The offender, they say, does not come into it. For instance, Margaret Holmgren says that "the appropriateness of forgiveness has nothing to do with the actions, attitudes, or position of the wrongdoer".[29] This of course means that repentance is not necessary for forgiveness, and Trudy Govier talks of forgiveness that is unilateral and unconditional.[30] In *Forgiving and Not Forgiving* (1999), Jeanne Safer, a Jewish psychotherapist in New York, says that the idea of universal, unconditional forgiveness is widespread among both Christians and Jews, and the statement that forgiveness is unconditional means that it does not require the repentance of the wrongdoer. "Forgiveness," she says, meaning unconditional forgiveness, "has become spiritually correct".[31] A Catholic priest told her that forgiveness is always obligatory,[32] and she says that "forgiveness is compulsory for most believers",[33] whether there is repentance or not. Christians can add that when we say the Our Father we say that we forgive those who trespass against us, not adding, "if they are sorry". Safer says that many therapists, acting on this principle, urge their clients to forgive people who have hurt them, whether they are repentant or not, in order to get the evil out of their systems. She tells of Henry, who was hurt by his mother when he was a child, and whose mother has never shown any sign of repentance. Safer goes on: "One therapist predicted that unless Henry forgave his mother, he would 'fall into a terrible depression when she died' and encouraged him to pay her a visit".

When Nelson Mandela was freed he seems to have expressed forgiveness of the whites for what they had done, without demanding repentance of them. In the United States Gary Wright saw a strange wooden structure in the parking lot of the place where he worked. He tried to move it and it exploded, injuring him severely. It had been put there by a man known as the Unabomber and Wright was his eleventh victim. Years later, it became known that Ted Kaczynski was the Unabomber. He was arrested and put on trial, during which he seemed to be proud of what he had done. Wright told him that he had forgiven him years earlier. That was forgiveness without repentance. Also, when John Paul II was shot and taken to hospital, he said later that on the way to the hospital "I said to Father Stanislaw [Dziwsz]

---

29   Holmgren, "Forgiveness and the Intrinsic Value of Persons", p. 342.
30   Govier, *Forgiveness and Revenge*, chap. 4, pp. 62-77.
31   Safer, *Forgiving and Not Forgiving*, p. 143.
32   Ibid., p. 22.
33   Ibid., p. 171.

that I had forgiven my assailant", and Fr Dziwsz said that when he and the Pope went to see the assailant "the Pope had already forgiven him publicly in his first speech after the attack". In Melbourne, a weatherboard church hall, connected to a Greek Orthodox church, was set alight in the early morning of 9 April 2009. The police think that it was deliberate. Asked if he was angry, Bishop Ezechiel said: "Not really. As Christians, we have to forgive everybody".[34] For all these people, repentance was not necessary for there to be forgiveness.

That repentance is necessary for forgiveness

Let us consider a fictitious example:

> James, a professional man in his mid-twenties met Susan, who was a year or two younger than himself, and they fell in love and got married. Living in Melbourne, they became moderately well off and had several children. After twenty years of marriage he, in his mid-forties, met Veronica, a stylish woman of thirty who, without encountering much resistance, seduced him and an affair began. After a complicated year, the details of which I will pass over, he left Susan and their children and set about obtaining a divorce. He said to someone: "They say you're only young once. I don't believe that and I intend to prove it's wrong". He went to a lawyer who specialised in divorce and prided himself on seeing to it that the person whom he represented would come out of the settlement with as much money as possible, which in this case meant that Susan and the children would get as little as possible. James chose him because he wanted to enjoy a high standard of living with Veronica, for which reason he wanted to have to pay as little as possible to Susan and the children.. He and the lawyer were successful, so that when he married Veronica he took her to the Club Med in Moorea for a month's honeymoon, after which, with his own and her money, they settled in an apartment in Sydney that had a harbour view, while in Melbourne Susan and the children had to adjust to life at a greatly reduced level.
>
> Five years later, Veronica was killed in a car accident. James was devastated. He felt alone, because his social circle in Sydney had been primarily Veronica's friends, who had accepted him only because of her.
>
> Ten more years went by. Then he met someone who knew Susan in Melbourne and this person gave him news of her, telling him that

---

34 *The Age* (Melbourne) 10-11 April, 2009.

she looked good, that she had not remarried but was not lonely as she had close friends and was popular in a wide circle. She never spoke bitterly of him. He wrote to her, along these lines:

"I had better say at the start that I am not sorry for what I did fifteen years ago. My marriage with Veronica was great while it lasted and I treasure the memory of it. I know that you suffered, both emotionally and financially. Indeed, I admit that what I did was morally wrong. However, all that is over now. As I am sure you know, Veronica died ten years ago, and I have lived alone since then. You were poor, but you are not poor now, so that's over, too. Let's put the past behind us and be reunited. Will you forgive me?"

Is it possible for Susan to forgive James? Some people to whom I have told the story have said: "If Susan refuses to forgive James, she needs to be helped to deal with her anger". Others have said: "I can understand Susan if she refuses to forgive James. If I were the ex-wife in that situation, I doubt whether I would have enough generosity to forgive him". It has been maintained that to make forgiveness conditional on repentance is wrong. Some authors have said that, in the case above, if Susan refuses to forgive James it is because, having suffered herself, she wants him to go on suffering the loneliness which he has experienced since Veronica died, or wants him to come crawling to her, humiliated. They believe that she wants revenge. I maintain that for reconciliation, after admission of guilt, repentance is needed so that it is impossible – not difficult, impossible – for Susan in that story to forgive James. This is because forgiveness is the restoration of a two-sided relationship and if one party has hurt the other and is unrepentant, he or she is maintaining a hostility towards the other party so that there cannot be a mutual relationship. Revenge does not come into it. Let us now suppose that when James wrote to Susan he said something like this:

"When I left you I was ruthless. I was cruel. I wanted a high life with Veronica, and I was prepared to hurt you in order to get it. As long as Veronica was alive I maintained that attitude. Since she died, however, I have come to see things in proper perspective, and I now see that I behaved badly. Badly? It's too weak a word. What I did was evil. And I am deeply sorry I did it. I'm sorry I had sex with Veronica the first time. I'm sorry that after it happened I didn't stop there. I'm sorry I left you and the kids. I'm sorry for what I did to you regarding money. And yes, I'm sorry I had those years with Veronica. We went to Moorea after the divorce, and now whenever

I see a South Sea island on television I feel terrible. I remember what you and the kids were going through while we were playing around there, and I feel foul. I deeply wish that all that had never happened. What I ask is: can you, and if so will you, forgive me?"

Let us suppose that in saying all this he is sincere and that Susan does not doubt his sincerity. Whether Susan forgives him on the spot, asks for time, or tells him that she will never forgive him, I believe that in this situation forgiveness is possible. In replying to the people whose words I quoted earlier I would have said: "Susan got over her anger long ago and it is not that which is the obstacle to forgiveness; neither is it lack of generosity on her part and it is not vindictiveness: the fact is that she judges that it would make no sense to say 'I forgive you' to an unrepentant James and the obstacle to forgiveness is not something in her, it is his attitude".

Other authors have said this. Scheler, for instance, says that the act of repentance is required for the victim, after receiving compensation, to forgive,[35] and John G. McKenzie says: "Repentance is the condition of forgiveness".[36]

Not forgiving

Like Jeanne Safer, I want to make a distinction between the refusal of forgiveness and simple not-forgiving. If someone has hurt another person, repents, says that he or she is sorry and asks to be forgiven, the hurt person is able to refuse and, if he or she does, this is a refusal of forgiveness. If, however, a person has hurt another and is not at all repentant, then if I am right there can be no forgiveness. This is not a case of *possible forgiveness refused*, but of *not forgiving because forgiveness is impossible*.

Ideally, in a case of not forgiving, the offended person should not nurse a sense of grievance, brood on how much he or she has suffered, hate the offender and wish sorrow and pain on him or her. Indeed, he or she might be at all times willing to forgive, while having a life – ideally, a good life – in which the offender has no part.

---

35   Scheler, *Formalism in Ethics*, p. 365.
36   McKenzie, *Guilt*, p. 179.

Where the wrongdoer is elsewhere

I have maintained that when a person has been wronged, he or she can forgive the wrongdoer if he or she (the wrongdoer) repents. There are, however, times when one person hurts another and then dies or goes one knows not where, so that further communication is impossible. For instance, a German woman may have been raped in 1945 by Russian soldiers, who have vanished. What I have said might seem to imply that for her forgiveness is impossible. However, a kind of conditional forgiveness is sometimes possible: a person who was hurt by a man can say, "I hope that he is sorry or, if he is dead, I hope that he repented before he died and, if he did, I forgive him". Whether there can be conditional forgiveness or not, not-forgiving is sometimes possible in these circumstances. Suppose that a man severely hurt someone and it is clear that he is not the least bit sorry for what he has done. Now suppose that without any warning he is suddenly killed. It seems unrealistic to suppose that he repented before he died.. It seems to me that the person whom he hurt cannot forgive him but should, instead, *not* think constantly of what was done, and not cherish the memory of it and often talk about it, but put it behind him or her.

An English woman doctor, a Catholic, went to live for a while in Chile, where she had a friend. Naturally enough, as an English-speaking Catholic woman she came to know the American Maryknoll sisters who were there. One day these sisters came to her: a revolutionary had been shot in the leg by soldiers and needed a doctor, they were hiding him and would she come? She went, being taken to the place blindfolded (with her consent), attended to the man, and was returned to her own place in the same way. Eventually the man was captured, the military recognised a professional job, tortured him, found out about her and arrested her. They then tortured her for information which she did not have, and a doctor stood by while she was tortured to stop the torturers, if necessary, before they killed her. Then she was kept in prison. Eventually, her release was obtained. Years later, she wrote an article in *The Tablet*, in which she said that she could not forgive the doctor who assisted her torturers and that this troubled her. I wrote a letter to her in which I set out briefly the position which I am stating here, and I said that, in the absence of any sign of repentance, of course she could not forgive and she should not feel troubled about it.

Forgiveness can be easy or difficult

Forgiveness can at times be difficult because once bitten one is twice shy. It is one thing to entrust yourself to someone who has shown you nothing but understanding and sympathy, and of whose present sincerity and future fidelity you have no reason to be suspicious; it is another thing to entrust yourself again to someone by whom, after you had given yourself the first time, your trust had been betrayed and by whom your happiness had been destroyed. Also, as I said earlier, a person who has been hurt may be unwilling to relinquish the role of victim; moreover, he may say to himself or she may say to herself, "Now I can take my revenge by saying no". More than love at its beginning, then, forgiveness always demands generosity and it may call into being a greatness of heart that is magnificent.

Forgiveness of oneself

We speak of forgiving or not forgiving ourselves for something we have done, and there is an analogy between self-love and self-forgiveness. If I have done wrong and have repented, then I should feel free of guilt and I should have a certain peace of mind: this is what is meant by self-forgiveness.

RECONCILIATION

Strictly speaking, the "re" in "reconciliation" implies that a relationship existed and has been broken, so that if one person wrongly hurts another, *whom he or she does not know*, and if he or she repents and is forgiven, this is not, strictly speaking, *re*conciliation. However, the word seems often to be used for the bringing-together of people one of whom hurt the other when there was no relationship between them at that time. In either sense, reconciliation is an element of the healing of the damage done by moral evil.

Pragmatic truces between individuals

There are cases of cessation of hostilities, no more. Neighbours who have had a dispute can reach an agreement ("We won't play any loud music after 10 pm if you don't use your lawnmower before 10 am") and abide by it without having any more to do with each other than they can help. A young woman whose father left her mother and herself when she was twelve might, as a young adult, occasionally deal with her father in a businesslike way if she needs to do so, but otherwise have nothing to do with him. Similarly, there are husbands and wives who never talk to one another but who live in the same house and arrive at public functions together, where they separate and talk to different people. In these cases there is neither love nor reconciliation.

False routes to reconciliation

UNDERSTANDING AND EXCUSING

I said earlier that forgiveness is not achieved through the understanding and excusing of the wrongdoer, and it follows that true reconciliation cannot be attained in this way.

FORGETTING THE PAST

I also said earlier that forgiving does not necessarily include forgetting, and if one person has seriously hurt another, repented and been forgiven, what happened is not forgotten. The persons concerned may rarely if ever think about it, and almost never refer to it in conversation. Each of them knows that the other knows what happened, and they both believe that the one has repented and the other has forgiven, so that they now love one another. People who have met them only recently may learn nothing about this part of their history or, if they have heard about it, they may wonder if the persons are pretending that it never happened. There is no pretence, however: what other people see is the persons as they actually are now. If they are a married couple whose children were small at the time of the hurt but are now older, one of them may, with the consent of the other, tell them the story, if they judge that not to do so would amount to a deception, but it is something that is over.

LETTING BYGONES BE BYGONES

It is sometimes thought that if an offended person cannot understand and excuse an action he can make up his mind to try not to think about it again, never mention it, and put the past behind him; and then, it is thought, he can be reconciled with the person who wronged him, for the present and the future. To this Jankélévitch says that an extremely superficial person, for whom only the recent past, the present and the near future seem real, may be able to go through life continually putting hurts and grievances aside, dismissing any thought of injuries that were done to him in the past simply on the ground that it was in the past that they were done, and being willing to associate with people who have injured him provided that it was not within the previous few days: such a person may be able to say that he lets bygones be bygones and mean it. A deeper person, however, does not let life fly by him into nothingness, but keeps his past; for such a person, to deny the present relevance of past deeds on the ground that they were performed in the past would be here and now to betray the values affirmed or denied in those deeds. For instance, if a woman were to say: "My husband was unfaithful, but because it happened last week" – or last month or last year – "it does not matter to me now", she would be untrue to her own ideal of marriage. The English cannot expect the Irish to let the Famine be a bygone, Chileans cannot dismiss from their minds all memories of the terror which was inflicted during the military dictatorship, and we white Australians cannot expect the aboriginals to let their sufferings be bygones, *simply because they happened in the past*.

Time, it is true, does have some healing effects. Anger subsides, for few can maintain a rage for years, even if they would like to. The shock one received when an offence was committed, or when one first heard of it, does not last, for one becomes accustomed to knowing what happened. What at first drove all other thoughts out of one's mind becomes something that comes to mind only now and then, and whereas for some time nothing could give one any pleasure, eventually one begins to enjoy life again. However, time does not heal all wounds. The state, it is true, separates a criminal from society for a certain period of time and then accepts him back when he has "done his time"; but if one has hurt another person one cannot return after so many days or years, claim to have "done one's time" and demand that the old relationship be resumed as if nothing had happened. Different principles apply.

True reconciliation

At its best, reconciliation restores the original relationship. It does not obliterate the past and cause the couple to be as if they were meeting each other for the first time. It takes them back to where they were before the break, with the memory of the good years which preceded it, and it enables them to face the future together with confidence in each other. However, sometimes, as we shall see, there is a difference. I shall give some fictitious examples of reconciliation and then make some general observations about it.

EXAMPLES OF RECONCILIATION

> A young man from a well-known, respected family became a drug addict and before long was being used as a supplier of drugs to young people in his social circle. Eventually he was caught and brought to trial. Sincerely, he told his parents that he was sorry and they did not disown him: instead, they forgave him for how he had made them suffer. They engaged a good lawyer to represent him and they were present in court when he was tried. He was found guilty and sent to gaol, where his parents visited him. When he came out they met him, took him home and tactfully looked after him. He for his part felt deeply sorry for the hurt he had caused to his parents and when he went home with them he was on his best behaviour, until one night they went out and came home unexpectedly early. When they came in, they could hardly hear each other because of loud rock music that filled the house. The father said, "I'll soon stop that", but the mother said, "Leave it. It means that our son is once more treating this house as his home. We are at last back to normal."

In my terms, reconciliation was complete. Here is another equally fictitious example:

> In West Australia, a man with a son aged twelve married a woman with a daughter aged eight and, unwisely as it turned out, the four of them became a family. Four years later the boy, now sixteen, went to the room of the girl, who was twelve, climbed into the bed and had sex with her, after which he swore her to secrecy and returned to his room. This went on for some years and then the son left home. Many years later the girl, who of course had become a woman and who now lived in Sydney, found herself suffering fits of depression and went to a psychologist, who asked her if she had been abused as a child. She told the story and the psychologist instructed her to go and talk to her brother-by-marriage, who was still in West Australia. She flew to Perth and went to see him. To her consternation, he said: "You enjoyed what we did, don't pretend otherwise, and you were lucky to have been initiated by me, who had already had some experience". When she returned to Sydney, her condition was worse than ever. More years went by and eventually she learned that her brother-by-marriage had about two months to live. Again she flew to Perth and went to see him. Other people were present when she arrived but he asked them to leave. He then looked at her and said: "I'm sorry". That was all, but it was enough. She felt as though an immense weight had been lifted from her. She burst into tears but

they were tears of relief, she said: "I forgive you", and the two of them hugged one another. When, later, she was beside her mother and step-father at the funeral, she felt that it was right for her to be there, since she and the dead man had been reconciled before he died.

Here is another example: I told the story of Marcel and Henry on p. 109 and I will here continue it.

> Henry and Marcel had been friends, then Henry had unjustly wronged Marcel and they had ceased to be friends. Years passed. Marcel's wife died. Henry did not go to the funeral but his wife went, and sat at the back. Then Marcel himself became seriously ill and was in hospital. Henry went to see him and said: "I've come to say I'm sorry for what I did. For a long time I managed not to think about it much but as I've got older I've come to see that my career took off from an evil deed, and I'm sorry. If I could have my life again, I would not do what I did. If my son were to be in the situation I was in, to get the idea of doing what I did, and to ask my advice, I'd say, 'For God's sake, don't do it'. And I've come to ask your forgiveness."
>
> Marcel did not then say to Henry: "It was nothing, don't worry about it". Nor did he say: "I'd have done the same if I'd thought of it first". He said: "When I found out what you had said, I was angry at the untruth and injustice of it. I was angry at being deprived unjustly of my right to be considered on my merits for the partnership which you got, and which by the way you would quite possibly have got anyway, in which case I'd have been happy for you. Also, I was sad because of your sacrificing our friendship to your career. Our friendship meant at lot to me and to my wife, and when it was broken there was a great hole in my heart. From today, that is past. I forgive you. We are friends again."

Jeanne Safer tells the story of a man who secretly watched his prepubescent daughter undressing and when she was a teenager paid her to take off her blouse for him. In later life the girl became a drug addict and went into therapy at the age of thirty-five. She evidently told the therapist about what her father had done, she and her father were brought together, he "listened to every accusation, acknowledged them all, wept with guilt and remorse", and the daughter forgave him, so that they were reconciled.[37]

In many marital cases where couples must either be reconciled with one another or separate, there is fault on both sides. Here is another fictitious example:

> A husband had culpably treated his wife badly, hardly ever talking seriously with her and making plain his quite irrational disregard for her; she had, also culpably, got half-drunk and spent a huge amount of money foolishly. When the husband protested about this, the wife, who was ready for the occasion, launched into a quite violent verbal attack on his behaviour over some years. They were on the point of agreeing to separate when their residual feelings towards one another made them agree to go a marriage counsellor. As a result, some time later both of them said that they were sorry, they forgave each other, they were reconciled and they stayed reconciled.

RECONCILIATION REQUIRES REPENTANCE AND FORGIVENESS

In all these cases, reconciliation is achieved through repentance and forgiveness, which I maintain are necessary. This is a problem with the South African Truth and Reconciliation Commission, which seems to have been working on the principle that if the truth is told, that will be sufficient for reconciliation. In practice, there has sometimes been repentance which has been followed by forgiveness and reconciliation. In other cases there has not been repentance, and in these cases there has not been reconciliation properly so called; instead, there has been what I have called a pragmatic truce.

REPENTANCE AND FORGIVENESS MUST NORMALLY BE EXPRESSED

Consider this story:

> A man who had been living in Melbourne with a good wife and several children one day left them and went to live with another woman in Sydney. After some years this woman threw him out and he then lived by himself in Sydney. One day he met in Sydney a Melbourne man whom he had known and who still knew his wife, and he told this man that he would like to return to her. "But," he asked, "would she take me back?" When the man returned to Melbourne he put

---

37 Safer, *Forgiving and Not Forgiving*, pp. 103-104. Safer says that the daughter accepted her father's apology, which I have taken to mean that she forgave him.

> the question to the wife and she said that yes, she would. The friend passed this information on to the man in Sydney, who phoned his wife and said: "Can I see you on Friday night?" "Yes," she said at once, "I'll expect you here", and she hung up. On the Friday evening the man flew to Melbourne and went to what had been their home. Much to his surprise his wife met him at the door as if he lived there and was returning home from work, and as she had always done in the past she proceeded to tell him what she had been doing during the day. After some time of this he tried to bring up the painful subject of his adultery and desertion but she took no notice and went on talking of other things. Eventually he understood that he could stay but that what he had done was not to be talked about.

If one imagines first that one is the husband and then that one is the wife in this story, one senses that they are not going to achieve a genuine reconciliation. The past cannot be ignored like that and it is now the wife who, by refusing to talk about it and to let the man admit his wrong and say he is sorry, is preventing a genuine reunion from taking place.

RECONCILIATION IS FOR EVER

Like forgiveness, reconciliation is for ever. If two persons, one of whom has hurt the other, come together for a limited time, on the understanding that they will resume hostilities when the time is up, they are not reconciled.

The idea that the post-reconciliation relationship is better than it was before

It sometimes happens that after an entire experience of offence, break-up, repentance, forgiveness and reconciliation, a relationship is better than it was before. The partner who did wrong may have been self-righteous before his or her fall and may now be cured of this fault. The innocent partner may have been naive to a fault and may now be wiser, more mature and more interesting. After the prodigal son returns home, the relationship between him and his father may be better than it had been before he left. In Faulkner's *Requiem for a Nun*, Temple Drake says:

> Love, but more than love too: ... tragedy, suffering, having suffered and caused grief; having something to have to live with even then, because you knew both of you could never forget it. And then I

began to believe ... that there was something even better, stronger, than tragedy to hold two people together: forgiveness.[38]

It is true that to have a deep relationship people need both to enjoy themselves and to suffer, to work and to play, to laugh and to weep, together; they need perhaps sometimes to find themselves surprisingly at one in their judgements and wishes, but also at other times to encounter disagreements, differences in temperament, misunderstandings and clashes of mood. I cannot believe, however, that it can be true in general that it helps if one of them maliciously hurts the other, even if he or she later repents and is forgiven. Also, if in a particular case a man could see that by deliberately hurting someone who loved him, causing a break in the relationship, then later repenting and obtaining forgiveness, he could bring about a deepening of the relationship, it would not be right for him to do this. The end does not justify the means, and moral evil is not something that can be taken as if it were medicine. Only someone with an incredibly superficial moral sense could possibly think of trying to use it to achieve some good purpose. It is not even right, if a relationship has been deepened by an experience of sin and reconciliation, to be glad that the sin was committed, for this would be retrospectively to will evil for the good that came of it, thus willing evil as a means to a good end.

The idea that reconciliation may sometimes not completely restore the original relationship

Consider this case:

> A good Catholic young woman was engaged to a young man, they were going to get married in three months time and, because she had made it clear at the start that she was against premarital sex, they had not made love. One day, when she was hanging her fiancé's jacket on a hallstand, a packet of contraceptives slipped out of a pocket and fell on the floor. Shocked, she concluded that he was having sex with another woman or women. She confronted him with the evidence, making it clear that she had found it by accident. He expressed sincere sorrow for what he had been doing, promised that he would stop, and begged forgiveness. She said, "You will hear from me", and sent him away. Some time later she said to him: "I believe that your sorrow is genuine and that here and now you intend not to have sex with anyone until we are married, and after that only

---

38 Faulkner, *Requiem for a Nun*, act 2, scene 1, p. 138.

> with me. I forgive you. As far as I am concerned we will be able to meet occasionally, quite amicably. But, frankly, I am not in love with you now, as I used to be, and I will not marry you."

In this case there are two actions, the forgiveness and the breaking of the engagement. Others may disagree, but I for one would not tell the young woman that the obligation to forgive entailed the obligation to go ahead with the marriage. Here is another story.

> A Sydney couple got married when they were in their twenties and they had some children. When he was about fifty and the children were grown up, the man left his wife, married a younger woman and settled in Melbourne, where he had no contact with either his ex-wife or his children. Many years passed, the ex-wife did not remarry and as old age approached she moved into a retirement village. A year or two later, to her surprise, her ex-husband, who did not know that she was there, also moved in. She avoided him but one day he came to her and said, "Can we talk?" She agreed and he began by informing her that his second wife, with whom he had had no children, had died about ten years earlier. Then, in a long speech about which he had obviously thought much and which equally obviously came from his heart, he said that, looking back over his life, he was profoundly sorry for what he had done and he now believed that the children had done the right thing in not keeping in touch with him. "I will not say," he said, "that I had no joy in my second life, but I will say that I repent of it." In conclusion, he asked her to forgive him. She asked for time to consider this and a week later she told him that she did. From then on they took most meals together, they talked amicably, she brought it about that he was reunited with their children and he met his grandchildren. The woman did not, however, feel that by forgiving her ex-husband she was committing herself to cohabitation with him, and they continued to live separately, like friends.

That seems to me to be not only credible but acceptable. If I am right, there is forgiveness here, not not-forgiving, but the story shows that reconciliation does not necessarily involve a restoration of the original situation as it was.

When attempts at reconciliation fail because there is no repentance: "not forgiving"

I have maintained that without repentance forgiveness is impossible. Since offending persons do not always repent, this means that it is not always possible to forgive and hence to be reconciled. I agree, then, with Jeanne Safer, who, early in *Forgiving and Not Forgiving*, says that "people need to be told that resolved, thoughtful unforgiveness is as liberating as forgiveness".[39] She says that "not forgiving *without vindictiveness* can be morally and emotionally right".[40] She quotes a woman, Sandy, who was seriously mistreated by her brother and who said: "Making up without apology or remorse on his part would have been another degradation of myself".[41] Therapists who urge victims to make contact with unrepentant offenders sometimes make things worse.

In practice, what the person should do is this: make a personal life for himself or herself in which the offender has no part. If a woman was abandoned by her husband some years ago, and if it is now clear that he is extremely unlikely to seek a reconciliation, she may have to deal with him occasionally about money or other matters, but she should set about making a personal life from which he is absent. Jeanne Safer herself says of a man who hurt her: "I can now encounter with equanimity a man I used to dread running into since he has not been part of my life for twenty-five years".[42] She says that a girl named Sandy says of the brother who mistreated her: "I've taken a strong position that he's out of my life".[43] And she tells of three women who did not forgive their unrepentant mothers and who felt no grief when their mothers died, because they were no longer personally involved with them.[44] There have also been women who, when they were young, were abandoned by their fathers who left their mothers and them, perhaps paying such support as they were required by law to pay for as long as it was required but otherwise having nothing to do with them; some of these women, when they became adults and were going to get married, did not allow their fathers to "give them away" or even come to the weddings, each of them saying of her father, "He is out of my life". If they had been nursing hostile feelings their fathers would have been in their lives.

---

39   Safer, *Forgiving and Not Forgiving*, p. 5.
40   Ibid., p. 8.
41   Ibid., p. 147.
42   Ibid., p. 44.
43   Ibid., p. 147.
44   Ibid., pp. 155, 163.

The reconciliation of an individual with a group and of countries, or groups within countries, with each other

Sometimes by doing wrong an individual separates himself or herself from a group, membership of which is voluntary. If he or she repents and asks to be forgiven and received back into the group, this is possible. For it to happen it is not usually necessary that absolutely every member of the group agree to it, but as a rule there needs to be a substantial majority. Also, whole groups may be hostile to each other, and the question is: is reconciliation between them possible?

Vatican II said that Moslems and Christians should "forget the past"[45] and be friends. Also, in El Salvador many people maintained that Christian morality demands that we put the past out of our minds and in 1993 the president said: "What is most important now is to erase, eliminate and forget everything in the past". Whereas it is impossible for individual people to forget important incidents in their lives, it is often possible for the people of one generation to say nothing about past wrongs and so to ensure that succeeding generations know nothing about them so that the group "forgets" its past. Indeed, where governments have control of the schools and media, they can prevent information about past wrongs from being passed on, in the hope that eventually almost no one will know about them. Elsewhere, it is seen that what is called "the truth" about the wrong which was done must be brought to light. I referred to the Truth and Reconciliation Commission in South Africa, where the truth about the crimes which were committed in the time of apartheid was made public. Unfortunately, as with individuals, publication of the truth does not by itself bring about reconciliation. It is, however, a necessary first step, and in most cases books and television programmes which show past wrongs fairly are to be welcomed. In Paris, at one end of the Ile Saint-Louis, there is a monument to the people who during the German occupation were deported, and the inscription says that what happened must be forgiven but not forgotten. Perhaps the author had read Jankélévitch, who says: "Those who preach forgetfulness are only seeking to exploit people's frivolousness, laziness and superficiality".[46]

---

45   Vatican II, *Nostra Aetate*, # 6.
46   Jankélévitch, *Le pardon*, p. 79.

Pragmatic truces between countries

Two countries which have fought can call a halt, make a treaty and observe it. Fighting stops but there is no love lost between the people of the two countries, any sporting contests are unfriendly both on and off the field, and it may be generally believed that sooner or later war will break out again. In each country intensely chauvinistic people make it their business to keep the memory of past wrongs alive and they tell atrocity stories in a way that suggests that the whole other country is guilty of horrible crimes, so that the hostility is maintained even if no actual fighting is going on. This is what I have called a pragmatic truce, which is not a reconciliation.

The repentance or regret of a group

Suppose that the directors of a drug company vote unanimously for the concealment of information about the danger of using a drug which the company produces. In such a case, each of them should accept responsibility and personally repent. I believe that the company as such should also express repentance. For this it is not necessary that absolutely all the directors should agree to do this, but on the other hand 51% would not be enough. In South Africa, what has been called the Kairos Protocol says that "no reconciliation, no forgiveness and no negotiations are possible without repentance" and Wilhelm Verwoerd, the grandson of the architect of apartheid in South Africa, has said that by forgiving whites without demanding repentance of them, Mandela "prevents our having to face up to what we have done". There are groups of persons who have no personal guilt but who have guilt by solidarity. Many English people are conscious of what England did to Ireland in the nineteenth and early twentieth centuries, and of the bombing of German cities, most of the people in which were civilians, in World War II. Especially in the years after that war, when what had been done to Jews by the government was revealed in its horror, many Germans who had not even known that Jews were being killed felt solidarity-guilt; and it was felt later by Germans who were born after the war. Finally, in Australia aboriginals were treated dreadfully. Also, many children of white fathers and aboriginal women were taken forcibly from their mothers and put in separate boys' and girls' orphanages, so that they would have children not with each other but with white women and men and "aboriginality" would diappear from their descendants. Many non-aboriginal Australians not only regret this but also feel a kind of guilt because of it.

In these cases, in which there is no personal responsibility, personal repentance is impossible, since there is no evil will to be reversed. However, when a whole country or group is involved, a leader whose position gives him the right to speak for the group as a whole can express what I might call group repentance. On 5 May 1985, speaking for all Germans, the President of West Germany gave expression to this. Tony Blair apologised for what England did to the people of Ireland. And on 13 February 2008 Kevin Rudd, the prime minister of Australia, with the general support of all parties and therefore speaking for the whole country, said "I'm sorry" to the aboriginal people of Australia.

Forgiveness by a group

Jewish people have said, "One cannot forgive a wrong done to another". However, if a group of people have been hurt and if the persons who hurt them are repentant, or if the group which hurt them is repentant, there can be forgiveness. Some German men who had been soldiers in Belarussia went back there in 1994, which is to say about fifty years later, when they were old men. One of them began to say how sorry he was for what he had done during the war and an old Belarussian woman took him in her arms and kissed him. He had spoken not only for himself but for the comrades who had come with him, and indeed for a vaguely defined group of thousands of others, while she expressed a forgiveness that was not only her own but also that of the community.[47]

Where the members of the offending group are not personally guilty, it seems to me that they cannot *repent personally* and *be forgiven*. However, the group can repent and when this is done there can be reconciliation. What is usually necessary is that there be someone who can speak for a large majority of the group. If a country is involved, it is normally a political leader whose position gives him or her the right to speak for the group.

---

47   Govier, *Forgiveness and Revenge*, p. 94. Govier says that she has taken the story from Geiko Muller-Fahrenholz.

Group reparation

After World War II the West German government gave a great deal of assistance to the State of Israel, and I have been told that some young Germans went to work on kibbutzim in Israel to make some reparation for what Germans of an earlier time had done to Jews. Also, let me tell a fictitious story.

> Some years ago I was the rector of a Jesuit college and one day, wearing ordinary clothes, I went to a book launch. There I met an elderly gentleman, we began to talk about books, we found that we had a lot in common and an enjoyable conversation developed. After a while he asked me what I did and I replied, "I'm the headmaster of …" and I named the college. He said, "Oh!" and then went on: "I went to that school until I was expelled. Unjustly". It was my turn to say, "Oh!", and he went on to say that he had gone to work in his father's printery, which he had subsequently inherited. He had later become a publisher as well, which was why he was at the book launch, and he had been successful in every way. "So," he said, "it did not ruin my life."
>
> When I returned to the school I looked up the records and found that, sure enough, this man had been expelled fifty years earlier, but there was no more information than that. I then went to a retired Jesuit who I knew had been in the school at that time and said:
>
> "Is it true that John Smiggin was expelled unjustly fifty years ago?"
>
> "Yes," he replied, "It is. One morning there were piles of printed leaflets in all the classrooms, with scurrilous allegations about some of the masters. No one knew where they had come from. The rector, who as you know has since died, was furious and announced that the boy responsible would be expelled when he was found out. Some time went by and then the rector announced that he had learned that John Smiggin, whose father was a printer, often worked in his father's printery in the holidays, knew how to work the machines and had gone into the printery one night and printed the leaflets. He expelled John Smiggin. Some senior boys came to me and told me that they were in a quandary. The leaflets, they said, had been produced by Ian Brown, a boy who came from a distinguished family and who was one of the school's best athletes. On the one hand, they said that John Smiggin ought not to be expelled; on the other hand, it was against all their schoolboy principles to tell on someone – telling me did not count because I had no power. I told them to leave the matter to me. I went to the rector and told

him that I had been told by some boys, who I was sure had told me the truth, that John Smiggin was innocent. I did not tell him about Ian Brown. He said, "Leave it to me and don't tell anyone else what you have told me". He did nothing. John Smiggin had gone and that was not changed. I, too, did nothing. I regret it now, but I felt then that I had done all I could do."

When I learned from the retired Jesuit about what my precedessor had done, I not only disapproved of it, I felt ashamed and as headmaster of the school I was sorry for it.

I asked myself what I should do. On the one hand, neither I nor anyone then working in the school had been personally guilty of any injustice. On the other hand, I felt, the school owed this man an apology and as the headmaster it was up to me to make it. Also, I felt that I ought to make some attempt to repair the harm that had been done. So I wrote to Mr Smiggin saying that I had learned that what he had said to me was true, and on behalf of the school I apologised. I also wrote to the president of the school old boys' association, telling him the story and asking him to invite John Smiggin to join the association, from which he had been excluded. "Tell him," I said, "that you will understand if he does not join, but that you feel bound to extend the invitation".

I believe that in that story "I" did the right thing. Incidentally, in case you were wondering, this story is entirely fictitious.

15 The Divine Forgiveness & Other Theological Matters

Catholic culture used to place an exaggerated emphasis on sin, guilt, purgatory and hell. Also, priests used to spend many hours in the confessional and religious were obliged to go to confession once a week. At that time, repentance, which was called contrition, was greatly stressed. Every Catholic knew an "act of contrition" by heart and said it whenever he or she "went to confession". Catholic theologians distinguished between perfect and imperfect contrition and all educated Catholics were familiar with this distinction (to which I shall come). Repentance was not analysed or stressed to anything like the same extent by Protestants, who had a lot to say about the divine forgiveness, which they said we should more or less passively accept. In Western culture at large scientific psychology has to a large extent replaced Christianity as the "theory" in terms of which people attempt to deal with anguish; being deterministic, modern scientific psychology tends to absolve people from blame because of what they have done and to regard guilt feelings not as a moral reality but as a pathological condition. Therapists may tell clients not to blame themselves, not to be hard on themselves, or to let themselves off the moral hook. I venture to say that, largely because of the influence of this kind of psychology, sin and repentance do not figure highly in present-day high Catholic culture. At the academic level, books appeared around 1950 with titles like *The Morbid Universe of Fault* and *Morality Without Sin*, and the non-consideration of repentance had a certain vogue. At the popular level, "going to confession" is no longer done frequently, and few if any priests "hear confessions" for hours; many Catholic religious and practising laypeople go to the sacrament of reconciliation once or twice a year, or never. There is little or no talk of perfect and imperfect contrition. Moreover, some modern Catholics maintain that no one deliberately does wrong, so that repentance has no place in their spirituality or "theory." A priest who has this idea turns what is left of personal confession into a counselling session and if someone comes to confess a particular serious sin, he sets about persuading the person that he or she did not commit a sin, which by the way is often the case, especially where practising Catholics are concerned. However, Jesus often said to people, "Go in peace, your sins are forgiven", and the ideas of sin, forgiveness and redemption are huge in Christianity.

That the divine forgiveness needs repentance

I said earlier that some counsellors maintain that forgiveness is entirely within the person who has been hurt, so that the person who inflicted the hurt, and who is forgiven, need not be involved. I denied this then and I now deny it of the divine repentance. In Jeremiah we read: "They will turn, each of them, from their evil behaviour, *so that I can forgive* their sinful guilt" (Jer 36:3 NJB). If the parable of the prodigal son expresses Christ's teaching on forgiveness, we must note that the son does not return home and say:

> I enjoyed myself enormously while the money lasted and I feel that my time in that distant land made a man of me, so I have no regrets, but the money ran out and I got a job that was hard work and paid badly. I thought then of the working conditions on this farm and decided to come back and ask for a job here.

He returns with repentance in his heart and on his lips and this, I believe, is essential to the parable. Journet, then, is in accord with the Bible when he says, "Sin without repentance *cannot* be pardoned, any more than God can annihilate himself".[1]

I have come across non-Catholics who imagined that when Catholics go to confession they tell their sins and emerge free of guilt, as if that were all there is to it. I have even seen a film in which a Catholic went into a confessional and told his sin, whereupon the priest said, "Go in peace" or words to that effect, closed the sliding door, and the person left. That was all. In Catholic teaching concerning this sacrament, however, persons must not only tell their sins but must also express repentance, which is why they are called "penitents"; and if a man were to go into a confessional, tell the priest of some sin he had committed and make it clear that he was not sorry for it, the priest would not be entitled to "give him absolution".

---

1 Journet, *The Meaning of Evil*, p. 209.

The controversy concerning attrition

The Fathers of the Church demanded of sinners that they be sorry for their sins *because they had offended God*. In the twelfth century, however, some people said that if they wished that they had not sinned *because they were afraid of hell*, this was enough. This came to be known as attrition as opposed to contrition, or as imperfect as opposed to perfect contrition. Albert the Great maintained that it was not sufficient, but discussion went on. Some authors maintained that if a person who was moved only by fear of hell went to confession, he would in the confessional be moved to be sorry because he had offended God (*ex attrito fit contritus*). Luther was contemptuous of attrition, calling it *Galgenreue* or gallows-regret and Trent said that, as far as it goes, it is good and indeed can dispose a person to have contrition. In the seventeenth century the Jansenists, who were the ultraconservatives of the time, said that attrition is selfish and only makes a person worse. Others, including the Jesuits, opposed this and between 1640 and 1670 there was fierce conflict between Contritionists and Attritionists. In 1667 a decree of the Holy Office said that Attritionism was permissible and it added that it seemed to be the more common view of theologians, but the Vatican did not come down clearly on either side. If I remember rightly, in the first half of the twentieth century it was commonly taught in Catholic schools and churches that attrition is sufficient for valid reception of the sacrament of penance, but if one has committed a mortal sin and is unable to go to confession one can obtain divine forgiveness by making "an act of perfect contrition" with the intention of later telling the sin in confession. Attrition alone was thought to be insufficient. This, incidentally, implied that when a person who has committed a mortal sin and *because of fear of hell* wishes that he had not committed it, if he goes to confession and dies he goes to heaven but if he dies before he can go to confession he goes to hell. Let us wish that attrition had never been thought of and affirm that repentance (which attrition is not) is needed for the divine forgiveness to be possible.

God's attitude towards unrepentant sinners

So long as unrepentant sinners are alive, God is hurt by their wrongdoing, still loves them and hopes that they will repent, so that he can be reconciled with them. I said earlier that if someone has been unjustly hurt by another person, who shows no sign of repentance, on the one hand he cannot forgive the person who has hurt him and so be reconciled with him or her; on the other hand he ought not to go through life nursing his hurt and brooding over it: he ought to have nothing of a personal nature to do with the person who has hurt him; he will not forget what has happened and will always feel a certain pain, but he will get on with life and enjoy it. Can it be that this is the divine attitude? Not that God refuses forgiveness to repentant sinners who ask for forgiveness, but that he loves those who have offended him and, as long as they are alive, hopes that they will repent of their sins so that he can forgive them; if their rejection becomes definitive, he is eternally hurt but accepts that they have gone away from him? He lives with a certain sadness. This may seem incredible to people who have been taught that God is perfectly happy, but can one combine the beliefs that there are some persons, angelic and human, in hell, the belief that God loves all his creatures, and the belief that he is perfectly happy?

Our obligation to forgive

Is what I said about not forgiving unchristian? It is true that nowhere in the Bible does it say that repentance is needed for forgiveness just as nowhere does it say that human beings have free will; it is, however, assumed, just as belief in free will is assumed. It is also often stated. In many New Testament passages we are told to forgive those who hurt us *if they repent*. For instance, in Luke we read: "If another disciple sins, you must rebuke the offender, and *if there is repentance*, you must forgive. And if the same person sins against you seven times a day, and *turns back to you seven times and says, 'I repent'*, you must forgive" (Luke 17:3-4). If that were to happen, I expect that "you" might doubt the sincerity of the offender's repentance, but obviously sincere repentance is meant here.

Also, Jesus said: "If your brother sins against you, go to him and show him his fault. But do it privately, just between yourselves. If he listens to you, you will have won your brother back." "If he listens to you" means if he admits his fault and says he is sorry, in which case you should forgive him. Jesus goes on to say that if your brother refuses to listen to you, you should try again, taking one or two other persons with you, and if that does not work you should tell the whole story to the church. He concludes: "If the offender refuses to listen even to the church, let such a one be to you as a Gentile and a tax collector." (Matt

18:15-17.) In his society, good Jewish people had occasional business dealings with gentiles and tax collectors, but they did not eat with them and they did not make friends among them, so that this means: if attempts at reconciliation with people who have hurt you fail, have nothing to do, socially or personally, with them. In 1 Corinthians Paul said that there was sexual immorality going on among Christians. He said: "You should not have anything to do with anyone going by the name of brother who is sexually immoral" and "Do not even eat with such a one" (1 Cor 5:9-11). This is "not forgiving". Let me say again that by "not forgiving" I do not mean refusing to forgive someone who is sorry, and I do not mean hating an offender or plotting revenge. I mean living with a certain sadness.

16 Retributive Justice

Revenge

In certain cultures, if anyone is hurt the other family members are obliged, as a matter of honour, to get revenge. Indeed, a family is understood as being, in the first place, a collection of people who will avenge a hurt inflicted on any of them. In some isolated peasant communities the rule is: "Never let anyone who hurts you get away with it; do not rest until you have got revenge, mobilise your whole family to help you and, if you die unavenged, bequeath your need for vengeance to your sons". In these communities, if one man takes some land from another, they become enemies for life; their sons usually avoid one another and, if they do meet, fight; grandsons inherit the feud, and the whole community knows that the Montagues and the Capulets, the Martins and the Coys, or whatever the names of the two families are, are enemies. In each family the wrongs committed by the other family are told over and over again, reconciliation is not even considered, and it is believed in each family that the conflict will end only when the other family is destroyed. This also goes on between ethnic groups and it can go on for centuries. Where there is love of some kind between persons, and one person, or one group of persons, wrongs another, there can be even greater hostility. As people say, "the best friends make the worst enemies".

It has been said that revenge is natural and good, and that its existence can be explained by the theory of evolution. If a particular animal were to be hurt by other animals of its species, and do nothing about it, that animal would not survive long, whereas an animal which, if it were to be hurt, would attack the animal which hurt it, would be more likely to survive. Also, if members of a group were to be killed by beings from outside the group, and if the group were to do nothing about it, it (the group) would probably not survive in the struggle for existence, whereas if it were to obtain revenge, it would be more likely to survive. That is, vengefulness is an element of Darwinian "fitness", either of the individual or of the group. It has then been deduced that when human beings appeared, before they developed intellectually and morally, revenge was in their nature. Eventually human beings developed societies and states, and as this happened the states reserved revenge to themselves, calling it punishment, so that if someone was unjustly hurt he or she was required to report the culprit to the state, which would carry out an investigation and, if satisfied that there had been a crime, it would inflict a proportionate penalty on him. And so we have retributive justice as we understand it now, using the word "punishment" for this particular kind of revenge.

To come to the present day, revenge is common in relatively uncivilised human beings, such as small boys in inadequately supervised school playgrounds and adult human beings in societies which (dare I say it?) are primitive. Some years ago an American Jewish journalist decided to write a book about revenge and she went to Sicily and Albania.[1] In Sicily she found that the rightness of revenge is a basic belief, so that even a Jesuit priest whom she met there told her that a man who does not pursue revenge is without honour. In Albania she found that revenge was codified by a certain man in the fifteenth century; his canon was not written but it was handed down for centuries in an oral tradition. Early in the twentieth century it was written and published. When Communists took over the country in 1945 they disallowed private revenge and the canon was put aside. However, when the Communist regime ended in 1991, the canon, copies of which abound, came back into force. A certain man had killed a man of another family during the Communist time and, when the Communist regime ended, a member of the second family killed a member of the first family, purely and simply to even the score. When Laura Blumenfeld's book was published, no one had talked to the police and the killer had not been arrested. According to the canon, this was right, and the people of the town accepted this.

Even in civilised societies, when people are seriously hurt they sometimes find themselves earnestly desirous of vengeance. If a woman was brutally raped and the rapist has been arrested and is being tried, she may say: "I want that man to suffer. Only an extreme punishment will satisfy me. The animal deep down in me wants revenge." When a policeman is killed, other members of the police force sometimes seek revenge.

---

[1] Blumenfeld, *Revenge*. Laura Blumenfeld was this journalist. Her father was wounded by a Palestinian terrorist in Jerusalem in 1986, she found in herself a desire for revenge and she decided to write a book about it.

In Shakespeare's *The Merchant of Venice* (a little before 1600), Shylock has been treated contemptuously by Christians in Venice and when he insists on obtaining a pound of Antonio's flesh he says: "If it will feed nothing else, it will feed my revenge". He also says:

> If a Jew wrong a Christian, what is his humility? Revenge. If a Christian wrong a Jew, what should his sufferance be by Christian example? Why, revenge.[2]

Nor is this entirely uncommon even now in highly civilised societies. According to Laura Blumenfeld, when World War II ended in 1945, fifty Jews called the Avengers believed that the entire population of Germany had collaborated in the Holocaust and they conspired to poison Germany's water, aiming to bring about the deaths of six million Germans, roughly equal to the number of Jews who died as victims of the Holocaust.

Also, the Bible attributes vengefulness to God, which it would not do if the authors regarded revenge as vicious, and many people have been quite happy to accept revenge when it seems to them to be justified. I shall discuss this later.

Punishment: the social fact

When human beings are together, they organise themselves into societies, which have rules. There are many and various kinds of society, and one thing which almost all of them do is have a way of dealing with wrongdoing in the society. (Some societies may also deal with wrongdoing that has no connection with the society, except that it brings discredit on it.) In most modern countries, wrongdoing (if detected) is punished and the state reserves to itself the right to impose it.

It should be noted that if someone steals some goods, is found out and obliged to give them back, this is not punishment. Also, if someone does wrong and subsequently suffers in some way that is not connected with his or her action – if, for instance, someone commits a theft and a week later is injured in a car accident – this is not punishment, either, though we may say it was "poetic justice".

---

2 Shakespeare, *The Merchant of Venice*, 3 1 ca. 48 & ca 65.

16 ॐ Retributive Justice

That punishment is a civil act

Punishment has taken different forms. In past times criminals were executed, sometimes in painful ways. Then the whipping of criminals was abolished and even capital punishment was made less painful, first by the guillotine and most recently by the use of lethal injection. In some countries punishment took the form, or takes the form, of mutilation. In Western countries it now generally takes the form of a fine or imprisonment. Prison as a form of punishment is only about two hundred years old, in its present form it has many highly objectionable features, and I do not intend what I will say about punishment to be read as a defence of prisons as they are now, or indeed of prisons as such.

In many countries there used to be public executions in the presence of hostile onlookers who hurled abuse, and Menninger quotes the distinguished jurist Sir James Stephen who as late as 1883 said: "I think it is highly desirable that criminals should be hated, that the punishment inflicted upon them should be so contrived as to give expression to that hatred".[3] Also, people were put in stocks in public places, exposed to the scorn of passers-by. Now, in advanced societies, if people are executed it is not in public and when they are imprisoned they are where few can see them. I am reliably informed that in Iran a relative of a murdered man kills the murderer and in the United States the relatives of victims are allowed to witness executions, but this sort of thing is now unusual.

Also, in a particularly revolting case the judge may speak in harsh tones as he or she sentences the culprit, and guards in gaols may show that they despise at least some of the prisoners. On the other hand, in civilised countries everything is done to make the procedure as impersonal as possible, the judge may restrain the expression of emotion by spectators, the members of the jury may be instructed to base their verdict solely on the evidence, and the judge may endeavour not to be influenced by emotion when deciding on the sentence. Everything is done to ensure that punishment is a civil act.

Retributive justice

The theory of retributive justice is that when people disturb the moral order by acting wrongly, they deserve to suffer; if they later suffer in a

---

3   Quoted in Menninger, *The Crime of Punishment*, p. 195.

commensurate way because of their actions, moral order is restored;[4] and there is a need for this to happen. It is definitely not part of this theory that deserved suffering causes a crime never to have been committed or the world to become exactly what it would have been if it had never occurred: the world will be in order again, but different.

The theory of retributive justice presupposes the existence of moral obligations and just as an action is not made moral or immoral by its practical consequences, so, according to this theory, it is not because of its practical consequences that retribution is necessary. As Ewing says, "the theory means that the punishment of the guilty is in itself something of value quite apart from the fact that it is a method of attaining other ends, like the deterrence or reformation of offenders."[5] J. L. Mackie states three principles, one of which is that a person who is guilty ought to be punished, and he says: "To yield anything worth counting as a retributive theory, such principles must be thought of as having some immediate, underived moral appeal or moral authority",[6] and in essence I agree with that.

Normally, if we see someone suffering in a way that, from a practical point of view, is useless, we are sorry for him or her and regret the suffering. If, however, someone does something wrong and suffers as a result, we may say, "He (or she) deserved it" and instead of regretting the suffering we are, deep down, in favour of it. If we ourselves or persons we love have been unjustly hurt, or if things in which we believe have been wrongfully attacked, we may be righteously angry. It is not demanded by justice that we hate the wrongdoer[7] and for that reason rejoice in his suffering, but we do believe that he or she ought to suffer. If retributive justice is a valid concept, it is immoral to help a wrongdoer to escape justice. This is in most legal systems, according to which it is wrong not only to help beforehand in the commission of a crime, but also to help a criminal to escape punishment afterwards.

---

4   I earlier mentioned primary moral order. This is secondary moral order.
5   Ewing, *The Morality of Punishment*, p. 13.
6   Mackie, "Morality and the Retributive Emotions" in *Persons and Values*, p. 208. Mackie does not accept the retributive theory: what I say above is that he has correctly stated it.
7   Jeffrie Murphy, in a book by himself and Jean Hampton, talks of "retributive hatred" and defends it (Murphy and Hampton, *Forgiveness and Mercy*, pp. 88-110), but I agree with his co-author, who says that "retribution is not a form of hatred at all" (p. 122).

Support for retributive justice

How might one prove that punishment is demanded by retributive justice? The deterrence theory of punishment can to some extent be tested empirically – one can examine statistics and see whether imposing stiffer sentences for this or that kind of crime has been followed by fewer cases of it occurring (in particular, one can see whether the abolition of the death penalty for murder has been followed by more murders, and whether re-introduction of it has been followed by fewer, or not). Rehabilitation can also to some extent be tested by seeing whether or not, when rehabilitation is made the aim of correction centres, fewer inmates return to crime when they leave. But a moral theory cannot be tested in this way, any more than one can find out by statistical analysis whether an action is moral or immoral. Moreover, it seems to me that the principle of retributive justice is not derived from any other principle and it is something which one either sees or does not see. What I intend to do is to show that it has been "seen" by generations of human beings.

PRIMITIVE HUMAN BEINGS

Paul Ricoeur says that in primitive human beings there existed a sense that wrongdoing ought to be punished and that order is restored by this.[8] He says that "suffering is the price of violation of order", and that this was a primitive notion, anterior to any ideas about avenging gods.[9] Indeed, he says, the idea of an avenging god did not give rise to the idea that crimes ought to be punished; rather, believing that crimes ought to be punished, primitive human beings attributed to their god or gods the punishment of them.

LITERATURE

The ancient Greek tragedies embody a belief in nemesis, or the idea that anyone who does wrong will inevitably suffer for it; and there was some idea that, when he or she suffered, order was restored. Unfortunately, it was explained in this way: a mortal who did wrong offended the gods, who reacted by afflicting him, her or the city. Retribution is to be found in Shakespeare's tragedies, which embody a world-view and a morality that have rung true for many people. For

---

8   Ricoeur, *The Symbolism of Evil*, pp. 39-41.
9   Ibid., pp. 30-31.

example, when Shakespeare wrote *Macbeth*, he established a happy situation in Scotland: there was a good king, there was peace in the land and moral order reigned. Then he had Macbeth deliberately commit a trebly evil deed: the murder of a man who was his guest; who was a wise, holy and old man; and who was the king. He had Macbeth go on to commit further murders, and as a result of his deeds Scotland became a hellish place. Then Shakespeare set about restoring order in Scotland, and he did not end his play with Macbeth sailing away to a comfortable exile on the isle of Skye, never to be heard of in mainland Scotland again, though that would have freed the land of him: he ended it with Macbeth being killed. The play has worked with audiences for almost four centuries, and it works now, because we *know* that for order to be restored it would not be enough for Macbeth to be sent away; he must suffer for his misdeeds. Similarly, we would be shocked if at the end of *Richard III* Gloucester simply sailed away. That is, we share Shakespeare's belief in retributive justice. C.A. Dinsmore says in *Atonement in Religion and Life* (1906): "The moral order always makes known its violation by the penalty it exacts, and the resulting woe reveals the authority of the ethical world",[10] and Helen Gardner says: "The idea of retribution, though not, as some would have it, the sole element in the design of a tragedy, is still an essential element in great tragedies".[11] It is also an essential element in almost all novels and dramas, since nearly always the wicked people who have been causing the trouble suffer retribution in one way or another: for an ending to be satisfactory, that has to happen. I will conclude by quoting from a film: in Jansco's *Elektreia* (Hungary, 1974) the following statement is made twice: "When punishment ceases to follow crime, the world is no longer a world and man is no longer man".

PHILOSOPHERS

For centuries, it seems to me, what I have called the theory of retributive justice was accepted by almost everyone, so that there was not much discussion of it among philosophers and it was assumed by theologians. Then discussion began. Kant said that the law concerning punishment is a "categorical imperative", which is to say that it does

---

10   Dinsmore, *Atonement in Religion and Life*, p. 164.
11   Gardner, *Religion and Literature*, p. 113.

not spring from practical considerations.[12] Hegel, too, held the retribution theory. In the twentieth century, Maritain talked of a "law of re-equilibration of being": when someone sins, he said, he disturbs being, and being turns against him and causes him to suffer; by his sufferings equilibrium or order is restored.[13] Ricoeur said that when human beings do wrong they disturb the moral order and "suffering is the price of the violation of order".

As I shall say at greater length later, many other recent philosophers rejected retributivism as a theory. Then, according to Kathleen Dean Moore, philosophers began to say that the wholesale rejection of retributivist principles should be re-examined, and in the nineteen-sixties "the voices of philosophers were heard across the land [the United States], advocating a return to the principles of retributive justice". A Committee for the Study of Incarceration was created and funded by two liberal foundations and included some distinguished liberal thinkers; in 1976 its report, *Doing Justice*, was published and in it the committee said: "Certain things are simply wrong and ought to be punished. This we do believe". Punishment, it said, "must be closely related to what the offenders *have done*, not to what they *may do*". Moore herself is a retributivist. And in *Philosophical Explanations* (1981), Robert Nozick discusses the idea that punishment is justified by its consequences, then says: "I wish to present a different view of retributive punishment, conceiving of it nonteleologically, so that it is seen as right or good in itself, apart from the further consequences to which it might lead".[14]

LAWYERS

I said earlier that when retributivism was rejected and the purpose of "punishment" was said to be the rehabilation of wrongdoers, this led to practical problems, as a result of which retributivism was reasserted by lawyers. For instance, Lord Justice Denning said:

> It is a mistake to consider the objects of punishment as being deterrent or reformative or preventive, and nothing else. ... The

---

12   Kant, *The Metaphysical Elements of Justice*, p. 138.
13   Maritain, *Neuf leçons sur les notions premières de la philosophie morale*, pp. 184-186.
14   Nozick, *Philosophical Explanations*, p. 72. This is from a chapter entitled "The Retributivist Backlash".

truth is that some crimes are so outrageous that society insists on adequate punishment, because the wrongdoer deserves it, irrespective of whether it is a deterrent or not.[15]

Charles E. Silberman, in *Criminal Violence, Criminal Justice* (1978), quotes this and on his own account says:

> We punish criminals, in short, because justice, i.e., fairness, requires it; punishment is a way of restoring the equilibrium [the moral order] that is broken when someone commits a crime. Hence punishment must be guided by the notion of desert, a less emotionally charged designation than the more familiar concept of retribution. This means focusing on the past – on what the offender has already done – rather than on what he may do in the future. It also means linking the nature and severity of the punishment meted out to the nature and severity of the crime that has been committed; if justice requires that criminals be punished, the notion of desert requires that punishment be commensurate with the severity of the crime.[16]

In New South Wales, Australia, a certain Portalesi was sentenced to be in gaol for a certain number of years before becoming eligible for parole, but a court of appeal later

> ruled that a judge in determining a non-parole period for a prisoner should not fix the minimum period of punishment which he thought justice required, but should, rather, fix a period no longer than the time considered sufficient to enable the Paroling Authority to form a proper opinion of the prisoner's prospects of rehabilitation,

and on that basis ruled that the Parole Board was free to grant parole to Portalesi before he had served his full non-parole sentence. If in a hospital a patient is told that he will be there for a month and after three weeks the doctors say that he is cured, he is sent home, and the above decision in effect said that a gaol is like a hospital. In 1974 the High Court in Canberra overthrew that decision, Barwick, Menzies, Stephen and Mason affirming in the majority decision that the legislation covering parole

> does not convert a sentence of imprisonment into an opportunity for rehabilitation. We cannot understand how a sentence of

---

15 Quoted in Silberman, *Criminal Violence, Criminal Justice*, p. 185.
16 Ibid., pp. 188-189.

imprisonment, either with or without hard labour, can, however enlightened the prison system, be regarded otherwise than as a severe punishment for a crime which has been committed.

Encouragement to reform, the court said, "does not and obviously is not intended to take the sting out of punishment".[17] In *A Capacity to Punish* (1984) Henry N. Pontell says:

> The retributive justification of punishment is based on the notion of "just deserts". Most legal theorists argue that this rationale for punishment is necessary, at least to some degree, as it is the only one that contains the elements of justice and reciprocity in sanctioning criminals. A recent study completed by a group of experts concluded that retribution should be the major purpose of punishment for similar reasons. They concluded that it was the strongest rationale, given the paucity of evidence on the effectiveness of other purposes of punishment.[18]

In its 1987 Discussion Paper no. 29, the Australian Law Reform Commission

> suggests that the primary goal of punishment ought to be to ensure that people receive their just deserts, at least to the extent that punishment is proportionate to and does not exceed the gravity of the offence and the culpability of the offender.

Simon Wiesenthal, who was mainly responsible for finding Eichmann, commented on the legal position in Austria:

> In Austria, as everywhere in the world, there were at one time prolonged arguments about the purpose of criminal law. The Minister of Justice Christian Broda ... took the view that a humane criminal law could aim only at resocialisation. On that basis Adolf Eichmann need not have been sentenced. He was fully integrated into Argentinian society – he was working, he was living within a well-ordered family framework, and he was a good father to his children. It was unlikely that he would ever again send Jews to gas chambers. Why then, Broda was asked in a television discussion, was Eichmann sentenced, if criminal law aimed solely at resocialisation? The Minister of Justice did not know what to say. If his theory had

---

17   The decisions are quoted in Hall, *The Real John Kerr*, p. 112.
18   Pontell, *A Capacity to Punish*, pp. 3-4.

been followed, all the Nazi murderers should have been allowed to live on in their villas in Argentina, Brazil, Uruguay and Paraguay.[19]

PEOPLE IN GENERAL

It is recognised by almost all writers, including many who do not agree with it, that the general public believes in retribution. Paton says: "The community as a whole places emphasis on the retribution theory, at least where certain crimes are concerned".[20] Ewing says that "the natural man is usually intuitively convinced of something that is at any rate like the retributive theory". The natural man believes that "punishment should be given primarily because a man has done wrong and so deserves to be punished".[21] And Mackie says that a retributive principle is deeply ingrained in us and persists as a feeling even when we have other intellectual convictions.

PARTICULAR CASES

In *A Rumour of Angels* Peter Berger says of the Holocaust that, first, we cannot accept that we think it was bad only because we have been socialised in a particular way; second, we believe that it demands retribution.[22] At the end of World War II, when what had happened in the concentration camps came to light, it seemed as though it might be impossible to take legal action against the persons responsible, since they had not broken any laws of their country or any international treaties, but it was quickly decided that their punishment was *morally* necessary. Gaylin says that if Hitler had survived, escaped to Argentina and spent the rest of his life there, quietly painting, this would have been intolerable, and he goes on:

> Even if it cannot be justified on purely utilitarian grounds, that man deserved to be punished with all the righteous wrath of an outraged community sensitivity. It cheapens the Holocaust to suggest that his punishment must be justified in terms of prevention of some future pain and destruction.[23]

---

19   Wiesenthal, *Justice Not Vengeance*, p. 94.
20   Paton, *Textbook of Jurisprudence*, p. 321.
21   Ewing, The *Morality of Punishment*, p. 14.
22   Berger, *A Rumour of Angels*, pp. 86-87.
23   Gaylin, *The Killing of Bonnie Garland*, p. 337.

16 ❦ Retributive Justice

On 1 March 2001 two Serbs and two Croatians were found guilty in The Hague of horrifying crimes against humanity and sentenced to long terms in gaol. The international community wanted the persons who had committed those crimes to be punished, not in the hope of reforming them and not so much (I believe) to deter people from committing similar crimes in the future, but mainly because it believed that, as a matter of morality, justice demanded that they be punished.

In the American South there had been many murders of blacks by Klansmen and others, and this intensified during the nineteen-sixties, when the segregationists were fighting what turned out to be a losing battle. For a long time, the black community was too weak to demand action and witnesses were afraid to testify, but this changed and in 1994 Byron De La Beckwith was convicted for the murder in June 1963 of Medgar Evans, a field secretary of the National Association for the Advancement of Colored People, and in 1998 Sam Bowers was convicted for the murder in January 1966 of Vernon Dahmer, president of the Hattiesburg NAACP. In June 2005 Edgar Ray Killen was found guilty of manslaughter for orchestrating the murder of three civil-rights workers in 1964. Many people, white and black, have called this "stirring up trouble" but the more general view has been that the convictions have been cleansing and will make it possible for the South to move beyond its past.

CHRISTIAN THINKERS

Throughout the centuries Christian thinkers have in general accepted, as an ethical principle, the principle that wrongdoers should be punished by civil authorities, and this was done in Christian countries. Augustine said: "The beauty of the universe may not be disfigured even for an instant by having the ugliness of sin without the beauty of a just punishment."[24] In *The Theology of Auschwitz* (1967) Ulrich E Simon says that the evil of Auschwitz "cries out for an atonement".[25] In El Salvador, where some Jesuits and another person were murdered and where it was proposed that an amnesty be granted for this and many other crimes, the rector of the university in San Salvador protested that it would be "an affront to justice", and in East Timor, Bishop Carlos Belo said: "Justice for the people of East Timor requires

---

24   Augustine, *De Libero Arbitrio*, book 4, chap. 15, 44.
25   Simon, *The Theology of Auschwitz*, p. 55.

that the perpetrators of the most serious crimes be identified and prosecuted".[26] These are only a few recent statements of what has at all times been accepted by Christians not as a peculiarly religious idea but as an ethical principle.

Rejections of retributive justice

Lord Justice Asquith on 11 May 1950 described retribution as "a theory now so discredited that to attack it is to flog a dead horse". This has been the view of many writers, especially empiricist philosophers, who think that retribution belongs in the trash can of outmoded ideas. Like free will, it is generally believed by the general public but it is denied in some academic circles.

EMPIRICISM

Empiricists reject all knowledge which is not from observation, or which cannot be tested by experiment. They therefore reject moral concepts such as retributive justice, for which they have a whole vocabulary of words of abuse, including "discredited", "unverifiable", "implausible", "arcane", "metaphysical", "moralistic", "dogmatic", "theological" and "mystical". Andrew von Hirsch says:

> The arcaneness of the benefits-and-burdens theory (and of various other retributive arguments of a similar nature) troubles me. It seems easier to accept the institution of punishment than to understand and accept the premises these theories propose as the basis for punishment.[27] Another author says that the concepts of responsibility and punishment are "theological and metaphysical anachronisms".

Herbert L. Packer says that the principle of retribution

> has no useful place in a theory of justification of punishment, because what it expresses is nothing more than dogma, unverifiable and on its face implausible.[28]

Some empiricists, on the other hand, especially if they are analytical philosophers, are more irenical and say that when a retributivist says that justice demands that wrongdoers be punished, *what he means* is

---
26 Belo, "The Path to Freedom".
27 Hirsch, *Past or Future Crimes*, p. 59.
28 Packer, *The Limits of the Criminal Sanction* (1968), pp. 37-39.

that the punishment of wrongdoers is beneficial to society or to the wrongdoers (or to both). He must mean that, they say, because anything else would be unintelligible. A.R. Manser says that, "like the modern philosophers", the members of the United Kingdom Royal Commission into Capital Punishment (held in 1949-1950) "searched for some plausible account of what the retributionists must have meant by what they said about punishment" and decided that deterrence and reform were "what the retributionists were really talking about".[29] For most retributivists, being told what you really meant, when it was not what you meant at all, is worse than having your theory called "unverifiable", "implausible" or even "moralistic".

DETERMINISM

I am not entering into an argument about determinism here, but I will remark that politically it seems to have moved from the right to the left. "Conservative" or right-wing determinists used to stress inheritance, maintaining that behavioural tendencies, among which they put criminality, are inherited and determine behaviour. They maintained, then, that if people have committed burglary (for instance), this shows that they are burglars by nature and their children, if they have any, will be burglars, too. Hence, they said, for the safety of ordinary people these people should be put away. Moreover, whether they are put away or not, they should be prevented, usually by sterilisation, from having children. It is to be noted that there is not here question of punishing people for what they have done in the past but of doing things to people to prevent them and their children, if there are any, from doing things in the future. "Liberal" or left-wing determinists generally deny that there is any inheritance of behavioural characteristics and they attribute behaviour, good or bad, to the environment. They maintain that if people have committed crimes the fault is that of their environment, of which they have been the victims, and that they should be "rehabilitated", not punished. For the future, they maintain that the remedy for crime is improvement of the environments in which criminals live.

---

29 Manser, "It Serves You Right", p. 296.

AN IDEA OF LIBERAL DEMOCRACY

Hyman Gross, in *A Theory of Criminal Justice* (1979), says that in past times people believed that a deity or a "universal moral law binding on all men" required that crime be punished, but this, he says in Chapter One,

> is alien to any modern political society in which democratic ideals are professed. In such societies there are no universal moral laws imposed by divine authority. Nor does the voice of the people itself create such a moral imperative when that voice is enacted as law. ... In modern societies of a democratic complexion there is no source of moral authority to command that crime be punished.[30]

Later in his book he refers to theories which, he says, "hold that repaying crime with punishment is simply doing justice and is a good in its own right", as opposed to being good because of its results, and he says:

> To the extent that a theory does not deem criminal punishment to be in need of justification [by its results] because punishment of the guilty is good in its own right, that theory is ignored here. It is ignored not because it is unworthy of serious philosophical attention, but because it cannot hope to be taken seriously as a justificatory theory of punishment in any section of the modern world that professes what might loosely be called liberal democratic ideals.[31]

He seems to be saying that a modern liberal democratic society cannot recognise a "universal moral law binding on all men", which seems to imply that if the citizens of such a society choose to adopt racist policies or not to do anything for poorer countries, no judgement can be passed on them.

HUMANITARIAN CONSIDERATIONS

Finally, in the minds of many liberals the theory of retribution is linked to harsh treatment of criminals in prisons and capital punishment for murder, that is, to a tough conservative programme based on deterrence and on ridding society of criminal elements. This is understandable, since retributivists, like tough conservatives, believe in punishment with a sting; and a belief that the punishment should fit the crime leads many of them to favour capital punishment for murder. During

---

30   Gross, *A Theory of Criminal Justice*, pp. 19-20.
31   Ibid., p. 378.

the Royal Commission on Capital Punishment various people argued for capital punishment on retributivist grounds – Manser remarks that while "there is no obvious contradiction in a retributivist opposing the death penalty for murder, ... it is rare that they do".[32] In *Joe Cinque's Consolation* Helen Garner tells of a trial which was held in Canberra, Australia, in 1999. A certain Joe Cinque had become involved with a girl in Canberra, who killed him in October 1997. Justice Crispin was both the presiding judge and the decider of the verdict. He found the accused guilty of manslaughter and sentenced her to ten years in gaol, with a non-parole period of four years.[33] This was to be reckoned from October 1997, when she was arrested, so that she could be (and was) set free in October 2001. Garner interviewed Crispin and he said:

> The real aim of sentencing is not retribution. The real aim is to try to protect the community by imposing sentences that are heavy enough to deter, but not so heavy that someone becomes institutionalised. And there's also the simple justice of it all. What would be a fair response under the circumstances? You've got to take some sort of hard line, but you can't throw humanity out the window.[34]

He seems to have begun by rejecting retribution and affirming deterrence as the purpose of punishment. Then by using terms like "simple justice" and "fair" he brought the idea of retribution in, but he did not impose what a retributivist would regard as a just sentence.

Punishment and revenge

There are at least three different views about punishment and revenge.

THAT PUNISHMENT IS BASICALLY REVENGE, WHICH IS A GOOD THING

Some people believe that revenge was not only natural and good when human beings were in their primitive state, but that it is the basis of all punishment even now. According to them, when punishment by the state was introduced, revenge was not outlawed but reserved to the state, so that if you say that, in essence, civil punishment is revenge, you are making an interesting observation but not offering an argument against punishment.

---

32 Manser, "It Serves You Right", p. 303.
33 The sentence was light and I shall deal with it later: see below, p. 195.
34 Garner, *Joe Cinque's Consolation*, p. 318.

THAT PUNISHMENT IS REVENGE, WHICH IS BAD

Often people who oppose punishment maintain that it is basically revenge, which for them is a bad thing, so that their belief is that it should be abolished. For instance, in 1957 Camus wrote "Reflections on the Guillotine", in which he said of capital punishment: "Let us recognise it for what it is essentially: a revenge".[35] He opposed it. In *Punishment: the Supposed Justifications* (1969) Ted Honderich says that the idea behind the retribution theory, rarely expressed, kept in the dark, is that when someone has done wrong someone else has a grievance and desires satisfaction;[36] he says that punishment of the wrongdoer "will give satisfaction equivalent to the grievance caused by his action"[37] and that *this* is why people are punished. He also says that this is what the retribution theory means. He says:

> We must in the end regard punishment as defended by the facts that it gives satisfaction to victims of offences and others, and that offenders have freely and responsibly taken the option of committing offences. This, fundamentally, is what the retribution theory comes to.[38]

This explanation is often proposed by psychologists, who naturally tend to have psychological explanations for social phenomena. For instance, Karl Menninger, in *The Crime of Punishment* (1968) said that the idea of retribution comes from "an irrational zeal for inflicting pain upon one who has inflicted pain"[39] and that the basic reason for punishment is "the persistent, intrusive wish for vengeance".[40] Erich Fromm says: "Not only blood revenge but all forms of punishment – from primitive to modern – are an expression of vengeance".[41] Robert

---

35 Camus, *Resistance, Rebellion and Death*, p. 197.
36 Honderich, *Punishment, the Supposed Justifications*, pp. 28-29. He says the same in "Punishment, the New Retributivism and Political Philosophy" (1984), p. 121.
37 Honderich, *Punishment, the Supposed Justifications*, p. 34.
38 Ibid., pp. 43-44.
39 Menninger, *The Crime of Punishment*, p. 113.
40 Ibid., p. 190.
41 Fromm, The *Anatomy of Human Destructiveness*, p. 272.

A Solomon says that "vengeance may be primitive, but it is still the conceptual core of justice".[42]

THAT PUNISHMENT IS NOT REVENGE

Other authors, with whom I agree, maintain that retributive justice is not vengeance. It belongs not to the animal in human beings but to the moral order, which is higher. Revenge is personal and individual whereas it is now generally understood that punishment is a matter for justice, which is impersonal and general. Lucas says: "Punishment is not revenge. Punishment is disinterested, revenge is self-regarding".[43] Scheler said that when primitive human beings learn of certain actions, they experience a revenge-impulse; civilised human beings, he said, desire retribution.[44] *Prison the Last Resort* says:

> Concern for justice for all means that there is never any justification for treating an offender on the basis of revenge. Revenge is emotional, often vindictive and cruel, usually destructive, and open to abuse.[45]

William Kneale says that sometimes rejection of retributivism

> is based on an assumption that retribution is identical with revenge. This seems to me to be a mistake. For although people who seek revenge often use phrases of moral accounting, such as "He shall pay for this", the hatred and anger that they show are not essential to the retributivist theory, and it is wrong to reject retribution merely because one dislikes hatred. There are versions of the doctrine in which retribution is simply a natural necessity independent of human passions.[46]

And Paton says:

> The retributive theory is not, of course, the narrow theory of vengeance, but rather the doctrine that the wrong done by the

---

42 Solomon, *A Passion for Justice*, p. 42.
43 Lucas, *On Justice*, p. 130.
44 Scheler, *On the Eternal in Man*, p. 52.
45 *Prison the Last Resort*, p. 33.
46 Kneale, "The Responsibility of Criminals" (1967), in Acton, ed., *The Philosophy of Punishment*, p. 181.

prisoner can be negated only by the infliction of the appropriate punishment.[47]

Simon Wiesenthal is clear about this and his book is entitled *Justice Not Vengeance*. Hegel anticipated these authors. He said that "prima facie, the objection to retribution is that it looks like something immoral, i.e., like revenge", and he said that "when there are neither magistrates nor laws, punishment always takes the form of revenge";[48] but, he said, a developed society is concerned not so much with the injured party and his or her feelings as with "the universal"; it has "a justice freed from subjective interest"[49] so that the avenging of crime is transformed into legal punishment.[50]

We may also ask whether when we see *Macbeth* we identify with Duncan, Banquo and others, we want revenge for what Macbeth does to them, and therefore we find the ending, in which Macbeth is killed, satisfying. Do we feel avenged at the end of *Richard III* and is that why we leave the theatre feeling that the play ended well? There are films which work by arousing and then satisfying a desire for revenge. In the first scenes of such a film we see a group of repulsive men killing all the members of an attractive family except one small boy; we then jump to when he is a young man and watch as he tracks down the killers, one by one, and kills each of them in a different and increasingly painful way, while we – or people around us – gloatingly relish every crunch, slash and groan. Are *Macbeth* and *Richard III* revenge Westerns in blank verse? No.

Some cases of non-punishment

After World War II, certain Catholic functionaries gave Vatican-city passports made out with false names to Nazi fugitives from justice and so enabled them to escape to Latin America. Bishop Alois Hudal, a German who was rector of the German Catholic church in Rome, is said to have helped many such persons with an "underground railway" and Eichmann is said to have been helped by a Franciscan in Genoa, who knew who he was. There were some trials of leading Nazis and Japanese who had not escaped and then, for a reason which I will

---

47   Paton, *Textbook of Jurisprudence*, p. 321.
48   Hegel, *The Philosophy of Right*, Additions, # 65.
49   Ibid., # 103.
50   Ibid., # 220.

state later, a halt was called. Daniel Lang, an American reporter, went to Germany in the nineteen-seventies, talked with people about the Nazi period, and said that after a time he realised that "an atrocity of unparalleled – and unprecedented – magnitude" had been committed for years and years, and it was going unpunished, apart from a relatively few cases, like that of Eichmann.[51] He need not have gone to Germany: as everyone knows, there were unpunished men elsewhere, of whom I shall list some.

In the American South, until surprisingly recently, white men were not punished for lynching blacks. At My Lai in Vietnam some American soldiers committed a massacre and only a lieutenant was sentenced to any punishment, which President Nixon reduced to three years of confinement to barracks, where a man's life is very different from his life in a gaol.. In *Casualties of War* Daniel Lang tells of another incident in the Vietnam War. A small group of American soldiers was sent out to make a patrol that was to last several days; they went first to a nearby village and, at gun point, forced a young Vietnamese girl to accompany them; they raped her at intervals during several days, then killed her before returning to the base. One soldier took no part in this but was unable to stop it. He later reported the others and in due course they were tried, found guilty and sentenced to terms of imprisonment. Then began a series of appeals, and, by finding technical faults in the court proceedings, later military courts drastically reduced the sentences, so that in the end the soldiers got off lightly. In Argentina it is estimated that roughly 30,000 people were subjected to torture and execution during the "dirty war" of 1976-1983. When that ended, the elected government which came to power passed "amnesty laws" in 1986 and 1987 and almost no one was punished for what had been done. In Germany, since the German Democratic Republic disappeared, there has been virtually no attempt to find and try people who were guilty of "crimes against humanity" in it, and in 2002 Anna Funder said "Not one of the torturers at Hohenschönhausen has been brought to justice".[52] In East Timor, in 1999, more than 1500 people were killed, thousands were raped and tortured, a quarter of the population was deported, and there was widespread destruction of power lines, irrigation systems, crops, livestock and public records.

---

51   Lang, "A Backward Look", p. 90.
52   Funder, *Stasiland*, p. 227.

As I said earlier, Bishop Carlos Belo has called for the punishment of the persons responsible for this, and in 1999 the United Nations Security Council called for trials, but almost no guilty persons have been punished.

Reasons for this

At times people who are guilty of wrongdoing are not punished because the persons who make the decisions concerning them approve of what they have done, even when they must admit that it was not legal. At the end of World War II, it quickly became clear that, while the USSR and the Western allies were not openly at war, they were enemies. The Western allies wanted West Germany and Japan to be on their side and for this reason desisted from the pursuit of justice. In 1974 in the United States, after Richard Nixon's resignation, the incoming president seems to have judged that if Nixon were to have been prosecuted for crimes which (it seemed) he had committed while he was president, the country would be divided into almost warring camps; therefore he blocked any proceeding against him. Since 1990 the non-punishment of people guilty of crimes against humanity in East Germany (mentioned by Anna Funder in *Stasiland*), seems to be because the German government thinks that it is practical to turn a blind eye.

A moral judgement on this non-punishment

It at least seems to follow from what I have been saying that there is a moral need for justice, so that the deliberate non-punishment of crime is immoral. After the French Revolution, the new government abolished pardons, because (it said) justice demanded that offenders be punished. (This was possibly because the kings had had a right to grant pardons, and had used it in an arbitrary way.) At around the same time Kant maintained that pardons involve offences against justice and he said:

> The law concerning punishment is a categorical imperative, and woe to him who rummages around in the winding paths of a theory of happiness looking for some advantage to be gained by releasing the criminal from punishment or by reducing the amount of it.[53]

---

53 Kant, *The Metaphysical Elements of Justice*, p. 138. See Moore, *Pardons*, pp. 28-34 for an account of Kant, who, she says, made exceptions.

I said earlier that at the end of World War II Bishop Hudal and others helped Nazi criminals to escape to Latin America, and they said that they were acting as good Christians, who believe in forgiveness and charity. John Paul II said:

> Not uncommon are countries whose leaders, looking to the fundamental good of consolidating peace, have agreed to grant an amnesty to those who have publicly admitted crimes committed during a period of turmoil. Such an initiative can be regarded favourably as an effort to promote good relations between groups previously opposed to one another.[54]

"A period of turmoil" seems to me to be an inadequate term for the Holocaust, for 1945-89 in East Germany, for 1976-83 in Argentina, and for the last years of the Indonesian regime in East Timor. Also, is amnesty morally just in all cases? Whatever of that, I feel sure that there is a place for mercy, and to this I now come.

Mercy[55]

In its legal sense, the word "pardon" as a noun means "a remission, either free or conditional, of the legal consequences of crime; an act of grace on the part of the proper authority in a state, releasing an individual from the punishment imposed by sentence or that is due according to law" (*The Oxford English Dictionary*). To which I would add that in a more general sense the pardoner might be a parent, the principal of a school, a bishop, the superior of a religious community or anyone else with authority to impose a penalty. Mercy, according to the same dictionary, sometimes means "the clemency or forbearance of a conqueror or absolute lord, which it is in his power to extend or withold as he thinks fit"; in this sense, if a rebellion has failed, the monarch might have mercy on the rebels. It is sometimes "kind and compassionate treatment in a case where severity is merited or expected". The word is used in this sense when a convicted criminal throws himself on the

---

54 Ibid., p. 829.
55 The word "mercy" used not to be specifically related to justice and punishment but meant pity or compassion towards people who were suffering in almost any way. "Works of mercy" were then works for people who were poor or sick, the Sisters of Mercy were founded to do such work, and mercy-killing was killing people in pain to end their suffering. I will not be using the word in this sense here.

mercy of the court and asks for a relatively light sentence. Mercy is also "forbearance and compassion shown by one person to another who is in his power and who has no claim to receive kindness". We use the word in this sense when one man hurts another in some way and the person who was hurt finds himself able to inflict some hurt on the one who hurt him and says: "I have you at my mercy". I shall use the word for not punishing, or not punishing as severely as expected, someone who has committed a crime.

I wish to propose here, as a suggestion, that mercy is at least not immoral when (1) the reasons are of a certain kind, (2) the offender is repentant, and (3) *some* punishment is imposed. Let me give a few examples. Consider this fictitious case:

> A man worked on international monetary dealings, and some criminals asked him illegally to launder some money for them, for which (they said) they would pay him. He agreed, did the job, was paid, then repented of what he had done but did not report it. They asked him to do the same again and this time he refused. To punish him and ensure his silence they shot him in the knees and told him that if he revealed their activity to the police, they would kill him. The first transaction was discovered and so was what happened to him the second time. He was charged and found guilty. The judge, taking into account his repentance and his refusal to commit the crime twice, chose to regard his lameness as to some extent satisfying retributive justice and gave him a suspended sentence.

Completely to ignore what the man had suffered and was suffering for his crime, and to send him to gaol for exactly as long a term as he would have been given if he had not been shot, would have been harsh. Since justice was here given its due and the man was sorry for what he did, it seems to me that the judge was both merciful and just.
Here is another fictitious case:

> Brown has a business in which Short is employed as the accountant. Brown discovers that, after years of honest service, Short has contrived to take for himself some money which should have gone to the firm. He confronts Short, who not only readily admits his guilt but expresses deep repentance, and asks to be kept on. Brown, who on the one hand does not want to dismiss his repentant employee but on the other hand wants to see justice done, says that he will think about it. While he is thinking about it, Short's wife comes to see him. She is highly repected by all who know her, and at various

times she has made significant contributions to the business. She pleads for her husband. Brown hears her out, says to himself, "That settles it", and tells the woman that he will impose some penalty but not sack her husband or report him to the police.

Is this immoral? I for one do not think so and I conclude that intercession can influence a person in authority to be merciful.

Mixed cases

There are times when a person has what I might call a private relationship with the offender, and at the same time he has a public role to play. Consider this fictitious case:

James, a priest, was the headmaster of a Catholic secondary school and his sister's son, Harry, was a senior student there. With the agreement of the school council and the staff, James announced to the students that anyone discovered with drugs at the school would be both expelled and reported to the police. Some time later a teacher came to James and said that he had been rearranging a classroom and in the process had opened Harry's desk to move the books in it to another desk. Among Harry's books he had noticed a book about chess and, being a chess player, he had glanced into it. He had then discovered that it was in fact a box disguised as a book and that it contained packets of what was probably heroin. It also contained a notebook with a record of sales. He had taken the box and he gave it to James, who had done a course on drugs and who quickly ascertained that the contents were in fact heroin.

James then sent for Harry, showed him the box and said, "Is this yours?" James admitted that it was, broke down and said that he was very sorry for the pain which he had caused to his uncle. He added that he would never have anything to do with drugs again. (For the sake of this story, let us suppose that he was sincere and that James saw this.) James said to himself that if Harry had come to him in confession, told of his drug dealing, said that he was sorry and would not do it again, he (James) would have given him (Harry) absolution and been able to tell no one about it. What he did, however, was this: he said, "Speaking as your uncle I accept your apology and I forgive you. When I visit your family I shall be your uncle in the same way as before. As the headmaster of this school and as a citizen of this state, however, I must respect justice and therefore I hereby expel you from the school and I will inform the police of what has happened, keeping you here until they arrive. I shall give them this box, which I am sure that they will use as evidence. I shall myself tell your parents what I have decided to do; I hope that they will understand."

In this case James has two distinct roles, that of the uncle and that of the headmaster. The first is what I have called private, the second is public. Also, there are two distinct judgements: as the headmaster he judges the past behaviour of the boy to have been bad, while as the uncle he judges his present repentance to be sincere. There is no contradiction between these judgements. Finally, there are two distinct actions: as the uncle he forgives the boy, as the headmaster he punishes him. Therefore, though the uncle-headmaster experiences anguish, he cannot be accused of being inconsistent. Also, if the headmaster in this story is right, and I believe that he is, forgiveness is not only not synonymous with pardon, it does not necessarily entail pardon.

Similarly, a bishop can find himself in a painful position. First, suppose that it is reported to a bishop that a priest was plainly drunk when he was celebrating a funeral, and suppose that the bishop knows the priest personally and sends for him. If the priest is repentant and promises not to offend again, the bishop as his quasi-father may be tempted to act as if he were hearing his confession: that is, to give him absolution and send him on his way. As the bishop, however, he might impose some penalty. Second, suppose that it is reported to a bishop that a priest whom he knows has sexually abused children. In this case he would have a legal obligation to report the offender to the police, but even if he has no such obligation he surely should be strict.

Consider also the following longer story, in which the private and public roles are not so clearly distinct. It is entirely fictitious.

> A deeply religious man gathered round him a group of followers and they became a religious order, which at that time consisted of one community. It grew in size, but it remained one community. In this community, one man, who had had some experience in the business world, was put in charge of the group's finances. He was given confidential advice by a man who knew a lot about what was going on in the financial world, and who admired the work which the community was doing.
>
> One day this religious, having been given a tip on a horse, put twenty dollars of the community's money on it, and it won. He put the stake back and kept the winnings in his room, saying to himself that he would decide later what to do with them. He began to use this to gamble and he won some more. The amount grew, and

he put it into a bank account which he opened in his own name. He received a letter which told him that he had inherited several thousand dollars, and enclosing the cheque. He should have put this money into the community account but he put it, "temporarily", into his personal account and told no one about it. Guided by the advice of the financial expert whom I mentioned, who did not know that the religious had money of his own, he invested the community's money, and also his own, with great success. Some members of the community suspected that something was going on, but no one had any idea of the scale of the man's operations until one day the community as a whole learned that it included a very rich man.

A grave community meeting was held, at which the man admitted his guilt. He also said that he was sorry, and that he wished with all his heart that he had strictly observed his vow of poverty; and he begged forgiveness. He then left the room.

Someone said, "I do not doubt the sincerity of his repentance", and everyone else loudly agreed with this. Someone else said, "Surely we must forgive him" and there was a slightly softer murmur of agreement. A third person, speaking somewhat hesitantly, said that he felt that it would not be right to call the offender back into the room, tell him that they forgave him and declare that the matter was now closed. "I hate to say this," he said, "but isn't this a case which calls for dismissal?"

The oldest religious, the only remaining one of the original group, then spoke. He said that the community owed a lot to the man who had looked after its finances, and who had done a tremendous amount of work for it. He went on to say that at one time, some years ago, when he himself had been the superior, he had learned of a layman whose business had failed and who was facing financial disaster. The man whom they were discussing had given this man some thousands of dollars, telling him to tell no one where the money had come from, and so had saved him. The speaker said: "I did not know how he managed to do what he did, I knew that he had not used community money but I did not know that he had used his own. Rightly or wrongly, I did nothing. What I wish to say is that we are not dealing with a case of utter selfishness." He went on to say: "I do not believe that we should dismiss this man and I ask for mercy for him".

Because of the eminence of the man who had spoken, and the respect in which he was held, these words made a deep impression. The third man who had spoken earlier said that he agreed with what had been said, but, he said, "Something, short of dismissal, needs to be done". There was a murmur of agreement about this.

At this point the man was recalled and told that he was forgiven. He broke down and told the others that they could not imagine the joy and peace that he was feeling. For years, he said, in his heart he had not really been one of them and his inner life had been that of a solitary; now, he said, thanks to their generous forgiveness he was inwardly as well as outwardly one of them again. Also, he had been a secretive, dishonest sinner; now, he said, he was open, honest and a good religious again.

The superior heard him out and then said that the community believed that a penance of some kind should be imposed. A worried look passed across the man's face but as soon as he had understood the spirit in which the proposal had been made he said, in effect, quoting Shakespeare, "Yes, please, 'tis my deserving, and I do entreat it".

A penance was imposed, and then the community asked itself, "What will we do with this man's money?" They decided not to put it into the community account but to give it anonymously to *Médecins sans frontières*.

In general, it seems to me that, while forgiveness is possible and morally good, it should not be understood as a rejection of retributive justice. Dinsmore says, "there can be no forgiveness in which the majesty of the moral law is not upheld",[56] and it is upheld here. Or is it not?

---

56 Dinsmore, *Atonement in Literature and Life*, p. 180.

17 Expiation & the Victim's Need for Justice

EXPIATION

I said earlier that restoration of the moral order after there has been wrongdoing requires that wrongdoers suffer, whether they are repentant or not. I will now add that if a wrongdoer has repented and been forgiven, his complete restoration requires that he accept suffering in the belief that he deserves it. That is, punishment or other suffering not only restores the moral order but can also heal the offender. For the first of these two purposes the repentance of the offender is not necessary, which is why, when someone is convicted of a crime and whether he is repentant or not, he is not set free. For the second, it is necessary: as Sir Walter Moberly says, "Punishment can accomplish nothing in the way of reclaiming a wrongdoer until he admits to himself that 'it serves me right'"[1] and as Frank Pakenham says, "The prisoner is far more likely to be reformed if he can recognise the justice of the penalty than if he cannot".[2]

I spoke above of "punishment or other suffering". I said earlier that retribution has other forms besides punishment, strictly so called, and I gave examples of people who suffered justly as a result of their misdeeds. People can make expiation by accepting such suffering and the examples which I shall give will include cases of suffering which is not exactly punishment.

I cannot prove this expiation theory. All I can do is point out how many people have believed it.

People who have believed in expiation

PRIMITIVE HUMAN BEINGS

Ricoeur says that primitive human beings admired order, felt themselves to be defiled whenever by wrongdoing they had violated

---

1 Moberly, *The Ethics of Punishment*, p. 143.
2 Pakenham, *The Idea of Punishment*, p. 59.

it, and believed that by suffering they could be cleansed of their defilement. They therefore both dreaded punishment, because it was going to be painful, and wanted it, because it would restore their personal worth.[3]

PLATO

In Plato's *Gorgias* Socrates maintains that to do wrong is the greatest of all evils, so that if someone obtains an advantage for himself by foul means he loses more than he gains and is in a bad state. If he escapes punishment he continues in this state, but if he is punished he is "less wretched"; "he grows better in his soul if he is justly punished" and "he is thereby relieved from vice of soul".[4] Socrates does not say that a wrongdoer is in a bad state because the gods will punish him, and that after punishment he is in a good state because he no longer has to fear them: that is, he does not derive this idea from belief in an avenging deity. For him, it is an ethical matter.

LITERATURE

The idea is in literature, as was shown by C.A. Dinsmore in *Atonement in Literature and Life* (1906). Dinsmore went through Greek literature, Dante, Shakespeare, Milton and other great authors and found the idea everywhere. It is, he said, not legal, mechanical or imposed from outside: "Suffering is demanded by the guilty ones themselves as the only suitable expression of the new temper of mind, and as an appropriate satisfaction to their own aroused feelings". He concluded: "It is an axiom in life and in religious thought that there is no reconciliation without satisfaction";[5] the guilty person, he said, needs to suffer. Jaspers, too, finds this idea in literature. In *Tragedy is Not Enough* he says:

> Tragedy becomes self-conscious by understanding the fate of its characters as the consequences of guilt, and as the inner working out of guilt itself. Destruction is the atonement of guilt.[6]

Helen Gardner says that "the notion that men are responsible for what they do and must accept the consequences of their acts and the

---

3   Ricoeur, *The Symbolism of Evil*, pp. 30-31, 42-44.
4   Plato, *Gorgias*, 472e, 477a.
5   Dinsmore, *Atonement in Religion and Life*, pp. 184, 226.
6   Jaspers, *Tragedy is Not Enough*, p. 52.

penalties they have incurred" is an essential element in great tragedies.[7] For instance, in Shakespeare's *Measure for Measure* Angelo says:

> *I am sorry ...*
> *And so deep sticks it in my penitent heart*
> *That I crave death more willingly than mercy,*
> *'Tis my deserving and I do entreat it,*[8]

and in *The Brothers Karamazov* Dostoyevsky has Dmitry recognising his guilt (actually not of the crime for which he was punished, namely murdering his father, but of wanting to murder his father) and saying: "I want to suffer and be cleansed by suffering!"[9]

PSYCHOLOGISTS

The testimony of Karl Menninger is of great interest at this point. His *Man Against Himself* was published in 1938, when he believed in determinism, and in it he said that people who have feelings of guilt often have a quite irrational belief that suffering will cleanse them of their guilt and they set about bringing suffering on themselves without being aware of why they are doing this. "By far the most prevalent method of relieving the unconscious sense of guilt is by atonement", he said,[10] and he told of people going from doctor to doctor until they found one who would amputate a limb, which on medical grounds did not need to be amputated, but which the person associated with his guilt – for example, the hand with which, having lost patience, he had slapped his aged parent or infant child. In such cases, he said, the person in his conscious mind thinks that he has a medical problem which amputation will solve, but his real motivation is subconscious and what drives him is his pathological and unrecognised desire for punishment. When in 1973 he published *Whatever Became of Sin?* he affirmed free will and said that while many cases of false guilt and pathological guilt feelings exist, some people actually *are* guilty, and if they *feel* guilty, so they should. He said, further, that guilty persons may have not a pathological desire for pain but a genuine need of it, and that we may need to accept that in order to work out their cure.[11]

---

7   Gardner, *Religion and Literature*, p. 113.
8   Shakespeare, *Measure for Measure*, 5 1 473-476.
9   Dostoyevsky, *The Brothers Karamazov*, book 9, ch. 9, p. 598.
10 Menninger, *Man Against Himself*, p. 378.
11 See ibid., p. 178.

Another psychiatrist who holds this view is Willard Gaylin, who in 1976 said:

> True guilt seeks, indeed embraces, punishment; it is alleviated or mitigated by such acts. The relief that confession and, even more so, expiation in penance bring to the guilty must have been experienced by every reader.[12]

In 1982 he said that after Richard Herrin killed Bonnie Garland a group of clerics and laypeople associated with a Catholic centre at Yale began to take care of him. They did not entirely deny guilt and the need for repentance: a certain religious brother told Gaylin that Richard Herrin had "a certain amount of remorse" – "he knew he had done something wrong and that he was sorry for it" – and that within weeks of the killing he had gone to confession.[13] This, however, was very much played down and the idea of retributive justice was dismissed entirely. This is part of a conversation between Gaylin and one of the clerics, Brother Thomas:

> Gaylin: Would you, personally, not send the person who killed in cold blood to prison?
> Thomas: No, I would not; I would try some form of rehabilitation. I would be concerned that a person regret what he had done.
> Gaylin: So a sense of regret and a sense that he would not repeat would suffice for you?
> Thomas: Yes. ...
> Gaylin: But some people feel it isn't fair. The concept of just deserts seems important to them.
> Thomas: Yes, but then we have the question of whether we take two lives. This sounds like foolishness. One life has been lost. Should another be wasted and lost? Or should we try to salvage that life?[14]

Gaylin commented:

> For the most part the clerics involved with Richard were peculiarly disinterested [not interested] in the concept of penance. "Whatever

---

12   Gaylin, *Caring*, p. 121. I am sure that the simple reporting of the facts is not what Gaylin means by "confession". Confession includes repentance.
13   Gaylin, *The Killing of Bonnie Garland*, pp. 139-140. See above, p. 94.
14   Ibid., p. 130.

became of sin?" Karl Menninger asked in another context. Perhaps the Church, like the State – influenced in great part by a psychoanalytic view of human behaviour (where all actions are determined and all individuals nonculpable in the broadest sense) – may have joined in finding "punishment" an unfashionable and uncomfortable concept. Or perhaps it was that we were dealing with that segment of the religious community (chaplains and teachers) that was "social worker"-oriented.[15]

He said that in his opinion these clerics leapfrogged from sin to forgiveness "over the neglected but hallowed principle of penance". They offered ready forgiveness themselves and wanted Richard Herrin to "feel good about himself". A result of this, he said, was that Herrin could not understand why society was hard on him. He might, said Gaylin, have felt differently if he had met a Church which emphasised sin and guilt, remorse and penance.[16]

OTHERS

Not many writers on punishment as a legal institution discuss the idea which I am proposing here, but one who does is Sir Walter Moberly, who in *The Ethics of Punishment* (1968) says that the true norm of retributive punishment is expiation.[17]

I will quote, finally, John Glenn Gray, who in *The Warriors*, a study of men in battle, says that a soldier, even one with no religious faith, can feel guilt because of wrong things he has done and accept death itself as "a way of atonement"; "he can greet it calmly and inwardly at peace as the path to a mind at one with itself". He tells of American soldiers in World War II finding the body of a young German soldier who had been hanged by SS troops, and who looked happy. Gray felt sure that the soldier had accepted death gladly, as a means of atonement.[18]

Group expiation

When a group of people are collectively, though not in all cases individually, guilty of wrongdoing, if some of them (not necessarily the personally guilty ones) suffer and if the group as a whole accepts

---

15 Ibid., p. 118.
16 Ibid., p. 140.
17 Moberly, *The Ethics of Punishment*, p. 120.
18 Gray, *The Warriors*, pp. 120-121.

this, saying in effect that "we" did wrong so that now "we" deserve to suffer, the suffering can be expiatory.

The right to punishment

Hegel says that a criminal has a right to punishment,[19] and from what I have been saying one can see the sense of this. It is extremely rare for criminals to give themselves up to the police claiming punishment as their right, and most of them, if they were told that they were entitled to be punished, would promptly say that they waived their right. This leads Ted Honderich to dismiss the idea, saying that "a right that cannot be escaped is an odd right".[20] It is not, however, so odd as to be unique, since a married man cannot validly waive his exclusive right to sexual intercourse with his wife, and if a man were to waive his right to freedom and sell himself into slavery for life for a lump sum for his children's education, the contract would be not only immoral but invalid.[21]

THE VICTIM'S NEED FOR JUSTICE

I shall here talk about the victims. By this term I shall mean not only the direct victims, who in some cases are dead, but also their families and close friends.

When a morally offensive crime has been committed, people generally, including people who do not know anyone involved in the case, feel that justice demands that the person who committed it be punished. They may also feel that society – the city, the country or even the whole human race – was dirtied by the crime and that punishment of the criminal will, at least to some extent, cleanse it. It has been said that courts often proceed on the supposition that in a typical trial the parties mainly concerned are the state and the accused person; the victim is either not called at all or is among many witnesses, and, whereas everything is done to protect the rights of the accused while searching for the truth, nothing is done about the rights, if any, of the victims. It has been said that religious ministers, too, often consider immoral behaviour only in terms of the relationship between God and the sinner,

---

19 Hegel, *The Philosophy of Right*, p. 97; S 100.
20 Honderich, *Punishment*, p. 47.
21 Morris, "Persons and Punishment" is almost entirely a defence of the right to punishment.

virtually ignoring the victim or victims. In some churches, victims of sexual abuse have found that when they reported what had happened they were questioned, sometimes aggressively rather than sympathetically, and then expected to fade away as if their role was only to give information. Victims, however, are often important persons in the story and I have been told by people who have counselled victims of crimes that they experience a need to know that their attackers have been punished. If, in spite of the best efforts by authorities, an attacker has so far proved impossible to identify or (if identified) to find, that is bad enough. If the authorities have neglected to pursue him or if he is found guilty but given a ridiculously light sentence, that is worse. In such cases as these, it is extremely difficult for the victims to come to terms with what they have suffered, to put the incidents behind them, and to become happy people.

I shall give examples of this, then discuss the explanation of the need.

Examples

In *Measure for Measure*, Angelo, the temporary ruler of Vienna, tells Isabella, who is a novice in a convent, that if she will have sexual intercourse with him he will pardon her brother Claudio, who has been condemned to death. She pretends to agree but another woman (whom Angelo had been supposed to marry) takes her place. Angelo does not notice the change, has sex with the substitute, and nevertheless orders the execution of Claudio. When the duke whom Angelo has temporarily replaced returns and resumes his authority, Isabella appeals to him:

> Justice, O royal Duke! Vail your regard
> Upon a wronged — I would fain have said, a maid.
> O worthy prince, dishonour not your eye
> By throwing it on any other object,
> Till you have heard me in my true complaint,
> And given me justice, justice, justice, justice![22]

She here demands that Angelo be punished, as a matter of justice. Consider this fictitious story:

> A young woman was brutally attacked and raped by a gang of youths. She reported the incident to the police, who found the

---

22 Shakespeare, *Measure for Measure*, 5 1 20-25.

youths and arrested them. At their trial, she gave evidence, recounting in a matter-of-fact tone what happened as she remembered it. This was painful to her, first, because it meant being in the same room as the youths and seeing them well-dressed and with their hair done, looking at her; second, because it meant telling her story with sexual details in a large room full of people, including reporters; and, finally, because she had to submit to being cross-examined by the defence barrister, who endeavoured to make the jury think that she had led the youths on, at least at the beginning. The youths were found guilty, and were sentenced to a surprisingly short term in gaol. At this the young woman was appalled, so were her parents and friends, and so was everyone who had dealt with her. An appeal was lodged against the lightness of the sentence, it was upheld and a higher court sentenced the youths to a term in gaol that by general consent was proportionate to the offence. Asked for comment, the young woman said that she believed that justice had been done and that in consequence she was a step nearer to "getting over" what had been done to her.

I will offer a judgement on this later.

In the Holocaust, millions of Jews were not only killed but, before being killed, they were humiliated and mistreated in ways that still inspire horror. Many Jewish people who have wanted Nazi criminals to be found and punished have felt that they owed this to the victims. They have also felt that the fact that many of the persons responsible for this huge crime have evaded punishment has been a crime against justice and against Jewish people who are alive now, making it even more difficult than it would otherwise be for them to come to terms with the Holocaust.

I mentioned earlier Helen Garner's *Joe Cinque's Consolation*, which is an account of how a certain girl killed Joe Cinque in Canberra in October 1977 and received a light sentence. Joe Cinque's parents, whom I had in mind when I said at the beginning of this chapter that "the victim" in the title includes people like them, believe that it was insufficient and are in pain because of it. Also, Helen Garner describes a Victims of Crime rally which was attended by people who were seriously distressed because there had been no punishment or it had been, in their opinion, too light.[23]

---

23 Garner, *Joe Cinque's Consolation*, pp. 275-279.

The need of the victim: what is its source?

IS IT A NEED FOR REVENGE?

In all the above cases it would be easy to maintain that the motive was revenge. Since the desire for revenge is an unhealthy or even immoral desire, it would follow that it ought not to be satisfied. Let us, to test this, consider the examples above, seeking as far as possible to enter into people's feelings and understand their nature.

In *Measure for Measure*, Isabella asks for justice, using the word five times; she does not speak of revenge. Is she moved by her moral sense to make this demand, or is she in reality demanding revenge and using "justice" as a euphemism for it?

Imagine that you are the raped girl of the second example and ask yourself: When you tell your story to the police, and when later you tell it in court, are you saying to yourself, "I wish I could make those men suffer as much as they made me suffer; unfortunately, that would be impossible; well, I'll make them suffer as much as I can – I'll get them, the bastards"? Or are you saying, "I need to know that justice has been done, and that is why I am doing this"? And if you are saying the latter thing, is it the same as the former, only in more high-sounding language? When the men who raped you are given a light sentence, are your feelings those of someone who has been deprived of vengeance, or does your outrage spring from your sense of justice, which is different?

When there has been a particularly brutal crime, or when there has been a heartless swindle of old, credulous people, one often reads in the newspaper that the victims or, if the victims are dead, the children of the victims or others who loved them have expressed a deeply-felt need to know that justice has been done. In 1994 a politician was murdered in Cabramatta, New South Wales, Australia. His fiancée appealed to anyone who had any information to give it to the police so that the murderer would be brought to justice, and it seemed to me that she was expressing a personal desire or need. Was this purely and simply a primitive and hate-filled desire for revenge, or was it a moral thirst for justice, a feeling that if the wrongdoers were punished, moral order would be restored? Are there sometimes two distinct desires, a base one for revenge and a noble one for justice, co-existing in hostile fashion in the psyche?

IS IT A NEED FOR DETERRENCE?

Some Jews do talk as though Nazi criminals must be punished to deter future antisemitic governments from ordering other Holocausts. Is this the whole justification of punishment?

IT IS A NEED FOR JUSTICE

The answer to all these questions is: the desire for justice is not a desire for revenge or deterrence. Few, I imagine, think that Jews wanted punishment of Nazis mainly because they wanted to deter possible future persecutors, or imagine that if a victim of gang rape wants the men involved to be put in gaol it is to deter them from raping again, and to deter men in general from raping women. The explanation which I am offering for their feelings is that they spring from a sense of justice, which is moral. May I say that I find this the only plausible explanation? The more moral the person is, the greater is the sense of outrage if justice is not done and the more difficult it is for the victim to find peace. If the attacker is found and punished, and if he is at least in some measure repentant, a generous victim may harbour no bitterness against him and will not be angry if, years later, he learns that after the attacker came out of gaol (if that was his punishment) he got a good job and became a prosperous and respected citizen.

Conclusion

18 Some Theological Reflections

The evolutionary theory

I can understand why some Christians, who believe that absolutely all our hope should be in God, find a secular hope unacceptable, but I, for one, believe that there are such things as secular truth, value and hope, and that we ought not to be dismayed by the thought of secular, even scientific, grounds for confidence in the material universe. It is true that I have denied that constant divine intervention has caused the evolution of the material universe, but I maintain that the universe reflects the nature of its creator, whose hand we do not see in particular events (such as the emergence of aquatic beings from the sea), but whose nature we see in the whole history of the material universe. Moreover, when Christians engage in such secular actions as building a bridge or cooking a meal, they co-operate with God in his work of creation, so that these and other actions have religious meaning. The theory, then, may be secular, but not in a bad sense.

Bright and dark mysteries

I said earlier that moral evil is ultimately inexplicable and I quoted some Christians who say this. I now add that, talking explicitly about sin, Emil Brunner says:

> Only he who understands that sin is inexplicable knows what it is. Sin ... is the one great negative mystery of our existence, of which we know only one thing, that we are responsible for it.[1]

and Karl Barth says of sin:

> It has, therefore, no possibility – we cannot escape this difficult formula – except that of the absolutely impossible. How else can we describe that which is intrinsically absurd but by a formula which is logically absurd? Sin is that which is absurd, man's absurd choice and decision for that which is not, described in the Genesis story as his hearkening to the voice of the serpent, the beast of chaos.

---

1 Brunner, *Man in Revolt*, p. 132.

18 ❧ Some Theological Reflections

Sin exists only in this absurd event. ... [If we understand sin] we lose all our desire to bring it into a final harmony with God and man. In all its forms – as enmity against God, as fratricide and as self-destruction – it is then seen as that which is out of place and will never be in place. Even the humblest being in the most obscure part of the created world fits in somewhere and has some potentiality and a God-given right of actualisation. But sin does not fit in anywhere and has no genuine potentiality and no right of actualisation.[2]

There are, it seems to me, bright mysteries and there is the dark mystery of moral evil. Bright mysteries, like the Trinity and the Incarnation, at first seem to be utterly strange, but the more we think about them the more we feel ourselves to be moving into the light. Moral evil, however, seems at first to be easy to understand but the more we think about it the more incomprehensible it becomes until we feel almost forced to give up. As we study it, we feel ourselves moving into darkness, which of course is a biblical symbol for sin. Bright mysteries are in themselves perfectly intelligible, and though they surpass the grasp of our minds they are understood perfectly by God; but the dark mystery of moral evil is in itself pure unintelligibility, it does not surpass our minds but is opposed to reason as such. Rosenbaum says that according to some authors the missing explanation of Hitler is "locked up tight in the inaccessible, indecipherable mind of God",[3] and he quotes the Jewish theologian Emil Fackenheim, who said: "Only God can account for such radical evil, and he's not talking".[4] If he is not giving us an explanation, it is because ultimately there isn't one. Which is not to say that moral evil is utterly irremediable. If it is committed by someone who has a personal relationship of some kind with the divine persons, it involves a breaking-away from them and an offence against them, but all is not lost. As Christ said again and again, if people repent God forgives them. The divine forgiveness was not, perhaps, an utterly original idea at the time, but his insistence on it was, to say the least, remarkable.

There has at times been what seems to me to be excessive emphasis on what I have called the dark mysteries. There has often been

---

2   Barth, *Church Dogmatics*, IV/1, # 60, p. 410.
3   Rosenbaum, *Explaining Hitler*, p. xlvi.
4   Ibid., p. 279.

enormous emphasis on sin, and many perfectly innocent actions have been judged to be evil. It has been thought that for "ordinary people" the main motive for being good is fear, and graphic sermons about hell have been preached by priests who clearly believed that only by frightening people can anyone inspire them to resist temptation and lead lives which, if not exactly good, are at any rate not immoral. Some sermons and writings were examples of the pornography of violence: one senses a perverse delight in the description of intense pain, and a sadistic delight in power as the preacher terrified his hearers.[5] There was often a similar perversity in horrifying descriptions of the passion of Christ. The cult of violence, if I may call it that, has persisted in spectacular processions with people walking along streets whipping themselves, climbing hundreds of steps on their bleeding knees, or in other ways "doing penance" for their sins.

Some people today believe in diabolical spirits which, they say, are active in pop music, indecent shows, astrology, spiritism and libertarian movements of various kinds. According to them, what they call Satanism is all around us, poisoning our culture. I will not waste time discussing this here.

When it came to explaining how we were redeemed by the passion and death of Christ, some retributivist explanations which were given in the past were, one suspects, thought up by preachers who sought desperately for some way of enabling their uneducated hearers to understand what it meant to say that Jesus died for us, and who grasped at analogies drawn from fairly primitive peasant life. They said, for instance, that, when human beings sinned, they slapped God the Father's face and he needed to slap them back; his Son said, "Slap me instead of them", God the Father did this and since then has felt better so that if we lead good lives he will be well disposed towards us.

The present situation

In fairly recent times, many Christian theologians have understandably been appalled by what I have been describing, they have felt, rightly, that it was a perversion of Christianity and they have, I believe, gone to an extreme in the opposite direction. They dismiss the whole idea of sin, or they say nothing about it, except perhaps to say that we should

---

5 The passage which I quoted from Fr Furniss (above, p. 32) is an example of this.

not worry about it since God loves us and his love is utterly unaffected by our behaviour. Influenced by the liberal view of retributive justice they have decided that it belongs in the trash-can of outmoded ideas. Stressing the divine mercy, they have said that forgiveness entails pardon so that when God forgives us he pardons us and that is that. Redemption has virtually no place in this world-view, and if these Christians talk about the sufferings of Christ it is to say that they show how much he loves us, since it was at the risk of being put to death that he freely came among us. It is a world-view that is full of sunshine and joy. It is better than the old "fire and fear" popular theology which I summarised above, but, it, too, is incomplete.

Some men were beginning their professional careers when World War II broke out and for some years they were away at the war. When it ended, they came home, resumed their family lives and careers more or less where they had left off, and from then on did not talk about the war. For them it had had no positive meaning and they wanted to put it behind them. After Jesus' death and resurrection his followers did not take this attitude. They thought about his sufferings and death and decided that they had been of immense benefit to his followers and should be talked about constantly, because by dying for us Jesus saved us. A theological question therefore is: how did Jesus' sufferings and death do anyone any good?

The Bible – vengeance?

Emil Brunner says that since Ritschl "juridical" expressions have been rejected by many theologians, but we could not imagine the Bible without them.[6] For their sin, Adam and Eve were expelled from the garden of Eden; for his sin Cain was condemned to be a fugitive; because of the evil which men had been doing God sent the flood:

> God said to Noah, "I have determined to make an end of all flesh [human beings], for the earth is filled with violence because of them; now I am going to destroy them along with the earth" (Gen 6:13).

But perhaps this is a feature of the Old Testament's idea of God, not that of the New? Not at all. In the gospels, Jesus does not propose retributive justice as a new idea but he constantly assumes, especially in his teaching concerning reward and punishment in the next life, that wicked people are punished as they deserve. For instance, he said

---

6   Brunner, *The Mediator*, p. 465n.

in a parable that when a king's servants were maltreated and killed by the people whom he wanted to invite to his son's wedding, "he sent his troops, destroyed those murderers and burned their city" (Matt 22:7). One might say that Jesus is here telling a story without necessarily approving of all that the characters in it do, but he also says: "The Son of Man will send his angels and they will collect out of his kingdom all causes of sin and all evildoers, and they will throw them into the furnace of fire" (Matt 13:41), and he says that when the Son of Man comes in his glory, people who have behaved selfishly will not be sent to a rehabilitation centre for therapy but, they "will go away to eternal punishment" (Matt 25:46). In Acts we have such events as the deaths of Ananias and Sapphira (Acts 5:1-11). Paul says that God "will repay according to each one's deeds" (Rom 2:6), and he goes on: "There will be anguish and distress for everyone who does evil" (Rom 2:9).

In many passages Old Testament authors seem to regard divine punishment as God's revenge. Moses in a song says that God says, "Vengeance is mine, and recompense" (Deut 32:35), Isaiah says, "The Lord has a day of vengeance" (34:8) and "Here is your God. He will come with vengeance" (35:4); Psalm 94 begins:

> O Lord, you God of vengeance,
> you God of vengeance, shine forth! (Ps 94:1)

and Nahum begins:

> A jealous and avenging God is the Lord,
> the Lord is avenging and wrathful;
> the Lord takes vengeance on his adversaries
> and rages against his enemies.

In the New Testament, Romans and Hebrews say that the Lord says, "Vengeance is mine, I will repay" (Rom 12:19, Heb 34:8).

A suggestion

I wish to maintain that we must dismiss revenge and similar ideas from our minds, but we should not dismiss the idea of retributive justice. This, I maintain, is not something which God has freely chosen to introduce into our world, but an intrinsically necessary element of it. Sins have been committed, and for this to be remedied there must be suffering. I will not here survey all the literature on this question, but I will say that Anselm's *Cur Deus Homo* did a great deal to establish a systematic understanding of redemption, and it used the idea of retributive justice. I will also quote two recent authors. Emil Brunner has written:

> The more seriously guilt is regarded, the more it is realised that "something must happen", just because forgiveness is not something which can in any way be taken absolutely for granted. The more real guilt is, the more real also is the gulf between us and God, the more real is the wrath of God, and the inviolable character of the law of penalty retribution. ... The more serious our view of guilt, the more clearly we perceive the necessity for an objective – and not merely subjective – atonement. To deny this means the *nondum consideravisse pondus peccati* [not to have considered the gravity of sin].[7]

In *Redeemer: Understanding the Meaning of the Life, Death and Resurrection of Jesus Christ,* Stephen B Clark said that the 'curses" of the covenant are

> God's promises to stand behind his covenant and back it up by punishing serious violations. This does not mean that God bears personal hostility toward those who violate the covenant. Rather, as the just ruler of his people, God will enforce the law contained in the covenant.[8]

Christ, he says,

> took upon himself the curse that should fall on law-breakers. This means that Christ underwent punishment stipulated by the curse of the law. As a result, we do not have to be subject to the curse by undergoing that punishment ourselves.[9]

Later he says:

> To say that Christ died "for us", therefore, means that not only was his death for our benefit, but also that he died "on our behalf" as our representative.[10]

---

7 Brunner, *The Mediator*, p. 451.
8 Clark, *Redeemer*, p. 103.
9 Ibid., p. 104.
10 Ibid., p. 159.

Our part in our redemption

Redemption is not a one-sided affair: that is, we are not purely passive in our own redemption, still less can we be redeemed against our wills. For one thing, as I said earlier, the divine forgiveness needs our repentance. Retributive justice demands that there be suffering and Christ has suffered for us – that his sufferings benefit us is to be explained by solidarity, not penal substitution. Also, for us to be completely cleansed, it is perhaps necessary for us to experience some suffering in this life and the next, short of perpetual separation from the divine persons and exclusion from heaven; and if we accept suffering in this spirit, it can be expiatory. Also, the intercession of saints and other holy people can help us. Faith, then, is an enormous help to believers when they experience effects of moral evil.

"The last things"

In an earlier book I suggested that when unrepentant sinners die they do not appear before the judgement seat of God, who condemns them to hell, into which they are dragged, screaming. Rather, they simply do not meet God at all but find themselves outside heaven. Those who are in a union of love with the divine persons while they are alive go into eternal joyful union with them and the community that is around them.[11]

---

11 See my *Personalism and Scholasticism*, pp. 177-178.

Bibliography

This is not a list of books about evil; it is a list of the books and articles to which references have been made in footnotes, with the facts of publication that were omitted there.

In general, classic books like Shakespeare's plays, Milton's *Paradise Lost*, Spinoza's *Ethics* and Thomas Aquinas's works have been omitted, unless a particular edition has been used. In footnote references, PG and PL mean Migne's editions of the Greek and Latin Fathers of the Church.

Acton, H.B., ed. *The Philosophy of Punishment*. London: Macmillan, 1969.

Aeschylus, *Agamemnon*, tr. Richard Lattimore. University of Chicago Press, 1953.

Ahern, M.B. *The Problem of Evil*. London: Routledge & Kegan Paul, 1971.

Anders, Timothy. *The Evolution of Evil. An Inquiry into the Ultimate Origin of Human Suffering*. Chicago: Open Court, 1994.

Anderson, Maxwell. *Winterset*. London: John Lane, 1938.

Arendt, Hannah. *The Origins of Totalitarianism*. New York: Harcourt, Brace, 1951.

Barth, Karl: Church *Dogmatics*, III/3. Edinburgh: T. & T. Clark, 1961.

———. *Church Dogmatics*, IV/1. Edinburgh: T. & T. Clark, 1956.

Basinger, David. "Human Freedom and Divine Providence: Some New Thoughts on an Old Problem." *Religious Studies*, 15(1979)491-510.

Baudelaire, Charles. *Baudelaire*. Selected poems edited and with introduction by Francis Scarfe. Harmondsworth: Penguin, 1961.

Beauvoir, Simone de. *The Marquis de Sade*. London: Calder, 1962. This consists of the essay, "Must We Burn Sade?" (72 pp.) and selections from Sade (120 pp.).

Belo, Bishop Carlos. "The Path to Freedom", *The Age* (Melbourne), 28 August 2001.

Berdyaev, Nicolas. *Freedom and the Spirit*. London: Geoffrey Bles, 1935.

Berger, Peter. *A Rumour of Angels*. Harmondsworth: Pelican, 1971.

Berkouwer, GC. *Sin*. Grand Rapids, Mich.: Eerdmans, 1971.

Bernanos, Georges: *Diary of a Country Priest*. London: Bodley Head, 1937.

———. *Joy*. London: The Catholic Book Club, 1949.

———. *Un crime*. Paris: Plon, 1935.

Blue, Lionel. "On the Couch." *The Tablet* (London), 13 November 1993, p. 1482.

Blumenfeld, Laura. *Revenge. A Story of Hope*. New York: Simon & Schuster, 2002.

Bonhoeffer, Dietrich. *Ethics*. This book was made from papers left by Bonhoeffer, which had to be arranged. It was published in German in 1949, then in a rearranged edition in 1963. This was published in English by Collins-Fontana (London) in 1964. It was rearranged again in German in 1998 and a new translation of this is in the *Works*, vol. 6 (Minneapolis: Fortress, 2005).

Bowker, John. *Problems of Suffering in the Religions of the World*. Cambridge University Press, 1970.

Bradley, A.C. *Shakespearean Tragedy*. London: Macmillan, 1957.

Brasnett, B.R. *The Suffering of the Impassible God*. London: SPCK, 1928.

Brunner, Emil: *Man in Revolt*. London: Lutterworth, 1939.

———. *The Mediator*. London: Lutterworth, 1934.

Buber, Martin. *The Knowledge of Man*. London: Allen & Unwin, 1965.

Buttrick, G.A. *God, Pain and Evil*. Nashville: Abingdon, 1966.

Camus, Albert: *The Fall*. Harmondsworth: Penguin, 1963.

———. *The Plague*. Harmondsworth: Penguin, 1960.

———. *The Rebel*. Harmondsworth: Penguin, 1962.

Resistance, Rebellion and Death. New York: Knopf, 1961. This collection of writings includes "Reflections on the Guillotine", which first appeared in Koestler and Camus, *Réflexions sur la peine capitale* (Paris: Calmann-Lévy, 1957).

Cardenal, Ernesto. *Love*. London: Search, 1974.

Caussade, Jean-Pierre (1675-1751). *Self-Abandonment to the Will of God*. As was said in the text, this used to be attributed to Caussade. It was edited and published, as having been written by him, in 1861. English translation 1933 by Algar Thorold. London: Burns & Oates, 1959.

Choderlos de Laclos. *Les liaisons dangereuses*. Penguin, 1961.

Clark, Stephen B. *Redeemer: Understanding the Meaning of the Life, Death and Resurrection of Jesus Christ*. Ann Arbor Mich: Servant, 1992.

Clarke, John. *A Defence of Natural and Revealed Religion*, the Boyle lectures 1691-1732, 3 vols. London: 1739.

Claudel, Paul. *Partage de midi* and *Le soulier de satin*. In Paul Claudel, *Théâtre*, Paris: Gallimard Pléiade, 1956.

Cowburn, John: *Love*. Milwaukee: Marquette University Press, 2003.

———. *Free Will, Predestination and Determinism*. Milwaukee: Marquette University Press. 2008.

———. *Personalism and Scholasticism*. Milwaukee: Marquette University Press, 2005.

Creel, Richard E. *Divine Impassibility: An Essay in Philosophical Theology*. Cambridge University Press, 1986.

Denziger-Schönmetzer. *Enchiridion Symbolorum*. 35th edition. Freiburg: Herder, 1973.

Dinsmore, C.A. *Atonement in Literature and Life*. London: Constable, 1906.

Doing Justice. Published by the Committee for the Study of Incarceration, 1976.

Dorner, Isaak August (1809-1884). *Divine Immutability: A Critical Reconsideration*. First published as three essays, 1856-58, then included in Dorner's collected works in 1883. English translation, Minneapolis: Fortress, 1994.

Dostoyevsky, Fyodor. *The Brothers Karamazov*. Harmondsworth: Penguin, 1958.

Eliot, T.S. *Collected Plays*. London: Faber & Faber, 1962.

Ellis-Fermor, Una. *The Frontiers of Drama*. London: Methuen, 1964.

Ewing, A.C. *The Morality of Punishment*. London: Kegan Paul, Trench, Trubner, 1929.

Fairbairn, A.M. *The Place of Christ in Modern Theology*. New York: Scribner's, 1893.

Farrer, Austin: *Love Almighty and Ills Unlimited*. London: Collins, 1962.

Faulkner, William: *Absolom, Absolom!* London: Chatto & Windus, 1960.

———. *Requiem for a Nun*. London: Chatto & Windus, 1965.

Fiddes, P. *The Creative Suffering of God*. Oxford: Clarendon, 1990.

Finance, Joseph de. *Connaissance de l'être*. Paris-Bruges, Desclée de Brouwer, 1966.

Flew, Anthony. "Compatibilism, Free Will and God." *Philosophy*, 48(1973)231-244.

Frankl, Viktor. *The Unheard Cry for Meaning*. New York: Simon & Schuster Touchstone, 1979.

Fromm, Erich: *The Anatomy of Human Destructiveness*. New York: Holt, Reinhart & Winston, 1973.

———. *The Art of Loving*. London: Allen & Unwin, 1957.

Funder, Anna. *Stasiland*. Melbourne: Text, 2002.

Furniss, J. *The Sight of Hell*. Dublin & London: Duffy, before 1869.

Gardner, Helen. *Religion and Literature*. London: Faber & Faber, 1971.

Garner, Helen. *Joe Cinque's Consolation*. Sydney: Picador, 2004.

Garrigou-Lagrange, Réginald: *God: His Existence and His Nature*. St Louis: Herder, 1936. Originally published in 1914.

———. *Providence*. St Louis: Herder, 1951.

Gaylin, Willard: *Caring*. New York: Avon pb, 1979.

———. *The Killing of Bonnie Garland: A Question of Justice*. New York: Simon & Schuster, 1982.

Geach, Peter. *Providence and Evil*. Cambridge University Press, 1977.

Genet, Jean. *The Thief's Journal*. Penguin, 1967.

Geivett, R. Douglas. *Evil and the Evidence for God. The Challenge of John Hick's Theodicy*. Philadelphia: Temple, 1993.

Govier, Trudy. *Forgiveness and Revenge*. London & New York: Routledge, 2002.

Gray, Francine du Plessix. *At Home with the Marquis de Sade: A Life*. New York: Simon & Schuster, 1998.

Gray, John Glenn. *The Warriors*. 2nd Torchbook edn. New York: Harper Torchbook, 1970.

Green, H. *Prolegomena to Ethics*. Oxford: Clasrendon, 1906.

Grisez, Germain. *Beyond the New Theism*. South Bend: University of Notre Dame Press, 1975.

Bibliography

Gross, Hyman. *A Theory of Criminal Justice.* New York: Oxford University Press, 1979.

Hall, Richard. *The Real John Kerr.* Sydney: Angus & Robertson, 1978.

Hegel. *The Philosophy of Right.* Corrected edition. Oxford Unversity Press, 1945.

Heim, Karl: *Jesus the Lord. The Sovereign Authority of Jesus and `God's Revelation in Christ.* Edinburgh & London: Oliver and Boyd.

———. *Jesus the World's Perfecter. The Atonement and the Renewal of the World.* Edinburgh & London: Oliver & Boyd, 1959.

Hick, John. *Evil and the God of Love.* London: Macmillan, 1966.

Hirsch, Andrew von. *Past or Future Crimes. Deservedness or Dangerousness in the Sentencing of Criminals.* New Brunswick: Rutgers University Press, c1985.

Holmgren, Margaret R. "Forgiveness and the Intrinsic Value of Persons", *American Philosophical Quarterly,* 30(1993)341-352.

Honderich, Ted. *Punishment, the Supposed Justifications.* Revised edn. Harmondsworth: Peregrine, 1971.

———. "Punishment, the New Retributivism, and Political Philosophy" in A Phillips Griffiths ed., Philosophy and Practice, supplement to Philosophy, CUP, 1984, pp 117-147. Read 1989.

Houghton, John. *Does God Play Dice?* Grand Rapids, Mich.: Zonderan, 1989.

Jankélévitch, Vladimir. *Le pardon.* Paris: Aubier, 1967.

Jaspers, Karl. *Tragedy is Not Enough.* London: Gollancz, 1953. This book is a translation of part of *Von der Wahrheit.*

Jenyns, Soames. *A Free Inquiry into the Nature and Origin of Evil.* London: Dodsley, 1758.

John Paul II, Pope. *Memory and Identity: Personal Reflections.* London: Weidenfeld & Nicolson, 2005.

Journet, Charles. *The Meaning of Evil.* London: Geoffrey Chapman, 1963.

Jung, Karl. *Aion in Collected Works,* vol. 9 part 2. New York: Pantheon, 1959.

Kant, Emmanuel: *The Metaphysical Elements of Justice.* This is a translation by John Ladd of *Tugendlehre,* part 1 of *Die Metaphysik der Sitten.* New York: Bobbs-Merrill, 1965 and Indianapolis: Hackett, 1999.

———. *Religion Within the Limits of Reason Alone*. New York: Harper Torchbook, 1960.

Kaufmann, Walter. *Without Guilt and Justice*. New York: Wyden, 1973.

Kekes, John. *Facing Evil*. Princeton, 1990.

Kendrick, Sir James. *The Lisbon Earthquake*. London: Methuen, 1956.

Kenny, Anthony. *The God of the Philosophers*. Oxford: Clarendon, 1979.

Knox, Ronald. *Enthusiasm*. Oxford: Clarendon, 1950.

Kondoleon, Theodore J. "The Immutability of God: Some Recent Challenges." *The New Scholasticism*, 58(1984)293-315.

Küng, Hans. *Justification*. New York: Thomas Nelson, 1964.

Kushner, Harold. *When Bad Things Happen to Good People*. London: Picador, 1982.

Landsberg, Paul Louis. "Le sens de l'action". *Esprit*, 73(1938).

Lang, Daniel: *Casualties of War*. New York: McGraw Hill, 1969. This was originally an article in *The New Yorker*, 18 October 1969.

———. "A Backward Look". *The New Yorker*, 3 October 1977.

Lautréamont, Le Comte de (Isidore Ducasse). *Les chants de Maldoror*. Translated into English and published as *Lautéamont's Maldoror*: London: Allison & Busby, 1970.

Lavelle, Louis. *Les puissances du moi*. Paris: Flammarion, 1948.

Lawrence, DH.: ———. *Lady Chatterley's Lover*. Harmondsworth: Penguin, 1960.

———. *Women in Love*. London: Heinemann Phoenix, 1954.

Lecky, William Edward Hartpole (1838-1903). *History of European Morals from Augustus to Charlemagne*. Originally published in 1869. I quote from a revised 3rd edn, London: Longmans, Green, 1877. There have been later editions: London: Longmans, 1911; New York: Appleton, 1913, and London: Watts, 1946.

Leibniz. *Theodicy*. London: Routledge & Kegan Paul, 1951. Originally published in 1710.

Letter, Peter De. "The Reparation of Our Fallen Nature", *The Thomist*, 23(1960).

Lewis, C.S. *The Problem of Pain*. London: Geoffrey Bles, 1940.

Lonergan, Bernard. *Insight*. London: Longmans, 1957. Reissued London: Darton, Longman & Todd, 1978.

Lovejoy, Arthur Oncken (1873-1932); *The Great Chain of Being. A Study in the History of an Idea*. Harvard University Press, 1936.

———. "Milton and the Paradox of the Fortunate Fall." In *Essays in the History of Ideas*. Baltimore: Johns Hopkins, 1948, pp. 277-295.

Lucas, JR. *On Justice*. Oxford: Clarendon, 1980.

McKenzie, John G. *Guilt*. London: Allen & Unwin, 1962.

Mackie, J. L.: "Evil and Omnipotence." *Mind*, 64(1955)200-212.

———. *Persons and Values*. Oxford: Clarendon, 1985.

Manser, AR. "It Serves You Right". *Philosophy*, 37(1962)293-306.

Maritain, Jacques: *Existence and the Existent*. New York: Pantheon, 1948.

———. *Freedom in the Modern World*. London: Sheed & Ward, 1935.

———. *God and the Permission of Evil*. Milwaukee: Bruce, 1966.

———. *Neuf leçons sur les notions premières de la philosophie morale*. Paris: Téqui, 1951.

———. *Redeeming the Time*. London: Bles, 1944.

———. *St Thomas and the Problem of Evil*. Milwaukee: Marquette University Press, 1942.

Maugham, W. Somerset. *Of Human Bondage*. London: Heinemann, 1937.

Menninger, Karl: *The Crime of Punishment*. New York: Viking, 1968.

———. *Man Against Himself*. New York: Harvest pb, originally published in 1938.

———. *Whatever Became of Sin?* London: Hodder & Stoughton, 1975.

Mercier, Desiré.-Joseph (1851-1926). *Métaphysique générale*. Seventh edn., Louvain: Institut supérieur de philosophie, 1923.

Metz, John Baptist, ed. *Moral Evil Under Challenge*. New York: Herder & Herder, 1971.

Moberly, Walter. *The Ethics of Punishment*. London: Faber, 1968.

Moltmann, J. *The Crucified God*. London: SCM, 1974.

Monden, Louis. *Sin, Liberty and Law*. London: Geoffrey Chapman, 1966.

Monod, Jacques. *Chance and Necessity*. London: Collins, 1972.

Mooney, Christopher. *Teilhard de Chardin and the Mystery of Christ*. London: Collins, 1966.

Moore, Katheleen Dean. *Pardons. Justice, Mercy and the Public Interest*. New York: Oxford University Press, 1989.

Moran, Mark. "Forgiveness may be Divine but also Health-Giving." *Psychiatric News*, 18 August 2000, pp. 33-34.

Morris, Hubert. "Persons and Punishment", *The Monist*, 52(1968) 475-501.

Morris, Leon. *The Cross in the New Testament*. Grand Rapids: Eerdmans, 1965.

Morris, Thomas V. "Perfect Being Theology." *Noûs*, 21(March 1987)19-30.

Müller, Julius. *The Christian Doctrine of Sin*. Edinburgh: T. & T. Clark, 1877.

Murphy, Jeffrie G. & Jean Hampton. *Forgiveness and Mercy*. Cambridge University Press, 1988.

Mythe de la peine, La. Acts of the colloquium organised by the International Centre of Humanist Studies and by the Institute of Philosophical Studies of Rome, Rome 7-12 January 1967. Paris: Aubier, 1967.

Niebuhr, Reinhold. *Beyond Tragedy*. London: Nisbet, 1938.

Nietzsche, Friedrich: *The Birth of Tragedy*. Garden City: Doubleday Anchor, 1956.

———. *Human, All Too Human*. tr R. J. Hollingdale. Cambridge University Press, 1986.

Nozick, Robert. *Philosophical Explanations*. Oxford: Clarendon, 1981.

Openness of God, The. A Biblical Challenge to the Traditional Understanding of God. By Charles Pinnock, Richard Rice, John Sanders, William Hasker and David Basinger. Downer's Grove, Ill.: Intervarsity, 1994.

Packer, Herbert L. *The Limits of the Criminal Sanction*. Stanford University Press, 1968.

Pakenham, Frank. *The Idea of Punishment*. London: Geoffrey Chapman, 1961.

Paton, George. *A Textbook of Jurisprudence*. 3rd edn., Oxford University Press, 1964.

Plotinus. *The Enneads*. Tr. Stephen MacKenna. London: Penguin, 1991.

Pontell, Henry N. *A Capacity to Punish*. Indiana University Press, 1984.

Polkinghorne, John. *Science and Providence. God's Interaction with the World*. Boston: New Science Library, 1989.

Pontifex, Dom Mark. *Freedom and Providence*, vol. 22 of *The Twentieth Century Encyclopedia of Catholicism*. New York: Hawthorn, 1960.

Pope, Stephen J. "The Convergence of Forgiveness and Justice: Lessons from El Salvador." *Theological Studies*, 64(2003)812-835.

Praz, Mario. *The Romantic Agony*. Second edn., Oxford University Press, 1970. Originally published in Italian in 1933.

Prison the Last Resort, published by a number of churches in Australia in 1989.

Rahner, Karl. *Spiritual Exercises*. New York: Herder & Herder, 1965

Raphael, David D: *The Paradox of Tragedy*. London: Allen & Unwin, 1960.

———. "Tragedy and Religion", in Sanders, ed., *Twentieth Century Interpretations of the Book of Job*. Englewood-Cliffs, N.J.: Prentice-Hall, 1968.

Ricoeur, Paul. *The Symbolism of Evil*. New York: Harper & Row, 1967.

Rodriguez, Alphonsus. "Treatise on Conformity to the Will of God", in *The Practice of Christian and Religious Perfection*. 3 vols. Dublin: Duffy, 1861. Originally published in 1609.

Rosa, Peter de. *God Our Saviour*. London: Geoffrey Chapman, 1968.

Rosenbaum, Ron: *Explaining Hitler. The Search for the Origins of his Evil*. London: Macmillan, 1998.

———. *The Secret Parts of Fortune*. New York: Random House, 2000.

Rostand, Jean. *The Substance of Man*. Garden City NY: Doubleday, 1962. This is a translation in one volume of two French books: *Pensées d'un biologiste* and *Carnets d'un biologiste*.

Russell, Bertrand. *The Basic Writings of Bertrand Russell*. London: Allen & Unwin, 1961.

Sade, Marquis de. *Justine, Philosophy in the Bedroom and Other Writing*. New York: Grove, 1965.

Safer, Jeanne. *Forgiving and Not Forgiving*. New York: Avon, 1999.

Saint-Exupéry, Antoine de. *The Wisdom of the Sands*. London: Hollis & Carter, 1952.

Scheler, Max: *Formalism in Ethics and Non-Formal Ethics of Values*. Evanston: Northwestern University Press, 1973. This was written before World War I and the first edition was published in 1916.

———. *On the Eternal in Man*. London: SCM, 1960. The first German edition appeared in 1921.

Schleiermacher, Friedrich. *The Christian Faith*. Edinburgh: T. & T. Clark, 1928. Originally published in 1821-22.

Schoonenberg, Piet: *Man and Sin*. Notre Dame University Press, 1965.

———. Contribution to *Mysterium Salutis*, 5 vols by many authors, ed. Joseph Feiner & Magnus Löhrer. Cologne: Benziger, 1965-1976.

Scullion, John, J. P. Kenny, John Cowburn & Harry Wardlaw. *Original Sin*. Melbourne: Dove, 1975.

Sereny, Gitta. *Albert Speer: His Battle with Truth*. New York: Knopf, 1995.

Sertillages, Antonin Gilbert:. *Foundations of Thomistic Philosophy*. London: Sands, 1931.

Shakespeare. Quotations are from *The Oxford Shakespeare* (1988).

Silberman, Charles E. *Criminal Violence, Criminal Justice*. New York: Random House, 1978.

Silvester, Hugh. *Arguing With God*. Downer's Grove, Ill.: Inter-Varsity Press, 1972.

Simon, Ulrich. *The Theology of Auschwitz*. London: Gollancz, 1967.

Smulders, Piet. *The Design of Teilhard de Chardin*. Westminster, MD: Newman, 1967.

Solomon, Robert C. *A Passion for Justice. Emotion and the Origin of the Social Contract*. New York: Addison-Wesley, 1990. This was republished by Rowman & Littlefield, Landham Md., in 1995.

Steiner, George: *The Death of Tragedy*. London: Faber & Faber, 1963.

Suhard, Cardinal. *Collected Writings*. Chicago: Fides, 1953.

Teilhard de Chardin, Pierre (often called by his shortened surname, Teilhard): *Activation of Energy*. London: Collins, 1970.

———. *Christianity and Evolution*. London: Collins, 1971.

———. *The Future of Man*. London: Collins, 1964.

———. *The Phenomenon of Man*. London: Collins, 1959.

———. *Toward the Future*. London: Collins, 1975.

———. *Writings in Time of War*. London: Collins, 1968.

Temple, William. *Nature, Man and God*. London: Macmillan, 1956.

❦ Bibliography

Tillyard, E.M.W. *The Elizabethan World Picture*. London: Chatto & Windus, 1943.

Van Steenberghen. *Ontology*. New York: Wagner, 1952.

Varillon, François. *The Humility and Suffering of God*. This is a translation of two books, *L'humilité de Dieu* and *La souffrance de Dieu*. New York: Alba, 1983.

Vereker, Charles. *Eighteenth-Century Optimism*. Liverpool University Press, 1967.

Villiers, Marjorie. *Charles Péguy. A Study in Integrity*. London: Collins, 1965.

Voltaire. *Candide*. Harmondsworth: Penguin 1947. Originally published ca. 1757.

Weinandy, Thomas G. *Does God Suffer?* Edinburgh: T. & T. Clark. 2000.

Weiss, Paul. *Man's Freedom*. Yale University Press, 1950.

———. *Nature and Man*. Yale University Press, 1950.

Wiesenthal, Simon. *Justice Not Vengeance*. Mandarin pb, 1990.

Wojtyla, Karol. *The Acting Person*. Dodrecht, Holland: Reidel, 1979.

Index

A
Aeschylus 112, 249
amendment 173
Anderson 47–48, 249
Anselm 247
Aquinas, see Thomas Aquinas 73, 116
Arendt 120, 127, 174, 249
Aristotle 77, 147
Asquith 216
attrition 201
Augustine 20, 28, 37–38, 87, 138–139, 215

B
Bañez 71–72
Barth 88, 96, 101, 124, 131–132, 172, 242–243, 249
Beauvoir, S de 45, 96, 249
Belo 215–216, 224, 249
Berdyaev 83–84, 124, 249
Berger 82–83, 214, 250
Bergson 54, 139
Bernanos 96, 107–108, 114–115, 250
Blumenfeld 205–206, 250
Bonhoeffer 86, 115, 132, 250
Brasnett 78, 250
Browning 26
Brunner 107, 118, 124, 132, 242, 245, 247, 250
Buber 105–106, 250

Bullock, A 126, 129–130
Byron 43–44, 97, 215

C
Camus 31, 48, 97–98, 100, 108, 133, 168–169, 220, 250
Cardenal 27, 146, 250
Caussade 18, 25–26, 76, 250
chance 27, 32, 47, 52, 54–57, 60–62, 69–71, 77, 122, 143
Chardin
see Teilhard 58, 60, 64–66, 151, 255, 258
Clarke J 139, 148, 251
Clark, SB 247, 249, 251, 256, 258–259
Claudel 101, 136–138, 251
condone 176
Craig, WL 74
Crispin 219

D
Darwin 58–59, 64
destroy 35, 72, 98–99, 101–103, 110, 122, 131, 141, 245
determinism 52, 55, 60, 73, 119–120, 126, 217, 233
Dinsmore 210, 230, 232, 251
Dorner 78, 251
Dostoyevsky 18, 31–32, 104, 233, 251

E
earthquake 24–25, 28, 30

Index

Eichmann 120, 213, 222
Einstein 69
Eliot 96–97, 114, 163, 251
Ellis-Fermor 42–43, 251
entropy 62
evil, moral 17–18, 20–21, 28, 31, 34, 37–38, 42, 44–46, 51, 63–66, 74, 78–79, 81–83, 86–89, 95, 97–98, 101–106, 108–113, 116–133, 135–136, 138–145, 150, 154–155, 157, 159, 161–163, 166–167, 169, 171–174, 179, 181, 184, 188, 191, 196, 200, 210, 215, 242–246, 248–249
evolution 52, 57–65, 67, 69–70, 77, 110, 151, 159, 204, 242
Ewing 208, 214, 251
excuse 128, 164–165, 169, 175, 178, 185
expiation 231, 234–235

F

Fackenheim 127, 243
Fairbairn 78, 251
fall 25, 46–47, 98–100, 108, 143, 179, 190, 247
Farrer 18, 117–118, 124, 251
Faulkner 48, 109, 190–191, 251
fear 39–40, 82, 108–109, 170, 201, 232, 244–245
Fiddes 78–79, 252
flaws 119–120
foreknowledge 70–77, 139–140, 146
forgetting 175, 185
forgiveness 17, 34, 38, 122, 128, 163–164, 168, 174–185, 188–192, 195–196, 199–202, 225, 228–230, 235, 243, 245, 247–248
Frankl 165, 252
free will 30, 32, 51–54, 56, 60, 68–72, 74–76, 83, 87, 91, 108, 121–123, 129–130, 143, 150, 202, 216, 233
Fromm 96, 102, 118, 120, 220, 252
Funder 223–224, 252
Furniss 39, 244, 252

G

Gardner 104, 125, 210, 232–233, 252
Garner 219, 238, 252
Gaylin 108, 114, 214, 234–235, 252
Geach 27, 252
Genet 108, 252
Goethe 100
Govier 166, 179, 196, 252
Gray, JG 101, 107, 235, 252
Greek Fathers 142, 144
Gross 218, 253
guilt 34, 37, 82, 86, 88, 93, 105–106, 108, 112, 132, 151–152, 154–157, 160–161, 163–170, 172–173, 181, 184, 189, 195, 199–200, 226, 229, 232–235, 247

H

Hegel 211, 222, 236, 253
Heim 131–132, 253
Heisenberg 61
Hick 20, 118–120, 123, 127, 252–253
Hill, J. 73, 254

Hitler 126–127, 129–130, 167, 214, 243, 257
see subject 126–127, 129–130, 167, 214, 243, 257
Holmgren 178–179, 253
Honderich 220, 236, 253
Houghton 69, 253
Huxley TH 64, 127

I

immaturity 158
impassibility 78–79, 149
implicit 95, 97, 99, 133
inexplicable 123–125, 127, 242
intention 86, 88–89, 99, 141, 169, 173–174, 201

J

Jankélévich 165, 175
Janssens 65
Jaspers 159–160, 232, 253
Jenyns 28, 135–136, 253
John Paul II 177, 179, 225, 253
Journet 73, 200, 253
Joyce 39
judging 160, 163
justice, see retribution 18, 37–38, 113, 151, 163, 165, 205–213, 215–216, 218–219, 221–227, 230–231, 234, 236–240, 245–246, 248

K

Kant 16, 28–29, 87, 120, 124, 210–211, 224, 253
Kenny, A 73, 254, 258
Kneale 221
Knox 24, 254

Kondoleon 148, 254

L

Laclos 98, 251
Lactantius 147–148
Lang 126, 223, 254
Lautréamont 43, 104–105, 254
Lawrence, DH 96, 98, 254
laws 18, 69, 89–91, 93–94, 110, 115, 117, 166, 214, 218, 222–223
Leibniz 23, 254
Lonergan 125, 129, 254
love 31, 45, 78, 85, 89, 96–97, 99, 103, 106–107, 118, 130–131, 133, 136–138, 147, 150, 172, 174, 178, 180, 184–185, 190–191, 195, 204, 208, 245, 248
Lucas, J.R. 74, 221, 255
Luther 201

M

Mackie 140–141, 208, 214, 255
Manser, AR 217, 219, 255
Maritain 54–55, 73, 116, 123, 211, 255
Marlowe 42, 132
Maugham 41, 255
McKenzie, JG 182, 255
meaninglessness 106
Menninger 83, 207, 220, 233, 235, 255
Mercier 21, 105, 255
mercy 38–39, 225–226, 229, 233, 245
Milton 23–24, 100, 104, 111, 145, 232, 249, 255
Moberly 231, 235, 255

Molina 71–72
Moltmann 78, 255
Monod 52, 60–61, 255
Mooney 65, 151, 255
Moore, KD 211, 224, 256
Murphy, JG 171, 177, 208, 256
mysteries 242–244

N

Newton 60
Niebuhr 55, 256
non-being 20–21, 116, 129
Nozick 211, 256

O

optimism 24, 26, 29–32, 41, 44, 139, 145–146

P

Packer, HL 216, 256
Pakenham 93, 231, 256
Pascal 157
Paton 90, 92, 214, 221–222, 256
Péguy 138–139, 144, 259
permission 35, 139, 145, 164
pessimism 41, 48–49
Philo 77
Pius XII 73
Plato 232
play (drama) 18, 29–30, 33, 52, 54, 56, 61, 63, 68–69, 75–76, 97, 105, 136, 138, 146, 159, 184, 191, 210, 222, 227
Poe, EA 104
Pontell 213, 256
Pontifex 116, 118, 129, 257
Pope, Alex 24, 135, 177, 180, 253, 257
Portalesi 212
possibility 51–52, 54, 67–68, 104, 140–141, 242
probability 56, 69, 77
punishment 37, 93, 108, 134, 205–226, 231–236, 238, 240, 246–247

R

Raphael, DD 34, 47, 257
reconciliation 34, 163, 168, 181, 184–187, 189–196, 199, 203–204, 232
repentance 17, 34, 108, 146, 164, 170–174, 177–183, 189–190, 192, 195–196, 199–202, 226, 228–229, 231, 234, 248
responsibility 32, 52, 85, 91, 105, 116, 121, 129, 140, 142–144, 150, 159, 165, 175, 195–196, 216
restitution 174
retribution 208, 210–214, 216, 218–222, 231, 247
revenge 174, 181, 184, 203–206, 219–222, 239–240, 246
Rickaby 123
Ricoeur 42, 102–103, 118, 141, 209, 211, 231–232, 257
rise 25, 34, 51, 209
risk 67, 90, 134, 142, 150, 245
Rivo, Peter de 71
Rosa, de 147, 257
Rosenbaum 126–127, 130, 243, 257
Rostand 42, 257
Russell 41–42, 47, 257

S

Sade 44–46, 96–97, 100–101, 104, 126, 131, 171, 249, 252, 257
sadness 34, 107–108, 132, 148–149, 202–203
Safer 179, 182, 188–189, 193, 257
Saint-Exupéry 108, 257
Scarfe 138, 249
Scheler 160–161, 165, 170–171, 173, 182, 221, 257
Schoonenberg 131, 160, 258
sensitivity 77, 147, 150, 214
Sereny 166–167, 172, 258
Sertillanges 20, 26, 123
Shakespeare 18, 41, 43, 48, 103–107, 110–111, 113, 125, 139, 168, 206, 210, 230, 232–233, 237, 249, 258
Silberman 212, 258
Simon, UR 86, 101–102, 213, 215, 222, 250, 252, 258–259
Smulders 66, 151, 258
solidarity 152–157, 160, 195, 248
Solomon, RA 221, 258
Speer 166–167, 172, 258
Spinoza 171, 249
subjectivity 82, 105, 169, 171, 177
Suhard 27, 258

T

Teilhard de Chardin 58, 60, 64–66, 69, 122–123, 130, 151, 158–159, 255, 258
Temple 21, 105, 190, 252, 258
therapists 105, 165, 179
Thomas A Kempis 157
Thomas Aquinas 20–21, 23, 28, 73, 96, 116, 147–148, 249
Thomson 41, 43, 46
Tresmontant 66

U

Unabomber 179
unforeseeableness 54
unpredictability 53

V

Varillon 78, 259
Vereker 28, 63, 127, 259
Vergote 132
Voltaire 28, 30–31, 41, 259

W

Weiss, P 74, 96, 259
Wiesenthal 86–87, 213–214, 222, 259